The Bond
A Novel

For Jaime Malamud-Goti

George P. Fletcher

The Bond
A Novel

HART
PUBLISHING

Oxford and Portland Oregon, 2009

Published in North America (US and Canada) by Hart Publishing
c/o International Specialized Book Services
920 NE 58th Avenue, Suite 300
Portland, OR 97213-3786, USA
Tel: +1 503 287 3093 or toll-free: (1) 800 944 6190
Fax: +1 503 280 8832
E-mail: orders@isbs.com
Website: http://www.isbs.com

Hart Publishing Ltd, 16C Worcester Place, Oxford, OX1 2JW, UK
Telephone: +44 (0)1865 517530 Fax: +44 (0)1865 510710
E-mail: mail@hartpub.co.uk
Website: http://www.hartpub.co.uk

British Library Cataloguing in Publication Data
Data Available

ISBN: 978-1-84113-983-8

Typeset by Tatiana Galarza
Printed and bound in Great Britain by
TJ International Ltd, Padstow, Cornwall

Contents

1

Identities

THE NAME ADAM Gross speaks history. His family name, meaning "large" in German, might be a sign that he is of German origin, but in the context of his life as a law professor in the United States it probably signals that he is of Jewish provenance, most likely with roots in an Eastern European country where everything German is held in high esteem. It may seem odd to us to name people "small" and "large," but it is often the case with Jewish names, perhaps because the terms are abbreviated references to the trades of wholesaler and retailer. Thus the name Gross tells us something, perhaps, about the way his forebears made a living in their small corner of Eastern Europe.

His first name also offers some clues. After the Second World War, after the Holocaust, after the Communist takeover of many of their governments, Eastern Europeans nurtured a fervent hope in a new beginning of history. The most popular names in Poland and Hungary at the time were Eva and Adam. These names signified that, although their world was supposedly liberated from religion, the new generation could think of themselves as though they were the first humans, not burdened by the horrors of past wars. They were free to decide for themselves whether they should taste forbidden fruit or create a world without the taints of capitalism, racism, or the other inhumanities of the past.

Adam's parents, Miklós and Leah, had met in Budapest immediately after the war, married, and had two children, Noga and Adam. During the heady revolutionary days of October 1956, they had taken advantage of the open border to emigrate. They could have gone to Israel, but Miklós had longed for a quiet, romantic place that was far from the Cold War and the military threats of the

Middle East. They had ended up in Buenos Aires, which had proved to be a happy choice—there they could connect quickly with other left-wing immigrants, make new friends and enjoy the open café life of the city. In Argentina, Adam had used the surname of Gross-Rand, Rand being the name of his mother, placed as a suffix in the Latin style. When he had started to have more contacts with the United States, however, the name had proved a source of confusion. The American universities answered his letters of inquiry by addressing them to Adam G. Rand, while the name of his mailbox and in the phone book was Gross. He found it less confusing to be called just Adam Gross.

We can trace this process of increasing engagement with American life in his curriculum vitae: BA from the University of Buenos Aires in 1973; MA in philosophy from Columbia in 1977; JD from Pace Law School in White Plains, New York in 1981; postgraduate certificate from Humboldt University in Berlin (East), 1984. On returning to the United States from East Germany, Adam had landed a teaching spot at Regina University in New York City. He had worked his way up the academic system and eventually become a full professor specializing in comparative law—a subject that had no real content, but which enabled Adam to demonstrate his unusual command of foreign legal systems.

We catch up with him on a warm Wednesday morning in August when the twin towers are still standing and the new millennium has just survived its fears of a global computer glitch triggered by the turning of the last three numbers of the date from 999 to 000. In the tranquil mood of that final summer of Bill Clinton's presidency, Adam was expecting nothing unusual when he approached lecture hall 104, ready for the first day of his annual introductory course for all the incoming graduate students...

At precisely 11 a.m. Professor Gross opened the door and strode down the center aisle, carefully checking out faces to the right and to the left, acting as though he had something to fear. When he reached the front of the hall, he turned slowly and announced, with a studied grin, "You look good to me." He had his entrance down pat.

From north, south, east and west, bringing 50 different accents and dialects, they came to Regina Law, the oldest and most prestigious of the city's law schools. Trained lawyers at home but novices in American law, they were about to begin their journey in the basics of the system that was new to them. They were 214 men and women, and nervous all. They took their seats in the amphitheater as though they were booking passage in an Ark that would carry them through the flood of legal minutiae and into a new world of money and prestige.

Adam took a breath, and began his scripted follow-up line. "We are going to talk about the differences between Continental civil law and common law, primarily American common law," he told the class. "I myself am not sure what these terms mean, but we will try to discover their meaning together." He paused and looked around. "So—what are your first impressions? What have you heard at home about the difference between these two great legal cultures?"

The students answered spontaneously from different sides of the room. Some said the common law was nothing but a series of cases— that it had no underlying principles. Others said that the civil law was based on codes. One French student even quoted Montesquieu's view that judges should be "the mouthpiece" of the legislated law: they should read the words of the code and apply them to the facts of the case.

"You're right," said Adam. "We are going to study cases more than we study statutes. But it is wrong to think that we have no statutes. There are many of them in the United States—the Internal Revenue Code, the Federal Rules of Civil Procedure... The United States Criminal Code defines something like 8,000 offenses. Later I will teach you that the greatest statute of all is the Constitution."

"Permission to speak, sir?"

Adam turned to a stocky, baby-faced student sitting off to his right. "Do you think this is the military, young man?"

"No, sir, but this is a classroom and you are the authority here," the blond young man replied, in perfect syntax but with a slight German lilt.

Adam suppressed a sigh. He had met this attitude many times before, and he was not about to play the part of the German or Argentine professor, spoon-feeding the law to eager note-takers.

"And your name, sir?"

"Joerg Mueller, from Berlin—or Miller, if you like," offered the young man obligingly.

"I like to use names as they are spoken at home, so, Mr. Mueller, what do *you* think about the common law?"

"My grandfather..." Joerg Mueller took a deep breath. "He thought there was a connection between race and legal culture. The common law expresses the spirit of the English and American peoples. Is this not an expression of their race?"

Adam noted several students shifting uneasily in their seats. "Do you think that as well, Mr. Mueller?"

"Well, I think that language has something to do with it. We on the continent of Europe do not understand the common law. It is like English. No grammar, no system, no structure."

Gross was nonplussed. He had felt the same thing when he had first studied law in the United States: he had longed for the orderly abstraction of the codes he studied in Buenos Aires. "Well, you have a point," he granted. "Something like the English love of empiricism. There's something in that. Some people like the facts; other people like theory."

"Yes, and I want to know about the theoretical dogmas of American law. Are we going to learn those on this course?"

Adam knew exactly what Joerg was talking about. He was familiar with the German term "dogma," which happened to be the same as the term used by the Catholic Church for the basic tenets of the faith. He had always thought this to be a remarkable indication of the connection between law and theology, the dominant subjects of medieval universities. He knew that French and Spanish lawyers used variations of the word "doctrine" to express the same point. But, in the Protestant countries of northern Europe, Great Britain, the USA and the most of the former Commonwealth, no one would dare suggest that the study of law was in any way similar to the study of theology.

"I understand what you are asking, Mr. Mueller," he said. "Let me put it this way. In a legal system, to make the system orderly and structured, codes are not enough, decisions by the judges are not enough; you also need input from scholars. But why should these scholars have any authority? Are they like the rabbis of old, or the priests of the Catholic Church?"

Joerg looked taken aback by the reference to the priests. As the word "rabbis" sank in, he seemed even more uncomfortable.

"In my part of Germany we are *evangelisch*—Protestants. Me too."

"Congratulations." Both fell silent for a few seconds. Adam regretted the remark but he did not bother to recant. "So you want professors to play the role of *rabbis*?" He emphasised the word. "You want them to tell you what the law is supposed to mean?"

Joerg looked as if he needed help. "Let me add something," a woman interjected from the top row. "My name is Chen Horowitz—from Tel Aviv. And I think you are picking on Herr Mueller."

Adam laughed, and then caught himself. He knew the danger. Adam Gross's standing as a scholar rarely translated into good relations with the students. Occasionally the students turned on him, complaining to the dean that his classes were too abstract and too far removed from their concerns as future Wall Street practitioners. At least 10 or 20 per cent would write "Fire the guy!" on their evaluations at the end of the semester. A few years earlier, a group of African-Americans had objected that all of Adam's assigned reading took the "white" point of view, and once, in a compulsory first-year class in jurisprudence, when a tattooed female student wearing a huge cross had claimed that the origin of property was theft from the Indians, he had burst out laughing. No doubt other teachers frequently wanted to do this when students made ridiculous comments, but part of the job for them, as for psychiatrists, was to listen patiently and to make the most possible sense out of the muddled assertions that came their way. Usually university teachers had the required discipline... but not always.

Professor Gross had paid dearly for his laugh. He'd made the mistake of writing a letter of apology to the whole class and sending it out over the newly set-up law school email network, which in an instant had broadcast the entire email directory, reserved at the time to the faculty alone, to everyone and anyone who wanted to engage in political organization. Suddenly the network of shared grievances had crossed the line from gossip in the halls to grass roots mobilization. The students had given vent to their anxieties and frustration in an escalating exchange of emails. In the face of the mounting anger Adam had lost his cool a second time and suggested that, if so many were unhappy with the class, they should ask the dean to set up an alternative section to it. This they had done, and the dean at the time, Rachel White, had complied. An older, easygoing black professor, Pat Graham, had stepped in to teach the alternative class. About half the students had transferred out. Adam had limped to the end of semester with his rump group, swearing never to let such a thing happen again.

Avoiding danger this time, Gross tried to ignore Chen and called on a dark-haired student who was waving his hand as though trying to hail a cab. "In Italy we say the same thing," said the young man, "but we use the English words. We don't say '*diritto civile*' but 'civil law.' We also say 'common law,' not '*diritto commune.*'"

"And what does this Italian habit of using the English terms tell you?" asked Adam.

"It tells me that it is an important idea—a little piece of American imperialism."

"Sort of like-a Coca-Cola?" The giggles confirmed that it was now OK to release a little nervous tension.

"Actually, we Italians do not care so much about what we have in common with the rest of the Continent. Some of us like French law, some like German law, but basically we are only interested in Italy."

"So why do you use these terms, 'common law' and 'civil law'?" Adam persisted.

"Not sure. Maybe the Americans want us to."

More laughter. This was starting to warm up, thought Adam. "I can understand Americans exporting their products," he suggested with a pensive air, "but why should we want to teach Italians to say 'common law' and 'civil law'?"

"Maybe you need to classify us," replied the Italian student. "You guys are Protestants; we are Catholics. We have a different language and we eat different food. You guys are on one side of the line, and we are on the other."

"We all love pizza." Adam thought it was a funny line, but there were only a few polite smiles.

"Yes, but we do not all love cases," Chen Horowitz countered from her lofty position. "We like the authority of the codes. When the legislature speaks, we listen. I am on Joerg Mueller's side. I want to hear about codes and about *dottrinas*—he called them dogmas—as explained by Professor Tedeschi in Jerusalem."

"Yes, I agree, my *capitán*, my *capitán*," called out a lanky, dark-skinned, handsome young man with curly hair.

Lord, thought Adam, who is this? The student caught his brief look of alarm. "Don't worry, my *capitán*, I am from Brazil—your neighbor. And you are the *capitán* of my legal ship. I do not know who this Tedeschi is."

Adam knew the Latin styles of speech well enough to recognize the Brazilian's sexual place in the world. "*Maricón*—gay," he murmured to himself, and felt dangerously on the verge of showing his irritation at this kid who was trying to profile him as the man with all the guns and all the answers. Hastily he looked around the room for more congenial company, and his eyes fell on a very beautiful young blonde girl gracing the bench in a strapless summer dress and sandals.

She saw his gaze pause on her and seized her chance to speak. "You and Joerg had an exchange about ze English language and ze common law. You think English and ze common law go hand in hand. But in Canada some schools teach ze common law in French. How about zat?" She seemed to be exaggerating her accent.

"And your name, Ms...?" Adam was tempted to add "...with the nice legs," but he stopped himself.

"Porte des Vaux. Charlotte de la Porte des Vaux."

"Mademoiselle de la Porte des Vaux—I love your name, so unusually French. Let me ask you: do you see a difference between the French used in discussing the *Code civil* and the French used to explain the basic concepts and terms of the common law?"

"First, let me say that I love your name too." She slanted her eyes at him. "It is so—what should I zay?—so ethnic."

The attack excited him. Nothing like a gorgeous blonde going after me, Adam thought, savoring the idea. He was slipping into one of the habits that had almost cost him his job several times. He could not resist flirting with good-looking girls 25 years his junior. I am just a little immigrant boy looking for love, he would say to himself.

"Give me a pause," Charlotte interrupted his reverie.

"I think you mean a break." Adam tried to direct the comment to her alone.

"I actually spent a year in one of those schools," Charlotte continued undaunted, "and I think the French words used to explain common law terms like 'estoppel' and 'fairness' and 'due process' are artificial. It is like a computer language."

"Excellent," responded Gross as he approached her in the front row, sat on her desk, and murmured to her quietly, "Talk to me after class."

Charlotte glowed in the public recognition. Twenty rows back, Chen Horowitz was watching. "I admit the French girl is attractive," she whispered to her neighbor, "but she's not *that* sexy."

"Back to business," the professor pressed on in a firm tone. "Ms. de la Porte des Vaux has reminded us that there are some jurisdictions, like Québec, that employ a mixture of common law and civil law. They have the language of one and the habits of the other. They speak French and use the jury system. If we are Coca-Cola, they are Coke Lite." He started roaming up and down the aisles—he couldn't help it; the attention from an attractive young French woman had emboldened him.

"What about Israel? Are we Pepsi Lite?" Chen got the class to focus back on her.

"Yes, what about Israel?" parried Gross.

"We too are a mixed system. Between the world wars, Palestine was a English colony. It was called the Mandate—I guess from the League of Nations, I am not sure. We acquired a lot of English law. But the land law is, or was based on, Ottoman law, and the newer statutes reflect admiration for Europe. For example, we now have a new basic law on human dignity. It is copied from German law. Maybe that is why we don't have the jury system—and we don't want it." Her voice rose in emphasis.

"Well!" said Adam. "You speak for the people of Israel?" Chen blushed.

Adam sensed that he was in trouble with at least half the class. Joerg wanted his dogmas, the Brazilian was looking for his *capitán*, Chen had become competitive, and he knew that he had been flirting with Charlotte. One of my typical days, he thought to himself. Maybe we need a little graceful walking, to use the language of tango—or straight lecturing in this lesser world—then some drama to end the class.

He fell into one of his pat one-minute routines. "True, the common law is case law. True, it is connected mostly to the English language. And it is also history, tied to the Norman conquest of Britain in 1066. The French brought their law to the little island off their coast and gradually it became the king's law, as opposed to local customs. The king had to establish the dominance of the common law, which he enforced in a court called the King's Bench. As one of the great colonizing nations in history, the English exported the king's law to their colonies. The English language followed the flag, and the common law went with it."

"So this is the dogma we should learn?" Joerg called out in tone of irony. "The common law is cases, it is language, and it is history? Are you serious? What is the content, what about torts, contracts, and property? What are the basic rules?"

Adam was tempted to imitate a technique he had observed Karl Llewellyn, the great American scholar of commercial law, use to shake up the students. Llewellyn believed in throwing the students into a "bramble bush" and making them find their way clear of the thorns. So, every so often, he would pretend to get very upset in class and storm out, slamming the door behind him. I'm afraid if I did it, reflected Adam, it wouldn't work. I like a little drama, but not that kind.

"Here it is for you, Joerg. The first rule of the common law is that there are no dogmas. You must read the materials and think for yourself. You have the first case in your materials. Study it as though you were looking for the whole world in a grain of sand."

Now I'm caught between roles, Adam realized. Am I the anti-authoritarian Protestant, or the English Romantic indulging in the irrational expectation of finding the entire body of law in a single case? In fact I'm a Hungarian Jew from south of the border. I don't blame them if they don't know where I'm coming from. He decided to be a little conciliatory.

"Let me end this first class on a personal note. I am resolved to teach in a way that is different from the lecture method they used to teach me in Buenos Aires. I sympathize with you; I know what you are going through—I've been there, done that. But I am convinced that you will get the hang of this new method, in which I speak and you respond and we try to engage in a dance together."

To the class, not knowing about Adam's youthful preoccupation with the tango, the reference to dancing came across as quaint and charming.

"You may be still curious about me. I will tell you more as the time comes, but I also want to know more about you. Do me a favor. Tonight, write me a paragraph about yourselves, your legal education—you can get as personal or stay as professional as you like. Send it to my email address, which you all have in your welcome notes. Perhaps that is going too far in a large class like this, but you should write something that you think it is important that your professor know about you. For example, you might think about some incident that made it meaningful for you to become a lawyer. Of course, your emails to me will be strictly confidential. I will share what I learn about you with no one."

As Adam assembled his books and papers in preparation for leaving, he reflected on this first interaction with the new students. He was absolutely committed to teaching by the Socratic method. That meant he asked questions and hoped that the students could intuit the right answers, exactly as Socrates might question a slave boy in the town square about the principles of geometry. This method had become famous in American law schools. It had started at Harvard, in the nineteenth century, when Christopher Langdell had invented the idea of teaching by the case method. He would assemble a bunch of cases from different jurisdictions and question students about their underlying principles. His assumption was that the common law—the customary law of the courts—was consistent and based on principle. By looking carefully at the facts of cases and the judge's reasoning for resolving them, one could infer the general principles of contracts, torts, or criminal law.

Gross also knew that European, Latin and Asian students hated this method. They wanted lectures about the codes—the codes of private law and criminal law; to take notes, and to be questioned in exams about the content of the lectures and readings—on the dogmas of the law, as Joerg Mueller described them. They were brilliant at doing just that. That was why they had been accepted to Regina. Adam was resolved to break their pattern of dependence on authority.

He had always hated authority. He remembered his parents' stories about the oppressive Communist party in Hungary before they fled, young Adam and his older sister Noga in tow, after the failure of the liberal revolution and the Soviet troops' entry into Budapest. Most of all he detested the authoritarian nature of Argentine politics, one military coup followed by another, finally topped off by a series of totalitarian generals who had their military underlings pick up people in the middle of the night for questioning and often for torture. Many of these never returned home. They were the famous *desaparecidos*, the "disappeared."

He even hated the authority of rhythm in dancing. When he was a student he had worked as a waiter in an offbeat cafés in San Telmo, one of the more bohemian neighborhoods of Buenos Aires. The right-wing governments of the time had frowned upon the tango that had flourished under the great composers of the 1920s. Yet a small group at the café had started dancing in the back room. It was not exactly a political protest, more an act of nostalgia for the elegant style of the *tangueros* in the time of Carlos Gardel, and a flirtation with radicalism by introducing the innovations of Astor Piazzolla. That was where Adam had learned to walk gracefully. He had often danced in "close embrace," as it is called in the tango, with his girlfriend Sara Kalvermann, a tall, gangly woman who wore knee socks all the time, even in the warm days of December.

Sara was a late version of what had been called a "beatnik" in the San Francisco of Allen Ginsberg. Her parents had in fact spent time in California in the late 1950s and tried to transplant their adopted style to Argentina. They continued to speak English and thought of changing their name to Calman, but no one understood what they were trying to say. Sara's parents had encouraged her to dissent from the habits of the people around her. Her anti-authoritarian sentiments and Adam's proved to be a good fit.

For Adam, the beauty of the tango was that the dancers did not have to stick to a rigid rhythm. Unlike the salsa or the rumba, where the beat of the music ruled your steps, on the tango floor you could dance as slowly as you liked, invent your own steps, and create the dance that best suited your mood. Learning the elementary steps like the *paso básico* was simply learning the grammar of the dance. Once you "spoke" tango, you could dance any way that made sense to you and your partner.

Leading your partner was, however, the key to grace on the dance floor. The man had to give the *marca*—the lead. It had to be gentle and clear. The woman would then interpret the *marca* and add flourishes of her own. Most of the beautiful steps were those executed by the woman supported by her partner as he remained fixed, to provide the frame for her kicks and her figure-eights.

At the outset Sara had had trouble with the male chauvinism of the dance. Why shouldn't the woman lead; why should they not dance independently, as was becoming popular on disco floors all over the world? Adam had had no good reply. Finally one of his professors, whom he'd encountered on the dance floor, had given them a good explanation. He had studied the tripartite division of legal authority discussed by the French philosopher Montesquieu: the legislature should lay down the law, the judiciary should interpret the law, and the executive should enforce it. The man, the professor elaborated, provided the law by leading; but the law in the bare form of a statute—an enactment by the legislature—meant nothing. It came to life only when the woman, as judge, interpreted it and put it into practice. This explained the beauty of the dance: two people, each with different roles, creating a display of unity.

"Is this the kind of government we have in Argentina?" Adam had sardonically asked Sara. Obviously not; the *juntas* were legislature, executive, and judiciary wrapped into one. They were ultimately dancing with themselves, a potentially deadly form of self-deception. When the military thought someone was dangerous, he *became* dangerous in their minds. Nothing anyone said could change their judgment. The only resolution was the suspect's disappearance.

When Adam had first started teaching law classes in New York, he'd thought of the Socratic method as something like dancing the tango. He would give the lead by asking a question, hoping that the students would go beyond his own understanding by interpreting the question and improvising their steps. He would provide the frame for their genius, just as he had for Sara on the dance floor.

This is my anti-authoritarian way of teaching, he thought to himself, as he reflected on the interactions of the class that had just ended. I encourage a free interpretation of my "leads" and therefore I must roll with the risk. He wished he could have used the tango as a method of explaining the law, particularly when in the first hour one student had slipped into the error, following Montesquieu, of claiming that the judge was just "the mouthpiece of the law." Adam knew from the tango floor that the woman was never merely the echo of the man's commands, and likewise the courts could never simply read the words of a statute and know how to resolve difficult cases. There will be a right time, he told himself, to explain this complex analogy.

Though carrying a large pile of books, Adam exited gracefully from the room, even stopping a few times without thinking about it, as he might in the tango, to place his right heel behind his left foot and then start off against with a repeated left step.

As they were walking out behind him, Joerg encountered Chen and said, "I don't know whether to trust this guy."

2

The Power and the Beauty

THE DEAN OF Regina was a fortyish Harvard graduate named Peter Levenger. Tall, well-built, with a shock of fair hair, he cut an attractive figure at faculty and alumni events. His uniform was a pressed navy blue suit, starched white cotton shirt, and brown Oxford shoes with neatly tied laces. His attire was almost the opposite of Adam Gross's. While the Argentine dandied his unkempt look for hours, the dean just grabbed another outfit off the rack. With ten identical sets hanging in his closet, each fitting his well-groomed body, he never had to think about what he was going to wear.

He had mundane taste in everything except women. Though vaguely Jewish, he had fallen in love with and married an olive-skinned, dark-eyed, liberal Turkish Muslim woman, Aschkin Yilmaz; her family name, adopted after the secular revolution in the 1920s, meant "dauntless." He had met her on a lecture tour in Europe. It was the greatest adventure of his life. He relished telling and retelling the story to others as well as himself.

Invited to give a series of lectures in Germany, he had made a planned two-day stop in Heidelberg, where Aschkin was writing her dissertation under a well-known professor of public law at the Max Planck Institute. At the cocktail reception after the lecture, Peter had noticed her looking his way. He had approached her with total indifference to his own performance and asked whether she thought "the whole field of human rights was a bit overblown." Though Aschkin had had trouble initially with the word "overblown" she had got the point and started explaining why she thought national legal problems, as modified by economic theory, were more solid and substantial than international issues. He had listened intently and kept staring. Both in the way he related to her intellectually and with his gaze, he had attracted her physically—he was probably the first man to have done so. With his strong build, his wavy blond hair and his charm, he was used to attracting woman. When he asked her to join him for dinner she said yes.

Aschkin had been nervous. She was not used to being alone with men who bathed her in physical energy. At dinner he continued to look her squarely in the eyes, but from time to time he allowed his eyes to drift down and follow the graceful lines of her curves and her narrow waist. She had grown up in a religious but intellectually free home in Istanbul, not far from the Bosporus, her environment defined by writers and intellectuals. There had never been a suggestion that she should wear the veil or hold back her intellectual potential. Her parents read the Koran in a liberal spirit, one that stressed the equality of all men and women. In fact, one reason they had named her Aschkin was because of its ambiguity: in Turkish it meant "transcendental" in the Kantian sense, as well as "thy love."

Aschkin was familiar with the basic stories of Genesis and had, despite her liberal outlook, absorbed their message—that woman secured power by having children. The maternal impulse was not just love of children but the pursuit of status. "Give me a child or I shall die," said Rachel to her husband Jacob, and the appeal had always resonated with Aschkin. In her world view, sex and having children were closely allied. Sexual experimentation without the purpose of procreation was definitely taboo. Pursuing her studies in Ankara, she had felt no need to rebel against her family and attach herself to a man. Besides, the young men of Ankara did not communicate the kind of respect that she thought was appropriate for a woman who was clearly their intellectual equal.

At the age of 28, when she had come to Germany for postgraduate studies and to write her doctorate, she was still a virgin—in mind as well as body. When the sexually well-exercised young German men dropped hints that they had "nothing against foreigners", she did not know what they were talking about. Her social life was limited to going out with colleagues from the institute in small group dinners, where they carried on serious conversations in German, Turkish and English.

Peter related to her in a way that was different from anything she had experienced. His love for the exotic appealed to her, as did his style of openness toward women regardless of ethnicity and religion.

His motives might have been complicated, but the cumulative effect on Aschkin was unmistakable. She was drawn in.

At dinner in the best hotel in town he ordered wine without asking. When Aschkin had first come to Germany she had adhered to the Islamic prohibition against alcohol, more as a matter of custom and identity than true subservience to religious law, but she didn't know anyone else who kept to this rule abroad so she had dropped it, and eventually developed a great love for the wines of Baden-Württemberg, particularly for the rieslings made from the vineyards on the hills sloping toward the Rhine. But, as Peter was served his pork steak, she laughed. "You are Jewish, aren't you?"

"Yes," he said, "but I regard myself as a universal man." He smiled at his own pomposity.

"Well, there are certain things I will not do." And she pointed at the white steak sizzling on Peter's plate.

"Oh, that's right—Jews and Muslims share their hatred for pigs. Well, for all their problems with other people and with each other, at least they have one hatred in common."

Aschkin could not tell whether he was trying to create a sense of common ground or just expressing his own unease about acting as an assimilated Jew. "I was taught that we were cousins, both children of Abraham," she answered.

"I never thought of it that way. So far as I know the Bible at all, I think of myself as the son of Adam and Eve, just like everyone else on the planet. We all have *human* rights—not rights as the children of Abraham."

Aschkin smiled both at Peter and herself, realizing that she was trying to get closer to him, to find points of intersection in their seemingly unrelated biographies. "Actually," she said, "I am not sure that we Turks are children of Abraham. The story is that Abraham had a son, Ishmael, with his wife's servant Hagar, then a son called Isaac with his wife Sarah. Sarah was jealous of Ishmael's status in the house and drove both him and Hagar into the desert. God protected them and Ishmael became the father of another great people in Middle East... Am I boring you?"

"Yes—I mean, no, not at all, it's interesting. But yes, I assume that you're talking about Arabs, and the question is whether Turks are really Arabs."

"Good point," she said professorially. "We share the religion but not this mysterious thing called ethnicity. We used to share the Arabic script with them. But since the Atatürk revolution we write in the Roman script, and therefore we feel cut off from the great literature of our Arab neighbors."

All of sudden she felt that she was becoming too intense, too unfeminine. She recalled the way Turkish men began to look at her when she got too serious about the material she was studying. Her words tapered off.

Peter considered her thoughtfully. "Do you want to pursue an academic career?" he asked.

"Of course," she said.

"Perhaps I can help you." Peter had the politician's gift for creating chits and getting others into his debt and then knowing when and how to call the chits in. And now he was creating one. He had never believed that women could love him for who and what he was; he had to do something to help them, something to generate gratitude. A grateful woman, he thought, would have more patience with him and not leave him. But, although his political skills worked in the academic arena, women eventually resented being in his debt. They did not stay with him, as he had expected, and he had never quite figured out why. His response to being disappointed in a woman was to redouble his efforts with the next one to make her feel grateful and dependent on him. Now he was nurturing fantasies of getting Aschkin a job with him in the law faculty in Wichita.

As they got up from the table, Peter put his arm around Aschkin, and she reciprocated by moving closer to him. She was unfamiliar with the moves women made in these situations, but his arm felt good and that was all that mattered to her.

There was a pool in the hotel, and Peter, emboldened by the wine, suggested they go down to the sauna that was attached to it. Aschkin replied, "Why not? I have not yet tried the saunas in Germany."

"It feels very good, believe me. Only one catch. Here in Germany, everyone goes into the sauna naked."

"Men and women together?"

"Yes."

"Oh! In my country men and women do not even pray together."

"So how do you feel about doing as the Romans do?" Peter challenged lightly.

Aschkin demurred. "They were a little decadent, weren't they? Anyway, we are in Heidelberg, not Rome."

He tactfully let the subject drop, and they sat in the bar next to each other and continued talking about their research and academic work. Aschkin was quietly enchanted at coming across a man who would take her studies of tax theory so seriously. It was a new field; there were not many people with whom she could discuss the implications of adopting the Coase theorem. As an experienced academic, Peter easily adopted the posture of someone who was genuinely interested in someone else's field. In fact he was more interested in her eyes and the slight curve of cleavage he espied between her breasts.

Aschkin basked in the attention and gradually came to the end of what she had to say about the Coase theorem. "You know," she concluded, "the most interesting thing about Coase is that he generated skepticism about the difference between causing harm and being harmed—in other words, between the active agent and the passive recipient."

"Am I the active one here?" Peter asked.

"It may look that way, but it was takes two to interact," she replied slowly, "and I was thinking... I should be wearing a veil. I am not doing that. So what difference does it make if I expose a little more skin? Let's go to the sauna."

They changed next to the pool in separate dressing rooms and then, wrapped in supersized towels, they met in the shower room. There were a few other couples coming in and out of the sauna. They all acted as though they had rediscovered the habits of people in the state of nature. Adapting quickly to the mood of the naturist colony, Aschkin gracefully turned her back to Peter, hung up her towel and followed one of the couples into sauna.

When Peter entered, Aschkin was sitting on one of the teak benches as women typically sit in mixed saunas, upright with legs tight together and bent at the knees, suggestively concealing her breasts. The trick of the sauna was to see while pretending not to look. Peter could tell enough from the outlines of her breasts to know that they were larger and firmer than they appeared under layers of modest clothing. He could not yet see her nipples and, for fear of his own body revealing too much of his interest, he did not try too hard to catch a glimpse.

Soon the other couples left. After a few minutes, Aschkin realized that it was too late in the evening to expect newcomers. She gradually relaxed her legs and lay back on the bench with her eyes closed. Peter devoured her with his eyes.

After 12 minutes in the 90°C heat they were both sweating, and went out together to cool off under the shower. Now completely at ease, Aschkin acted as though she were alone, throwing back her hair in the rushing cold water. Moving abruptly, Peter put his hands on her shoulders and kissed her on the neck. In response she could not help but grab him around the waist and press her naked body against his. Now there was no way for Peter to avoiding violating the sauna taboo against insubordinate flesh. He pushed her up against the wall. She didn't quite know what to do. She was not even sure how to respond to the feel of Peter's tongue in her mouth. Should she pull her tongue back or meet his with hers? The same with the lower half of the body. What should she do to embrace the hard flesh pressing between her legs? Just as she started to enjoy the new presence inside her, the door to the shower room creaked open. They jumped apart, back into the shower spray. Aschkin felt both rescued and abandoned. She wanted to end her isolation from men, and Peter was the most convincing candidate who had come along.

Peter prolonged his stay in Heidelberg and they devoted the extra time to trying to complete the act they had started in the shower. However willing both were, it was not easy to overcome the many years of Aschkin's unawareness of certain parts of her body. Before Peter left to return to the States, however, she had learned how to respond both to his kisses and to his body's hard desire. The overwhelming pleasure of their mutual discovery created a bond that Aschkin believed was unbreakable.

Sensing that her life was about to change, she redoubled her efforts to finish her doctorate, and before the year was out Peter called her and proposed marriage. Soon afterwards, he called again to say that the faculty in Wichita was going to consider her for a junior teaching position. She was so caught up in the excitement of Peter's attention, she failed to notice that her future husband was depriving her of the opportunity of looking for a job herself. It would take her years to feel the resentment of never having had to fend for herself in the academic world.

From the very beginning of their sexual connection, Peter encouraged Aschkin to use a diaphragm as a mode of birth control. At the time the Pill was raising concerns about its side effects, and Peter thought it an imposition to don a condom. Aschkin complied, and neither of them much minded the inconvenience of interrupting their caresses for Aschkin to skip into the bathroom to install the contraption.

They started teaching together in Wichita, and Aschkin felt satisfied professionally, but gradually she began to notice that something was missing in their daily life. Peter could not take seriously her being a Muslim; indeed, he seemed not to take any religious affiliation seriously. "We're human beings," he kept saying, as one might expect from a professor who lectured every day on human rights. With her family far away and virtually no Muslims in university positions in the USA, Aschkin felt isolated.

And then she began to notice something else, some slight differences in culture between her Turkish and European background and Peter's highly defined American personality. They worked hard, they had seminars over dinner, they went to conferences; but after eight years of marriage Aschkin could not recall a single laugh they had enjoyed together. Peter had a fiercely serious approach to his field. Once he got into a major dispute with an African scholar about whether female circumcision was a violation of human rights. The African insisted that Westerners should defer more to the local customs of African tribes. Peter was outraged. He insisted that Western values should prevail.

Aschkin was unsure about the basis of his strong convictions. She pointed out to him that both Jews and Muslims believed in male circumcision, and recalled a joke she had heard in Germany about a moel, the rabbi who circumcised the foreskin of Jewish males on the eighth day after birth. The moel set up a shop, and in the shop window he displayed a bunch of watches. A customer went in one day to buy a watch. The moel said he did not have any.

"Then why do you put the watches in the window?"

"What would you put in the window if your were a moel?"

Peter did not laugh. "This is serious business," he replied.

"Oh, really?" Aschkin said. "And you personally are going to make all those African women grateful to you for their improved sex lives?" She suspected that Peter's commitment to African women was in fact very thin. She felt strongly about the issue, largely because the circumcision of young adults was a big issue for orthodox Muslims. But she was dubious about Peter's taking the conventional line of favoring individual sexual gratification. Aschkin knew that the balance could shift away from respect for the rights of women toward greater appreciation for communal autonomy. Peter was, she thought, a fair weather human rights advocate.

But Peter had little patience for these conversations and easily lost his bearings. "Who else is supposed to change the world—God?" he snapped.

"Look," Aschkin said, "I feel lucky if two colleagues read my articles on tax theory. I refuse to take myself so seriously, and besides, what do you think an intellectual is? Someone who knows better than everyone else what's right and wrong? An intellectual—that is you, my dear, and that is me—is someone who likes to play with ideas." Once the word "play" came to her lips, it haunted her. She started translating into the languages she knew. *Spielen, oynamak, jouer, jugar.* That was what life should be about, she thought.

And then there was the subject of children. Peter typically avoided the question by talking about the sorry state of the world. "No place to bring up our child," he would say. Then later, when the child question came up after several years of a stable *modus vivendi*, he would say, "Why rock the boat? We're getting along fine as it is."

For a few years, Aschkin did not mind the deferral and the constant hassle of inserting the diaphragm before having sex. But then she decided secretly to stop using it. She would go into the bathroom and come back out and eagerly join Peter in bed. Her plan was to get pregnant and then present him with a *fait accompli*. This was not so very different, she told herself, from the wiles displayed by women in the book of Genesis, when the important issue was to secure the children they needed to be full members of the community.

While Aschkin saw her path toward fulfillment in classical Biblical terms, Peter readily accepted the values by which modern men proved their valor and gained respect. He was ambitious in the conventional corporate sense. For him, the next best thing to changing the world was to get a job at a higher-status law school. He angled for a job on the East Coast. This required publishing articles in prestigious journals, attending conferences in New York and Boston, developing email ties with the leaders in the field. It was not cool, however, to speak openly of his ambitions.

Eventually the call came. "Would you like to come as a visiting professor for one year to Regina Law School?" These were the words he had waited to hear. He responded coolly and negotiated with Dean Rachel White to secure an offer for Aschkin as well. When he broke the news to her, she asked, "Both of us?"

"Yes, both of us."

But she had not had the call herself, and this time, so many years on from their first meeting, her sense of being dependent was beginning to nag at her. She said she would go, but resolved to herself that this would be the last time that she would let herself be treated as his tag-along.

The move to Regina temporarily made her secret agenda to become pregnant less urgent. There was the new apartment, the new people to meet, the adjustments to the new city. Their circumstances at Regina turned out to be more engaging than expected. Aschkin found bright, motivated, Wall Street-bound students who were drawn to her courses. She became a popular teacher, and Peter flourished by mimicking the lines he heard from the other human rights advocates at Regina.

The deanship unexpectedly became vacant when Rachel White received a call from the White House and agreed to a judicial appointment. Two veteran members of the faculty started competing for the deanship, but both had accumulated so many enemies over the years that neither had a chance of securing a majority vote from the faculty. The centrists, led by the international law group in coalition with the clinical professors, hit upon the idea of appointing Peter as a compromise. In fact, he was the ideal candidate: charming, sociable, just good enough a scholar to protect the reputation of the deanship, and, most importantly, wearing a patina of intellectual conviction. The power-brokers in the faculty sensed that his moods would shift with the majority and therefore his candidacy caught on quickly. Even Adam Gross, though he belonged to no particular block on the faculty, supported him. And then, after Peter's election by a strong majority, there was little controversy about appointing Aschkin to an associate professorship. In some people's view she was a better scholar than her husband.

Over the next two years they began to feel some strains in their marriage. Perhaps Peter was disturbed that he could not do much more on a professional level for Aschkin. It did not occur to him that trying to foster her independence with a child might awaken their dormant erotic life. For Aschkin's part, the absence of eroticism in daily life ate away at her spirit on many levels. She did not know how to describe this spare and *spröd* way of life—she needed the German word for Peter's dry and prudish manner. Then she recalled reading about the earnest, joyless life of the Protestant work ethic. Perhaps they were lost in a culture in which material success would reveal whether they were among the chosen for salvation. Whatever it was, the style of life differed from everything she had known in Turkey and in Catholic southern Germany. There wasn't even a naked mixed sauna in Manhattan.

In the summer of 2000, as the graduate students arrived for their introductory courses, Peter and Aschkin had just returned from their regular two weeks at a summer rental in Sag Harbor. Peter loved vacations on Long Island because they gave him a chance to hobnob with the well-connected. Aschkin detested the bourgeois routine. She could not understand the attraction of playing tennis on private courts, strolling on the beach and dressing for cocktail parties. She longed for the solitude of wandering among the old churches of Italy or even for the familiarity of revisiting the grand mosques in Istanbul that she had seen so often as a child. One day it occurred to her that there was something else about the churches and mosques that she missed. They were the symbols of a mood, a disposition toward the world—of openness at the end of a dark vault. Life was closing in on her, as though she were in a tunnel groping for an opening, struggling to be born.

3

Law and Birthing

WHEN ADAM ARRIVED in his office after his first class there was a message on his phone from the dean's secretary. "Dean Levenger would like to see you this morning as soon as you get in." Adam was amused by the formality of the notice and pondered what it might be about as he walked up to the seventh floor, where Peter held court. As he walked into the inner sanctum, he saw Peter Levenger sitting with Ann O'Sullivan, professor of legal history and adviser to the law review. Adam clicked his heels in mock-Germanic style and said, "*Jawohl, mein Dekan.*"

"Not funny," said the blue suit. Ann gave him the same message with a frown.

Professor O'Sullivan was a tall woman with thick red hair, a flat chin and ruddy complexion. She strode rather than walked, and she had great charm and could turn a clever phrase. She had grown up in Boston, the daughter of a Boston University law professor and granddaughter of a Boston cop, and had worked summers in admin jobs at Harvard Law School. She frequently dropped allusions that eluded Adam; he was never quite sure what she meant with her smart English idioms and Irish colloquialisms. Once she had referred to the library's display case of recent faculty publications as "Snow White's glass coffin." Adam had pondered the expression several times but he could not get it. Like Peter, Ann O'Sullivan had a sense of where the power lay, and always seemed to be allied with the many against the few. Adam's strong-minded will to be original often put him in the category of the few—sometimes even a minority of one pitted against the majority vision of teaching and scholarship. Even if he had wanted to, he could not make the feminists on the faculty to trust him.

Dean Levenger stood up and walked toward Adam, waving a piece of paper at him. "I'm not happy about this criminal law exam," he said. Adam was surprised: the dean almost never expressed a personal opinion in faculty matters. "Many students are about to come in here and complain."

"They're 'about' to come?" Adam asked, with a philosopher's attention to logical connectives.

"I mean, they are coming any minute."

"Oh, really? What makes you think that?"

Ann O'Sullivan looked nervous. She uncrouched herself and, sitting up tall, spoke as though from the judicial bench. "Well, they have complained to me on the law review."

"Which exam are you talking about?"

"Criminal law from last spring," the dean and Ann replied in unison.

"Give me a pause—I mean, a break," says Adam, recalling Charlotte with a sense of pleasure. "It was the first time I taught the course."

"They are not complaining about your competence but about the tone of your exam. It is perverse and anti-female."

"Why should they complain to you and not to me?" Adam asked, in feigned puzzlement.

"We have a gender consciousness-raising group on the law review," answered Ann. "The women get together and discuss their experience of oppression in the law school. They found your exam about submissive males killing fetuses both offensive and oppressive— sado-masochistic. They were so upset during the exam, they couldn't concentrate."

"The women you're talking about all did well or they would not have made law review," Adam parried. "They must have gotten a good grade in the subject."

"We are also concerned about the women who did less well," Ann replied.

"Oh, are you speaking for all women? I wish you had made that comment in my class. It would have given me an easy target."

Ann looked at Peter as if to say, Didn't I tell you about this guy? "Let's face it," she persisted, "your exam is degrading to women. I'm particularly offended by the question in which the victim tells her doctor she wants to send her attacker a thank-you note."

"What's offensive about that?"

"Please! This man attacks her, kills her baby, and she wants to send him a thank-you note? Do you think women are sick?"

"Some women must be, otherwise there would be no work for psychologists," Adam said flippantly. "And for the record, I want to note that you said 'baby.' Don't you think 'fetus' is the correct word?"

"OK, fetus—but we think you enjoyed indulging in the idea that the victim was willing to have an abortion even if it meant being assaulted and beaten by a stranger."

"Well, it's possible, isn't it? There are cases like that. I just read about one in which a girl in Minnesota asked her boyfriend to hit her in the stomach with a baseball bat. She was too ashamed to go to an abortion clinic. But you think I enjoy these stories more than a normal person would? Ann, I didn't know you were trained in psychology. Shall I lie on the couch and tell you how I feel about women? We can start with my older sister Noga. She gave me baths when I was a child. Do you want to hear more?"

Peter was getting exasperated. "Can't you take this seriously for a minute? We live in an age when we don't offend certain kinds of people—minorities, blacks, women, gays. We *do not offend them*, get it?"

"What about Jews?"

"Don't be ridiculous!" Ann raised her voice. "Half the faculty is Jewish. How many of our colleagues are black or female or gay?"

She had a point—the numbers were embarrassingly low, maybe ten per cent altogether. Adam tacked with the wind. Ever the philosopher, he could not resist. "Well, how do we know when they are offended? Is their saying so enough to prove that they are, in fact, offended?"

"No, but in this case I think the delight you display in killing fetuses and portraying the female victims as perverse is enough to get a reasonable woman very upset and make it difficult for her to concentrate in an exam."

Adam began to glimpse the twilight zone between reason and slapstick. He didn't know exactly what he was feeling. Was it anger and outrage? Or was it amusement at the absurdity of the situation? Finally, he inquired, "Do you know anything about the issues being tested by the exam?"

Levenger patted his brow with a paper napkin left over from his morning coffee and stood up. "It doesn't really matter. We have these complaints and I have to do something about them. For the time being I don't want you to talk to any of the students from that class. I'm going to consult university counsel about whether this exam constitutes sexual harassment."

"You've got to be kidding. What the hell does this have to do with sexual harassment?"

"Professor O'Sullivan and Kathy Kong, our new colleague, claim that an exam probing matters embarrassing to women puts them at a disadvantage in the grading process. This is a form of unequal treatment made unlawful by Title IX of the Civil Rights Act prohibiting discrimination in the workplace. Haven't you read your MacKinnon?"

Adam felt two breaths away from a guffaw. "And you, Peter, what do you believe?" He forced himself to observe the scene as though he were writing a novel about academic life. The confrontation gave him delicious material.

"I don't know what I believe. That is why I want to talk to counsel."

"And what if this poor Argentine immigrant can show you from the grading sheet that the women performed just as well in the class as the men?"

"That wouldn't prove anything," interjected Ann. "And please try not to be so macho about all this. Perhaps the women should have performed much better. After all, their LSAT scores are, on the whole, higher."

Adam realized that Peter would not take a stand before he saw how the faculty lined up on the two sides of the dispute. The dean walked over to the desk and patted a stack of papers as though gently reassuring them. "No macho here, no macho here," he said in a mockingly gentle tone. He smiled at Ann as he passed her, but she pretended not to notice.

When Adam opened the door to leave, he found Chen Horowitz waiting in the anteroom. This was the first time he had seen her standing up; she appeared taller and slightly more imposing than she had in her seat at the back of the amphitheater. "You're waiting for the dean too?" he asked with an avuncular smile. Chen nodded in embarrassment, and he wondered if she was there to complain about his flirting with Charlotte.

As Adam drifted down the halls back toward his office, he began to wonder why he had gotten himself caught in this crossfire about abortion and feticide. As if the exam were not enough, he was concerned now about his next class, scheduled to start in little over an hour. He had time for a quick sandwich in his room while he was reviewing his notes for it. The students were required to read his translation of a 1927 German case on abortion. It was the subject of abortion that had drawn him to the case. But he had a larger point in mind—about the role of moral principles in overcoming legislative rulings. This was precisely the point that Joerg had raised when he'd asked him about the "dogmas" of American law. Adam too was concerned about these dogmas—but he would formulate the concern in a different idiom: as moral principles that could override legislative judgments. This is what I intend to teach, he said to himself over and over again.

But am I kidding myself? he began to wonder. The case is still fundamentally about abortion and the value of human life. How can I avoid these subjects and pretend that I'm only interested in the power of the courts to make judgements overriding the legislative prohibition of abortion? Am I just standing still and enjoying the power of my tango partner to decide for herself whether she will kick in a *gancho* or execute an *ocho*? If I'm interested in the basic values of our culture, in issues of life and death, what is the point of all my analogies about legislature and courts? This means I have to deal with religion in class. How can we talk about life and death *without* addressing the influence of religion? This is the first question asked in every religious culture: what is the nature of a human being? What is our purpose on this planet?

He paused and asked himself, Why am so confused about this? I haven't been in five years of analysis for nothing. In the 20 minutes remaining before class, Adam began to reflect on why—out of all the questions he might ask on a criminal law exam, out of all the cases to pick for his class—why did he dwell on issues of abortion and feticide?

His mind drifted back to Sara, her questions about the meaning of life, and his own struggle over the morality of abortion. After they had been dancing together for a year, she had made it clear to him that she was keen to take their relationship further. Her friends in the beat scene had already offered up their virginity to willing takers, and in the way of young people she was worried that she would be ostracized if she could not talk about her own adventures in bed. Adam was her best prospect. He was equally inexperienced and hungry. One evening they had gone for a walk along the Rio de la Plata and, after kissing a few times, Adam had got past her knee socks and managed to get her prone on the stone path by the river. It was over almost before they got their clothes off. But the first compact, made with dispatch, enabled them to relax and to explore each other's bodies in the quiet of Sara's apartment near the tango cafés in San Telmo. She had a double bed in a little alcove off her main room. That alcove was where Adam discovered his sexual prowess, testing his abilities and his limits, but he never thought much about whether these gymnastic sexual acts were gratifying for Sara.

She hadn't complained, though, seeming more interested in instructing Adam about the books he should read than in her own sexual pleasure. She had told him he must read the philospher Martin's Buber's *I and Thou* without delay, and she would raise metaphysical issues of the sort that Adam had never heard before. The meaning of life and death was always on her agenda.

Many years later, on a lecture tour in Poland, an elegant old woman who called herself the Princess Marissa had asked Adam, flirtatiously, why he had become an intellectual. He had answered, almost without thinking. "To get girls, of course." Now he realized that perhaps it was the other way around. The girl had got him first, and then seduced him a second time with the power of ideas. Perhaps she is the only authority I have ever accepted, he conceded to himself as he roamed the corridors before the beginning of his class.

Little rituals reminded him constantly of Sara. Once, when she had read one of his English papers, she'd circled every use of the word "such." "Don't say 'in such a situation,' tell me what the situation is." Though Adam had by now published thousands of pages in English, he systematically avoided the word. Every act of omission reminded him of the way his English grammar was born in a little alcove off a main room in San Telmo.

When the college term had come to an end, Adam had reluctantly given up his multi-layered tutorial with Sara to return to his parents in Palermo. She had gone to the family ranch in La Pampa for her vacation. As the summer passed, he tried to think about what it meant to be different and whether he had it in him to choose a life of spiritual "otherness." He read and read all the Buber he could find and then turned to Hermann Hesse. Bolstered by his high school study of the language, he even read *Narcissus and Goldmund* in German. He found himself identifying with Hesse's monks, who had retreated from the world in order to search for the meaning behind seemingly pointless games like *Das Glasperlenspiel*, the "glass bead game." For Buenos Aires in the early 1970s, this was about as thorough an education in mysticism as you could get.

One day, when Sara was at her *campo* with her family, Adam had received a letter from her. A strange feeling of foreboding had made him put off opening it. When he finally did, he gasped and exclaimed, "*Señor del Mundo!*" His mother overheard him and gently probed. He admitted that the letter was from his girlfriend. His mother intuited, correctly, that the issue was pregnancy.

In those days, in Church-controlled Argentina as elsewhere, the first thought that occurred to an honorable young man in these situations was marriage. To his relief, though, Sara had written that she was not interested in any contract of permanency. What self-respecting beatnik would have been?

So what could they do? Together they went to see a friend of the family, Leo, who was a doctor and a lawyer, and explained the situation. Leo said, "Get an abortion. You pay for it, but don't put anything in writing." These words had made a deep impression on the young romantic who thought of himself as an "intellectual," above the games that common people played. "Wow, a crime," he had thought. "This guy is telling me to commit a crime." In the language of Hesse, it had brought him from the plane of Narcissus down to the earthly level of Goldmund.

They had gone ahead with the illegal abortion. Adam sent the money and then heard nothing. His mother inquired and expressed concern, but there was no news. Two years later, as Adam was beginning to fear that he, like his sister Noga, would be picked up and questioned for nothing but being a Jewish intellectual, Sara had showed up at the university and found him in front of the library. She had a new boyfriend, she said—an officer in the military. The guy was furious about the loss of the child. It was never clear to Adam whether it was really Sara or the beau who was enraged, but either way Adam felt guilty. He would never forget her indictment. "You made my child *disappear*; you are no better than those thugs in this dirty war." The combination of being forced to face the issue of losing the child and his own fears of disappearing made a permanent groove in his moral sensibility.

Several years later, after law school, after studying in Berlin, after starting to teach, Adam had begun to address the question of abortion in his conversations with colleagues and in his classes. He found himself taking a very conservative but logically rigorous position. He could not understand how the proponents of abortion distinguished between the fetus one month after birth and one month before birth. The line of birth seemed totally arbitrary to him, as it did to some radicals who contemplated the possibility of infanticide for defective infants. Of course, the pro-choice people could easily turn the tables in this kind of argument. Instead of defending their own position, they would attack the opposition by driving the inquiry into the beginning of life further and further back until they reached birth control. Many people thought the Church opposed birth control for the same reason that it opposed abortion, but Adam felt that, although the anti-abortion argument was about protecting human life, the birth control argument was not. Rather it expressed a certain, he thought peculiar, attitude about the purposes of sex. Sex had to be natural, the Church decreed: the natural function of the male organ was to procreate, not to provide enjoyment. This position seemed to reflect so much guilt about sex that Adam could not take it seriously. But the Church's view on abortion seemed, to him, to deserve much more respect.

As he pondered these thoughts, the words "Sara, Sara" flashed across his mind. My God, had she really accused him of having made her baby disappear?

He had always thought that the major figure shaping his views on abortion was Father Robert Drinan, a professor and dean at Boston College. While the debate was raging about terminating the incipient life of defective fetuses (called "eugenic abortion"), Drinan had been quoted in *The New York Times* as saying, simply, "I like ugly Americans." With this single phrase, which Adam had read in the paper, the imaginative priest had captured an unlikely convert to the cause: a young, impressionable Argentine immigrant. As far as Adam was concerned, Drinan had refuted the view that it was better not to be born at all than to be born blind or deaf or "damaged."

When he had finally met up with the anti-war priest, then running for his second term of Congress, Adam had been impressed not only by his intellect but his physicality. Father Bob, as his friends called him, exuded male libido. Drinan would speak about his visions of civil rights and social justice and then in the next breath talk about meeting a girlfriend of his youth and finding that she had grown old. Adam had seen many priestly collars on the streets of Buenos Aires, but this was the first that had seemed to restrain the sexual energy surging from a man's body. Sometimes when he eyed a priest's collar after that, his fantasies turned to an imagined secret priestly sexual life, as rich and ornamental as the Catholic altar with its pinioned naked male, dripping blood.

Christianity had never appealed to Adam in his youth. He had grown up in a secular Hungarian Jewish home where it was normal to regard priests as agents of conversion and of the destruction of the Jewish people. They were typically regarded as in league with the right wing. When Cardinal Mindszenty, one of the leaders of the 1956 uprising in Budapest, had taken refuge in the American Embassy, Adam's father Miklós had been convinced that the old prelate was a spy for the Americans.

Yet lately some aspects of the Catholic Church did beckon, with its rituals and its vaguely homoerotic brotherhood of priests and monks. Perhaps he was drawn by the possibility of sanctifying hypocrisy—espousing certain rules, like the abortion taboo, to keep the masses in line, while at the same time tacitly permitting the élite to make exceptions for themselves. Adam was savoring these thoughts of a clandestine world when he glanced at his watch. It was nearly time to go to work. In a few minutes he must speak about the 1927 German abortion case. He feared that Sara and Father Bob would flood his mind and he would end up speaking aloud his fantasies about fetuses lined up like dogs, held in place by priestly collars around their necks.

4

The Aviary

TO GET TO grips with his fears of an involuntary, embarrassing confession to the class, Adam felt that he needed a couple of shots of whisky. None was available, so he decided that a quick caffeine fix would have to do. He diverted his course via the faculty lounge, the place he privately called "the Aviary." In the course of the day, there gathered there birds of all feather and plumage, all neuroses and pathologies. Most came for distraction, the newspapers, or the machine-made java. As Adam entered on this tense day he realized that he might eventually have to call on some of these faculty, fair and fowl, as political allies.

As he grabbed a styrofoam cup he thought nostalgically about the elegant cafés in San Telmo, where no one would dream of using paper and plastic. He heard the melodies of Piazzolla in the back of his mind as he positioned the cup under the machine's espresso nozzle. Argentines had less money, he thought, but they appreciated a proper style of life. That was what the tango was all about—posing and giving a good show with the other dancers. No paper and plastic there—not even in the more modest cafeterias in the Boedo or Almagro districts, where the children of the working class danced upstairs, day and night.

He felt recurrent nausea in coping with the inelegancies of American life. The garbage left behind was too much for him. He recalled his time studying in Berlin, when the Germans had already started recycling with a gravity appropriate to religious ritual. They separated their trash and recycled with as much devotion as Orthodox Jews spent separating meat from milk. But this was not the mood of throwaway America. All the paper cups stacked up, the plastic forks supplied at every faculty lunch, the disposable paper tablecloths—it all made Adam vaguely sick.

He could not resist the mental drift back to abortion, feticide, women and the related issues. Maybe the American willingness to generate garbage was a response to the wave of feminist thought in the 1970s. The obsession then had been who was doing the dishes at home. He remembered the scorn of a feminist scholar who had once accused her colleague of "having his meals prepared for him." And if truth be told, the men of the faculty still felt the workplace was a refuge from egalitarian home life. They were not going to do more than they had to do at home—and the female members of the staff were certainly not going to come into the faculty lounge and wash the cups the men had used that day. The solution was to use real crockery as infrequently as possible. "Better a full trash can than an angry woman," Adam muttered under his breath as he filled his styrofoam cup.

The Aviary offered up a distinguished flock that early afternoon. Joining him in line was Paul Keskemeny, an emigrant from Adam's parents' home country after the defeat of the 1956 revolution. Paul had adapted well to the American scene. He specialized in American constitutional law, even though most of the Americans on the faculty were skeptical about whether any foreign-born scholar— Adam or Paul—could master the mystical essence of American constitutionalism. They might have a little trouble defining what that essence was, but they believed fervently that there was something that only they, the native speakers, understood. In his aristocratic way, Paul never allowed any of this to bother him. He walked about with his Hungarian green paisley scarf topping off his collegiate tweed sports coat. He affected perfect English, dotting his sentences with the latest expression culled from some anthology of modern idioms. He was known for paying more attention to the latest gossip about Carnegie Hall than to the rumblings of faculty intrigue.

Adam had tried to get close to Paul and even ventured an occasional phrase in Hungarian remembered from home. Paul would respond politely but always kept his distance, as though, as a "real" Hungarian, with a perfect command of the language, he was in a different class from this porteño wannabe. With his ostentatious show of culture, Paul always made Adam feel like a Jewish Latino who could never quite understand European culture. In the Aviary, rank and status became readily apparent.

Sitting nearby in a corner, drinking tea, was Ariel Colline, one of Adam's favorite colleagues because he had no comprehension of the games others played around him. Having grown up in Israel as a gay man on the margins, he had served in the army and then emigrated to France, where he had changed his name back to the French original borne by his grandfather. For a while he had run a furniture boutique on Rue des Rosiers in the Marais district in Paris; for the first time he felt comfortable with who he was. In his spare time he would go to the Sorbonne and listen to lectures on law. He realized that the entire subject of discrimination, in particular discrimination against gays, had yet to receive much attention in conventional French law faculties. Then he heard that in New York several scholars were working in the new field of "queer law." He had to find out what they were saying. He came for a year and ended up staying five, writing a doctorate at a law school near the Village—the neighborhood closest in character to the Marais that he could find. Even though he was now prospering in his academic career, Ariel still had some tics and habits he had picked up in his self-doubting youth. He still hounded his friends, self-deprecatingly but disarmingly, with the question, "Do you think I am the worst scholar in the world?" Adam thought of him as a lovable child.

In a far corner of the lounge, curled up with a book, sat the half-Nigerian, half-Turkish Nkwame Mavioglu. Tall, slender and well-groomed, he acted as though he came straight from the lecture halls at Oxford, always dressed appropriately, always ready to maintain his distinctive Oxonion accent. He supposedly spoke five African languages, but no one at Regina was known to have heard them. He spoke English with his Irish wife. He came across as the consummate liberal, the man who believed he could define himself, regardless of heritage, nationality, language or family. Adam found him enchanting, largely because he was the mirror opposite of the self-indulgent Hungarian Argentine Jew who could never escape from his mix of historically determined identities. Nkwame and Adam had an unexpected affection for each other, derived largely from their mutual recognition as opposite species in the Aviary. Neither thought of the other as "fowl;" they were as close as they could get without their well-defined plumage coming between them.

Adam cherished these characters, bird by bird. He needed them from time to time as an audience, and, the way things had gone this morning, he knew that he might have to call on them more than in the past.

That afternoon Adam noticed the foreigners present in the Aviary, all residents or visitors to the United States. But there was another side to the room, less appealing to him. Almost as though it was all occurring behind his back—as if he was invisible—Ann O'Sullivan was engaged in conversation with a close colleague, a philosopher named Julien Wright. Joining them were assorted other Americans who constituted her political base. They made up the core of the faculty—the ordinary people, like Pat Graham, decent people with no special pretensions, no special claims of difference. They would share Ann's views about the "correct" politics of avoiding offense to minorities.

As much as Adam tried to concentrate on his friends, one person from the other side of the room never escaped his range. No matter which way he turned, Aschkin Yilmaz was there. He noticed the way she prepared her coffee calmly, with no sign of repulsion at the uniquely American combination of machines, paper, efficiency and waste. He focused on the way she wore her hair pulled back in a schoolmarm bun, prim and proper. She belonged to neither clique in the lounge. She was totally absorbed in her own world of thought. The others seemed not to matter, and Adam least of all.

Professor Gross hurried off to his next class. The demands of his intensive introductory course required him to teach twelve classes over eight weekdays with a weekend in the middle, which meant two classes most days—it was something like boot camp for new graduate students. His colleagues, teaching on the average of five hours a week, had more time to perch and gossip in the Aviary.

5

Dogmas We Live By

A S HE APPROACHED the classroom, Adam felt less afraid now of a spontaneous confession. He would concentrate on the topic at hand—trying to explain the difference between the civil law and the common law. The students were already gathered and chatting animatedly as their new professor walked down the center aisle. He noticed Chen engaged in an intense conversation with Charlotte. Was she questioning how the French girl would defend herself if the professor tried to make another advance in class? Joerg Mueller was talking to a young Japanese student. Was this a postwar Axis? How absurd, thought Adam. My paranoia is showing again. But little groups are forming, and this means that drama is brewing. Good.

He began, "In the last class Mr. Mueller asked me whether I was going to teach you the dogmas of American law. Yes, I am, but first I want to give you a feeling for why lawyers in Germany and Christian theologians are both drawn to the word 'dogma.' The term refers simply to the teachings of the wise. The question is whether those with wisdom have a role in defining and interpreting the law. After all, isn't the law simply the command of the sovereign, the command of the Parliament or the local legislature?"

"That is what many people think in France," injected Charlotte: "*La loi* is the command of the state, no more, no less."

"Yes," said Joerg, "but these are not the dogmas of the law that I had in mind. They are about the law but they do not help to learn the law." He was refining his position to great effect.

"I agree," replied Adam. "A great philosopher like H.L.A. Hart would not think of himself as developing dogmas about the law. He had theories about the meaning of the word 'law' and the structure of the legal system. But he would be offended at being described as laying down dogmas. To get closer to the idea of dogma as ideological premise of the law, we have to turn to areas of the law where religious beliefs are implicit and indispensable. That is why I have chosen this German case on abortion."

He looked around. "Is anybody familiar with section 218 of the German Criminal Code?" Several hands went up. "What did the statute say in 1927?"

Another German student, named Grigor Krysztal, responded to the open question. "This is a famous provision. Every German woman has associations with the number 218. In those days it said that if you underwent an abortion you would be punished by a minimum of six months in jail. No defenses."

"You say 'no defenses.' What about if the mother's life was in danger?"

"Actually, you are right," Grigor conceded. "The law did provide for an excuse called 'personal necessity.' It applied only on behalf of the person in danger. But it did not help the doctor who prescribed and executed an abortion to save the life of the mother."

"Why not?"

"Well, 'personal necessity' applies only on behalf of the person who has a gun to his head or who must steal a loaf of bread to survive. The doctors are not in personal danger. They commit the abortion because they think it is the right thing to do."

"Very good. But what about self-defense? One person is entitled to defend another against unlawful attacks. Isn't the fetus like a gunman threatening the life of the mother?" Adam asked.

Gad Menachem, a Hasidic student from Lakewood, New Jersey, almost leapt out of his seat. Adam had a hunch what was to follow.

"One of the greatest scholars of the law, Maimonides, wrote that in this situation the fetus is 'like an aggressor.' Not exactly an aggressor, but *like* an aggressor. Self-defense requires a real aggressor. Abortion then is, strictly speaking, not self-defense. But the highest value in Jewish beliefs is the saving of human life, and therefore it is all right to kill a fetus threatening the life of the mother." As he finished speaking, he swept his right earlock behind his ear.

Marga Estevez, from Colombia, spoke up for the first time. "Why is saving the life of the mother the only thing that counts? I think it is equally important to save the life of the fetus." When Adam looked her way, she flashed him a knockout smile. The mood was heating up. He seized the moment to get everyone involved.

"In this situation, as in many others, you must consult your intuition before you think about the law. What do you *feel* is the right answer? Let me ask for a show of hands. How many of you think that in this situation it would be ethically proper for a doctor to prescribe and perform an abortion whether the statute allowed it or not?"

Many hands shot up—it seemed like the majority.

"What if I told you," said the professor, "that I had reservations about the decision?"

"You have to be kidding," Chen Horowitz called out from the back of the room. The cactus style of some Israelis—thorns on the outside, sweet on the inside, the reason they were sometimes called Sabras after the prickly pear—amused Professor Gross. I will have faith in her sweet side, he told himself, as she continued, "The fetus is just an organ of the body that sometimes needs to be removed—like the appendix."

"Now I think you must be putting me on, Chen. What would you say if someone came along and maliciously kicked a woman with the intention of killing her fetus?" The controversial exam question had popped into his head.

"That's different," said Chen. "That is a malicious attack. The guy is guilty."

"But what is he guilty of? Is it an attack solely against the mother, or against the fetus as well?"

"Well, it's more serious than an assault against the mother," Chen replied. "It's an attack against the fetus too."

"You mean it's an attack against the appendix?"

"No," conceded Chen, getting the point of the Adam's Socratic questioning. "I guess you're right. The fetus must be worth something on its own terms."

"Yes, that is the view of the Supreme Court in *Roe v Wade*. The closer the fetus gets to birth, the more valuable it becomes in its own right. At the beginning of pregnancy, for the first trimester, the woman has the right to abort. That is implicit in the constitutional concept of privacy. In the second trimester the rights of the fetus are balanced against the rights of the woman. In the third trimester, after the fetus is viable—i.e. can exist outside the womb—the protection of the fetus is the greatest interest. This is all the 1927 German case is saying. We have to balance the rights of fetus against those of the mother."

Joerg was startled. "But where do they get the authority to do that? There is nothing in the German Penal Code to permit this balancing. Since 1975 we have had a special provision called 'necessity.'"

"Yes, precisely: the 1975 code is based on the 1927 abortion case. First the court decided, and then the legislature wrote that decision into the law. It was something like a reverse tango." Adam enjoyed the analogy, though he was not sure the class was ready for it.

"We know about this," interjected Rodrigo from Brazil. "Our professors, our captains of the law, wrote about it. It is called *justificación supralegal*." This time Adam was more amused than irritated by the reference to his fictitious military rank. He let it pass.

"You are right about the Spanish term *supralegal*. What does it mean?" asked Adam.

"It means 'above the written law.' It comes from higher principles."

"How is that possible in a codified system of law?"

This, as Adam saw it, was the key question. His purpose was to wean students away from the simple-minded view that the civil law, the Continental European system, was based exclusively on the law laid down by the legislature in a code. He believed firmly that judges made law in the so-called civil law countries just as much as in the common law world, but that they did it in a different way, by elaborating the basic dogma of the legal culture. He could have said this directly but he held back, wanting the students to discover the point themselves.

"Note that opinion in the 1927 case discusses two different theories of possible justification for the abortion," he continued therefore. "One is called the policy theory, and the other the balancing theory. Where do these theories come from?"

Adam looked around the room to see whether he could engage a new voice in the discussion. He noticed Charlotte in the front row looking decidedly less fetching than in the first class. The subject of abortion seemed to have struck close to home. Then his eyes caught a quiet, fortyish man sitting pensively on the far right side. The lines on his face and his earnest gaze reminded him of Father Bob.

"May I ask your name and your opinion, sir?"

"Yes—my name is Jaime Sullivan. As a former priest I have a particular perspective on what is going on here. Before the Catholic Church decided that life begins at conception, there were many different theories in play about when the fetus becomes a human being. Some scholars defined the idea that the soul was implanted at quickening; others said that life began at the time of implantation. These and other opinions competed for attention in the higher echelons of the Church. Finally the ruling bishops opted for the view that the soul is implanted at the time of conception.

"Something similar is happening here. The scholars have advanced various theories for justifying conduct beyond the statutory law. One theory is based on good motives—that is called the 'policy' theory. The other theory is based on the objective 'balancing' of competing interests. In this case the court chose the balancing theory and it thereby killed off the competing theories, very much as the Church had made a choice among the competing scholarly theories on the origins of human life."

Adam was stunned by this shared understanding. Rather than slip into effusive praise, which would have distracted everyone from Sullivan's message, he followed up with a linguistic point. "Do you know how German scholars refer to their various theories?"

Jaime Sullivan paused and Mueller shot up his hand. "We call it *Lehre* or *Dogmatik*. These terms refer to the teachings of the scholars. That is why I wanted to know whether you will teach us the dogmas of American law."

"The only problem is that, here, we don't talk about the teachings of scholars with the same respect. Where do you think this idea comes from in German law?"

"I'm not sure," Sullivan jumped in, "but I *am* surprised at how much the development of German law resembles the evolution of Church doctrine. The priests debate an issue, form differing schools— say, about the virgin birth—and then the choice is ultimately made by the Pope."

"It is the same thing in the Talmud," added Gad Menachem eagerly. "The school of Hillel debated everything with the school of Shammai, and at a certain point the tradition opted for Hillel on most points. But we retain the memory of Rabbi Shammai's unaccepted teachings, just as the 1927 German decision honors the policy theory by mentioning it before rejecting it."

"Hmm," murmured Jaime to himself, "you don't kill off the alternative, rejected theories as heresies. Would that the Catholic Church were so tolerant!"

Chen frowned at the shared understanding of the religiously sensitive members of the class. But Adam was pleased. "You know I don't come here to teach but to learn. It's worth listening to you."

Joerg looked over at Chen as if to say, we shared our doubts about this guy but maybe he is OK? Most of the Japanese and Chinese students were puzzled by the conversation. They had never heard of professors who came to class for the sake of learning from the students.

"We have developed an important argument," Adam continued. "The civil law traditionally does, in fact, resemble the culture of the Catholic Church, and the Church itself builds on the rabbinic tradition of scholars developing the law and guiding the people in their daily behavior. Modern Islam uses the same model of following the teachings of scholars. The scholars today are called professors and writers of civil law treatises. Imagine that: in the Continental legal culture people really respect the professors. They are bearers of the tradition. When they teach, the law listens."

Professor Gross loved making this point from the front of the room. It gave him a great sense of power to think that he was among the élite defining the law—formulating the "dogmas" of the law. And yet he hated everything authoritative in legal culture. His own anarchistic tendencies made him suspicious of anything that looked like orthodoxy. He wanted to be part of the élite defining the law—but only if that élite was the vanguard of revolution.

Several students of the English-speaking common law looked confused. They whispered among themselves, and one leaned forward. "But we all thought that in the common law we say that scholarship is a secondary authority. Statutes and cases are primary. This stuff about the learned people teaching dogmas seems undemocratic."

"You are right about the common law," said Adam encouragingly. "That *is* what we say. What we do might be different. We will have to see in practice who defines the basic concepts of the common law. The common law—in the Protestant tradition—is a decentralized system of authority. There is supposedly no hierarchy to tell us what is right and wrong." That is the way it is and I like it, Adam allowed himself to reflect a little distractedly. It makes me feel free.

"Yes," interjected Joerg, "but sooner or later some authority must decide. In the 1927 abortion case, the court decided that the balancing theory was the correct theoretical basis for recognizing the defense of necessity. That was the final word."

"Was it?" probed Adam. "Why did the German *Bundestag* affirm the result and write it into the code in 1975?"

"I guess the Parliament had the final authority, didn't they?"

"But then how could the court dare in 1927 to amend the statute by allowing a new defense of necessity?"

Adam was riding high. He was never happier than when he caught students in contradictions, forcing them to squirm in their inconsistencies. Was the fetus like the appendix or was it like a human being? Did the legislature have the authority to define the crime of abortion or not? There had been a time, in his youth, when these logical briarpatches had frightened him. If you fell in, you could never get out. He understood the need for clarity, and the fears, of those soldiers of the law who were willing to follow the orders of their lawgivers. That was the way most of his colleagues thought, he believed. For them the law was like the military, like the more militant hierarchal modes of religion. The lawgivers laid down the law and the foot soldiers followed, saying softly, "My captain, my captain."

Whatever his colleagues might really have thought, for him law was revolution. It was the opportunity to overturn existing dogmas. If he was at forefront of change, he did not mind.

"Recall the great transition in American society in the 1960s, when the courts led the Civil Rights Revolution," he said. "On a smaller scale we have this 1927 German abortion decision. Most lay people thought that Section 218 of the Penal Code defined the crime of abortion including all the reasons for relieving doctors of liability. Then came the court, backed by the scholars, and overturned the legislative judgment. Next time I will tell you more, and eventually I will show you how the 1927 German abortion case resembles the famous American case of *Marbury v Madison*. Don't forget, tonight I want you to write me your personal reflections. If you want to take a position in our discussions so far, please do so."

The students were on the edges of their seats. Some wanted more. Some looked down at their empty notebooks and wondered what they had learned. Joerg felt moved by the fast pace of the argument. Marga, Charlotte and Chen fell into step on their way out and agreed to a cup of coffee. Jaime lingered in a mood of spiritual reflection. The reactions were as varied as the hotchpotch of cases that most of them thought was the characteristic feature of American law.

As Adam exited the room among the milling students, he noticed a stranger standing 50 feet away standing in a posture of anticipation. The self-confident student stepped forward. "Hi, I'm Charlie Fairfield. I write for the *Law School Report*."

"Oh, that testimonial to the freedom of the press," teased Adam with a sardonic smile.

"OK, we're not *The New York Times*, but we're trying to beef up the paper by carrying more cutting-edge news. And I just got an assignment to write about your exam."

"Which exam?" said Adam warily.

"You know what I'm talking about. You and the dean discussed it this morning."

"What did you hear about it?" Adam suspected that Peter had leaked the story.

"Some of the feminist professors are complaining about your criminal law exam. Some of the women working over the summer spoke to the review adviser, Professor O'Sullivan, and she conferred with Visiting Professor Kathy Kong, who as you know is active in this area. They are particularly upset about the idea of a lesbian sado-masochistic cult that worships the Big Monkey and then one of the women tells one of their dependent males that they have to go out and kill fetuses in order to prevent the Big Monkey's wrath."

"Do you realize that this idea comes straight from an actual German case?" Adam asked. "The Big Monkey was called King Cat and there really was a cult that worshipped him." He paused. "I admit the Germans are sometimes pretty kinky."

"Professor Kong seems especially upset."

"I'm not sure why." Adam knew that Kathy Kong was a lesbian but did not see why this should make her less supportive. Adam always tended to think that anyone who was cast as an outsider should be his friend. The major reason he liked and supported feminists was that they too were fighting the dominant orthodoxy of society.

"Well, she thinks that this hypothetical case puts lesbians in a bad light," Charlie elaborated, "but really, that's only part of it. You give an example in which this submissive male, David, attacks a pregnant woman on the street, kicks her fetus to death, and then changes his mind and takes her to the emergency room. Then she tells her doctor that she wanted to have an abortion anyway. Don't you think that's a little over-the-top?"

"Maybe you don't realize it," Adam explained patiently but with obvious restraint, "but this case has a deep point to it. It raises an important question in the law of consent. If the woman tells her doctor after the act that she had wanted the abortion, is that the same as having consented to the attack?"

The two of them stared at one another.

"You know," said Adam, "casting for roles in exams is a little like casting in television. You can't have one group of people appearing as the bad guys all the time, but nor can you go to the other extreme and treat certain groups of outsiders as too pure ever to be evil."

Several of Adam's students caught a word or two as they passed by. They looked back over their shoulders.

"Are you actually interested in these legal and philosophical issues, Charlie?" Adam challenged, since the young man still seemed to have nothing to say.

"Not really. I'm just writing the story."

Adam was reminded of an incident several years earlier, when a group of black students had complained that he was paying too much attention to the "white" point of view. When the *Report* had threatened to run a story, he'd told them point blank that he would sue for libel. He had soon had a line of students at his door apologizing for any possible misunderstanding. He tried the same gambit now. "Look, Fairfield, if you a run a story claiming that I gave a sexist or misogynist exam, I'll sue you and your paper for defamation."

Charlie Fairfield did not look impressed. "Thanks for your time, Professor," he said blithely as he darted past him down the hall. Adam was slightly shaken. He began to think he might need advice from a wiser person. And there was only one person he knew who qualified.

6
Domestic Scenes

WHEN ASCHKIN RETURNED home in the late afternoon and opened the door to the apartment, she was overwhelmed by sights she had barely noticed for years. Near the door there was a picture of Peter and his family when he was ten, set in a wide gold frame with the names of the family etched on the sides. On the other side, a floor-to-ceiling bookcase housed many of the books that they had bought together, including some they had read and discussed in Germany. A richly textured red and blue Persian rug stretched from the entrance to the living room, where Aschkin looked with new eyes at the furniture she and Peter had chosen together. There was the slightly comical, ornately arched armoire she called *Schränkchen*, or "chest" in the German diminutive, a prize found in a flea sale in Ulm when they were traveling in Southern Germany. They had bargained fiercely, got it for a song and, gleeful about their business acumen, lugged it on top of their car all the way to the shipping company office in Hamburg. There were cushions in red and white embroidered slips, souvenirs from a trip to Hungary. The pile of glass cherries spread out seductively on a large serving dish was an idea they had conceived together upon seeing the cherries in a shop window in Venice. Aschkin treasured the reminders of their many adventures.

And then there was her collection of bottles of all different shapes and colors. Wherever they traveled Aschkin tried to find a bottle or jar characteristic of the local culture. Some of them were just milk containers, a few Coca-Colas written in different scripts; there was a tulip-shaped and a turquoise jar, and an opaque, squat bottle used for carrying incense in a Buddhist temple. All these material things held their memories. Peter and Aschkin spending nights in different beds in different lands, sometimes making love, sometimes not; their moments of contact, of anger, of disappointment—these artefacts had witnessed all.

Aschkin realized that her emotions were probably being affected by the hormone shots she was taking. This sudden sentimentality must be one of those reactions. At the beginning of the summer, before they'd gone to Sag Harbor, she had confessed to Peter that she had not been using the diaphragm for several years, but still had not become pregnant. Typically, in his all-understanding style, he had not been not angry. He'd even agreed to go with her to see his friend Roger Bluestone, a gynecologist and fertility specialist on East 76th Street. He did not really want a child, but he recognized the principle—women had a right to bear children—and was smart enough not to get in her way.

Roger had examined both of them and run tests on Peter's sperm. He had concluded that, while Aschkin was perfectly capable of conceiving, Peter's sperm were of borderline motility. It was extremely unlikely that Aschkin could conceive by any means other than *in vitro* fertilization. Aschkin had thought it was worth a try, and begun a series of medical tests to determine whether she was a sound candidate. She'd passed the stringent tests and, after her last period, she had started receiving FSH hormone shots to stimulate the growth of follicles in her ovaries and increase the production of eggs. When she reached the stage of ovulation, Bluestone's staff would remove the eggs and attempt to fertilize them in a test tube with Peter's sperm, several samples of which they would already have collected, treated to remove inactive cells and fluids, and the best samples frozen. The whole thing needed close supervision. Though it was not easy for her to check in every morning in Bluestone's office, she got there and managed to keep up with her regular obligations.

Because of the pressure on her schedule, she was grateful as she arrived home to notice that Peter was cooking dinner. It was a simple meal of pasta and salad, but it was welcome nonetheless. True, his cooking was bland in comparison to the rich dishes she could get on the streets in Istanbul or even the good home cooking she had enjoyed and learned in Germany, but the gesture meant something to her.

She went up to him in the kitchen and put her hand on his back as he washed the salad leaves. "I'm feeling very close to you, Peter, but something is missing," she said. "I'm getting these hormone shots on a daily basis, I feel my moods changing, my body is preparing to conceive new life..."

"What is it you want to do?"

"I know this will sound strange to you, but I think we should pray together."

"Oh, really? Where, in a mosque?"

"No, we couldn't sit together in a mosque anyway. I heard there is a very hip Jewish congregation on 88th Street. They sing a lot, they dance the way I remember the Sufis dancing at home. Will you go there with me? If not, we could pray right here in the living room."

"My God," he said, appalled. "No—I mean, *your* God. I don't know any prayers, Aschkin. I'm afraid if I tried to pray I would look like the kneeling Christians you see in movies. What is going on in this country? Billy Graham prays at the White House. And now professors have started devoting their classes to religious themes. An Israeli student came to to see me today and told me she was very offended by it."

"What did you tell her?"

"That the professor can do what he wants in his class. You know who it is, don't you?" She shook her head. "Who else but Adam Gross? And he's already in enough trouble over his exam last spring. Exams are one thing—I have the right to question those; they influence the way people get jobs. But his classroom is sacred."

"Do you really mean *sacred*?" She was still thinking about prayer.

"Not really—academic freedom and all that. I mean, the classroom is his business. Now you come home and tell me you want to pray with me. There's a religious revival passing over the law school—a wave of irrationality gripping all of us. Just when I've gotten sick of all the fundamentalists like Pat Robertson in politics..."

* * * * *

As Adam left the law school building and crossed the campus, he passed the focal point of Regina Law School: the sundial that had become the scene of many demonstrations over the years. He recalled stories about the great rebellion in 1968 in which the students had occupied the administration building. His friend Sydney Morgenbesser—then a youthful, energetic philosophy professor, now aging and sick— had been one of the leaders in the days when the Regina students were in the vanguard of protest against the university's building plans, perceived as encroaching on the black neighborhoods to the north and east of the campus. As a student in Argentina, Adam had sympathized with the student riots in France and later in the USA. Even before he came to study with Sydney he had known of Sydney's courageous stands against the police in the riots of 1968.

He headed south a few blocks to where Sydney now lived, though "living" was a generous word to describe Sydney's state of infirmity. He had been bedridden for several years, and lately could no longer digest his food. His daily survival depended on the coils, tubes, tanks and masks of medicine supporting the last stages of life. There was no way of knowing on any particular visit whether Sydney would be alive or dead. Every time he rang the bell, Adam trembled. The visits reminded him of his calling on his mother in the Palermo district of Buenos Aires. She too had been confined to her bed and her wheelchair for years before she died in the late 1980s. After Adam got his American passport he had felt safe going back to visit. But each time he left to return to New York he had been worried about the call that would eventually come. When he got that final call, he was on a plane to Paris. The pilot had announced his name over the intercom after the plane landed, and he had boarded the next flight to Buenos Aires. With his father dead too and no older relatives in town, Adam now looked on Sydney as his tie to his parents' generation.

During the 1968 riots, when a lanky Sydney with flowing hair had mounted the sundial and incited the students to burn the place down, there had always been one woman who was his closest ally. This was Alice Janks, the daughter of a famous Communist labor lawyer and an activist in her own right. Where else could a leftist find love but at the sit-ins? After the end of that tumultuous time, however, they had lost each other as they both heeded other calls.

After he became a public figure, at least in the limited world of the university, Sydney had incessantly wandered the campus, cornering students and faculty on their way to class, stumping them with unanswerable quandaries, making them laugh, winning and breaking the hearts of many of the women who came under his spell. He was the local Socrates, revered as a gadfly in a campus that was growing increasingly conservative and self-centered. Almost 30 years later, after her four children and two divorces, Alice had found Sydney again. The political climate had changed, but not their shared view of the world, nor the bond born of their willingness to risk arrest and police brutality. After a fall had injured his spine and robbed Sydney, as he put, of his 'ability to run away,' he had moved in with her on 111th Street.

His 75th birthday party had been a star-cast event. He could no longer walk, but he could sit and enjoy his chocolate cake and bask in the attention. The editor of the *New York Review of Books*, Robert Silvers, was there, chatting with Edward Said, the English scholar and Palestinian activist. The philosophers Edna Margalit and Robert Nozick flirted over a nostalgic conversation about the old Jerusalem, when immigrant scholars were the role models for the young. There were Arabs, Israelis, Europeans, Americans. In the life of Sydney's mind there was not just one "people of the book." His were the people of all the books.

That was the universalist way he talked sometimes—a view of the world befitting a philosopher. Other times, he slipped into Jewish parochialism. He had grown up speaking Yiddish and loved to drop these exotic words into everyday conversation and even into his classroom spiel. His favorite word was *meshuggah*, which meant, with some affection, "crazy;" its variant, a *meshuggenah*, was a crazy person. Before he had got sick, Sydney had thought of himself as the court Jew on the Regina campus. His colleagues had seemed too assimilated to take on the part of telling Yiddish jokes all the time, or quoting the Bible as though it were *The New York Times*. He was the only one, in his eyes, who was totally to free to think and speak as he wanted. All the others, in the language later used by gays and lesbians, were "in the closet." Once he had confronted Lionel Trilling, one of the top literary critics of the 1960s and an *armoire Juif*, and said to him over a couple of drinks, "Oh, I understand your philosophy. You believe *incognito ergo sum*." This play on Descartes' famous "*cogito ergo sum*" had meant to imply that only by hiding his identity did Trilling come alive. The jokes had made Sydney a celebrity in an academic world where humor was rare; and yet, as Adam knew, it was easy to get a laugh in class. In his prime Sydney had been the best that the university had to offer—devoted to teaching, to talking, to cultivating friends. No one had cared that he did not write or publish very much. His legacy was his students.

Interested in all fields, Sydney had made a friend of his younger colleague in the law school, once his graduate student in philosophy, and tried to keep up with Adam's growing sophistication in the law.

Adam had always very much appreciated the attention. Sydney said that he was a misplaced philosopher trying to survive in the law.

As Adam entered the apartment that Wednesday afternoon, he found Sydney sitting barely propped up in a chair by his window overlooking 111th Street. He was wearing an oxygen mask, but he still could talk. He was emaciated, his body barely supporting his head, but his mind seemed as clear as it had been when in 1968 he had taken the hustings and exhorted the students to rebel. Every time Adam saw him in these bedridden years, he was reminded of the thought experiment devised by Robert Nozick, one of Sydney's star pupils. Think, Nozick had said, of a brain floating freely in a vat. The brain had all the experiences imaginable in human existence but it could not do anything. The question was whether the brain in the vat could tell the difference between actually having had an experience in the world and merely having the sensation of experience. What, in the end, would be the difference between really doing something and just feeling that you were doing it? The question stumped people because everyone knew there was a difference. The trick was explaining it.

Sydney was not exactly a mind in a vat, though his experiences were limited to those that came to him in his feeble state. Nonetheless it was apt to think of him as a perfect mind, floating free, as it were, from all physical constraints.

Seeing the oxygen mask, Adam said immediately, "I can tell you all my views about philosophy and life and you have to listen. No interruptions."

Sydney smiled and squeezed out a few words. "Yes, but before you begin, I want to tell you one thing."

"What's that?" asked Adam naïvely.

"You're wrong."

Adam laughed and started recounting his fears of a political attack based on the criminal law exam. The feminists were going to skewer him for his "insensitivity." They could not understand, he claimed indignantly, the intellectual subtlety of his exam. Sydney listened patiently, and then said, "You know the Jewish telegram? Here's how it reads: 'Start worrying now STOP. Letter follows STOP.'"

"Do you think I am too worried?"

"No, but you do not understand the issues."

"Actually," said Adam, "there is a slight problem. I think they might have a point—the feminists, that is. Some of them claim that I express a perverse interest in sado-masochism and the brutal killing of fetuses. Perhaps they're right."

"Oh...you are feeling guilty already."

"Yes."

"No need for that. Jews feel guilty about large social causes—slavery in the United States, the genocide of the Indians, the treatment of the Palestinians. This kind of small-potatoes guilt is not Jewish. You have to think big!"

"OK—what is big for women?"

"Start with the Bible." This was where Sydney always started.

"I get it," Adam said slowly, going along with his old teacher. "The men are the players. Abraham enters into a pact with God; the heirs are Isaac, Jacob and Joseph."

"Right, and you have heard about the twelve brothers but how about the sisters?"

"Only about Dinah who gets raped."

"*Voilà*," said Sydney, and closed his eyes, appearing to rest.

"I thought the issue in the law school was simply whether women were made to feel too self-conscious and could not perform on equal terms with the men."

"Yeah, yeah."

Adam could not help but clap his hands. Sydney was invoking one of his more brilliant moments in the world of philosophical debate. At a conference on linguistics, a speaker had claimed that it was very puzzling that a double negative created a positive, but that a double positive never created a negative. Sydney had stood at the back of the room and replied, "Yeah, yeah." It was probably the shortest, most effective refutation in the history of philosophy.

"Well, do you mean, 'Yeah, yeah,' you believe me or 'Yeah, yeah,' you don't believe me? I think you don't believe me."

Sydney never gave a direct answer. "Well, do you think women in the law school are going to understand the subtle message of their always being cast into the role of victims."

"Should I feel guilty?" pondered Adam.

"You don't get it. Jews always feel guilty. This proves nothing. If there were Jews on Mars, they would feel guilty?"

"Of course they would. They would be worrying about possible attacks from the feminists. Are there feminists on Mars?"

"Of course," said Sydney, "How could there be Jews without feminists?"

Adam did not like it, but he was beginning to get the point. His exam had to be understood as part of a general pattern of speech—beginning much earlier than the Bible—in which the men were the active doers, the bearers of history, and the women stood by, either applauding or suffering. "But I did not mean to demean women in writing the exam," Adam protested.

Sydney smiled. "Would that people could control the way their words are understood!"

"So am I guilty?"

"Of course you are. But that is not the important question."

This was Sydney's way. It was not psychoanalysis. It was not the teaching of a Zen master. It was the Socratic method, brilliantly conceived. He managed to direct questions back to their source. The mind floating free in space enables others to connect better with their own lives.

It was time to leave. Adam bent over and kissed Sydney on the brow, as he had used to do with his mother when parting, and slowly left the front room, winding his way through the long corridor to the door. Feeling refreshed and at peace, he descended the stairs and embraced the warm August air.

7

Returns of the Day

AFTER GRABBING A BITE of dinner at one of the local eateries, Adam walked home to his modest flat in the Regina district. He had two rooms, which always reminded him of an Oxford don's flat. One was a small sitting room, the other a bedroom with a vast view of the Hudson River stretching out before it. He liked sitting at the desk overlooking the park and the water stretching to the south.

He had an enjoyable task ahead of him. He was going to read the students' email descriptions of themselves. I wonder if any of them will tell me anything really juicy, he thought with a sneaking relish as he booted up his laptop and launched his email program. About 50 students had already responded. He surfed through them to see which ones might be interesting, and paused on the names he already knew.

His eye landed first on the notes of Marga Estevez, the woman from Colombia with the warm smile who had made a passionate defense of the fetus's rights in the last session.

Dear Professor,

My native language is also Spanish. I did my undergraduate work at the Universidad de los Andes. It is a private university in Bogota, considered the best law school in the country. The reason I mention it is that there was a professor who reminds me very much of you, or at least I hope the similarities come to life. He was named Eduardo Alvarez-Correa. If you walk into the law faculty you will see a life-size painting hanging by the entrance to the dean's office.

Professor Alvarez-Correa was like no other law professor in the history of the country. He was supposed to teach us Roman law but in fact he taught the deep relationship between spirituality and the law. He talked more about Buddhism than about Roman law. I sat there every day, transfixed. The course did something for me that the Catholic Church could never do: it made me into a religious person. That is why I now understand the position of the Church on the life of the fetus, on the equal dignity of all human life. The very existence of human life is a great gift of God, and therefore I cannot choose so easily between the life of the mother and the life of the fetus.

I know that most of the students in your class were trained to read statutes and codes and to apply them as they read them. But this is not the way of Professor Alvarez-Correa. He taught us to appreciate the inner spirit of the law, and it is this that I always now try to seek, and that I hope to learn more of from you.

Adam was stunned. He had not expected that he could evoke feelings of this depth with the discourse in class. But the expectation that all the emails might be of a similar revelatory tone was dashed as he opened one mundane message after another. Many wrote to the effect of: "I took one degree here and another degree there and I want to specialize in corporate law and get a job downtown."

But there were also some more surprises. The Chinese student Jiong Chen, who had not yet spoken in class, wrote:

When I was a teenager I witnessed Chinese officials come and take my uncle away to prison. He was a local politician of some standing and he must have done something to irritate the party bosses. This was the last we saw of him. No charges, no trial, no information from the government about his status. I cried for weeks and resolved that I would devote myself to fighting injustice of this sort. I am here to learn to how to do that. Also, another important fact about me is that, as a result of my quest for justice in China, I met some underground Christian students. They expressed their political dissonance by adopting the front of religious exercise. We thought we would be safe so long as we said we were a purely religious organization. But in the course of time I began to take the dogmas of Christianity more seriously. I now wear a cross, as you will see in class. I feel part of the Protestant evangelical movement. This is very meaningful to me. It provides me with some security in a world that I feel is very dangerous and is likely to collapse on me at any time.

By the way my name is pronounced with a soft "ch" as in "church." The Israeli girl pronounces her name with a guttural "ch" as in Chanukah (that is what they say, isn't it?). To avoid confusion, I like to use the name Holly.

Adam resolved to be gentle with this committed but fragile warrior for human rights. But his concerns shifted rapidly as soon as he encountered Joerg's letter.

Dear Herr Dr. Gross,

I am very pleased that we have begun engaging with each other's issues in class. I have the feeling you already know the truth about my grandfather, Ulrich Mueller. He wrote books defending the absolute rule of the Fuehrer. I did not realize this until I went to law school and was exposed to his works in the library, in a special section set aside for National Socialist books.

But you have to understand something. I loved my grandfather. And he explained to me why he assumed views that are now regarded as despicable. He was an ardent follower of Carl Schmitt, who, as you know, has now become popular with the political scientists in the USA. Schmitt taught me that the fundamental characteristic of sovereignty is the ability to distinguish between friends and enemies. The sovereign is the person who can do that. Germany had enemies in the 1930s. The *Fuehrerprinzip*—the "leader principle"—enabled us to understand where we stood in relation to our enemies. Also my father worked closely with other leading scholars who still influence German law: Edmund Metzger on criminal law, Karl Larenz on contracts.

The Nazi party was very hostile to religion, as you know. I share their views in this regard. Government is always based on secular authority and the ability to decide. Take the question of whether abortion should be allowed in the 1927 case. The question here is of who has the authority to decide. Once the leader decides, that is the law. Then the court was claiming *it* was the leader of the society. There is no point in asking why or for what reasons. The court assumed the authority to decide. No wonder many politicians reacted against this usurpation of authority.

My grandfather died a few years ago. This was one of the greatest losses of my life. I never got along too well with my parents, who were always slightly embarrassed by the family name. I am not embarrassed. I know who I am and I am proud of it.

I also have to add that in Germany I cannot always express my opinions on these matters. People immediately classify me as a neo-Nazi. Nothing could be further from the truth. I think the Nazi party was disastrous for Germany. History has shown that to be true. Perhaps it is better that we are a more homogenous people now than we were before, but that unity is being rapidly challenged by the immigration of Turks and other minorities.

Adam felt a cold chill pass down his spine. He eyes returned to the phrase "perhaps it is better that we are a more homogenous people now." It sounded to him like a veiled apology, if not a justification, for the Holocaust. Joerg Mueller and I have much business to do, he thought. God knows how we are going to do it. But this is surely one of my challenges for this course. Mueller is daring me to confront him. I cannot just ignore him. But I must wait for the right occasion to make a move.

He was beginning to think of the class as more like a game of chess than a harmonious tango.

The heterogeneity of his class was accentuated by two more letters, one from Chen Horowitz and the other from Charlotte de la Porte des Vaux. He expected Jaime Sullivan to have something profound and supportive to say, so he decided to save that email for last.

Chen had clearly hit the keyboard with both hands firing.

Dear Prof,

I don't want you to get the idea that I don't respect you because I do, on first impression, as much as any other teacher I have had. But I have serious problems with you talking about religion in our law class. I come from a state where we believe in the strict separation of synagogue (church or mosque) and the state. Of course we have many religious people—of all stripes and uniforms—but we know who they are. A serious Jew wears a *kippah*—skullcap, I guess you say here. We have them in the law school; they taught us *Mishpat Ivri*, Jewish law. But in my home town, Jerusalem, an ordinary teacher—one like you, one who does not wear a religious uniform—would not dare talk about religion or the Bible.

You have a very strange country here. You have all these different religions and you write "In God We Trust" on your currency. Don't you think that is outrageous?

Anyway I object very strongly to your introducing religion into our class. Frankly, I cannot stand it. I feel threatened by the black coats and the fur hats, these Jews who do not serve in the Israeli army. You are bringing them into our midst with all your talk about the religious foundations of law. I have already complained to the dean (forgive me) but he said I should work it out with you.

"Ugggh!" Adam said out loud. He felt as though he had been hit in the stomach. At least he knew where to watch his step, though, and could predict that Marga and Chen were likely to disagree about any issues that came remotely close to religious ones in the law. Before continuing with Charlotte's epistle, he thought he should see what some of the other Jewish students thought about the class. He did a search for Gad Menachem, the Talmudist from New Jersey, and found a short comment.

I cannot tell you how thrilled I am to be in the class. This is the first time in my life that I have sat either with women or secular students in the same class. I am able to communicate with them. This amazes me. I hope they are interested in what I have to say about the Talmud. I will try not to make my comments "too Jewish" but I won't be able to resist. I have no desire to convert anyone, I just want to express myself. The world outside the *yeshivah* is rich and exciting, I feel I have come from a monastery on a hill to live among real people.

At this point Adam was not sure whether he should just read the thoughts of Jaime and call it a night. Maybe it would be better not to know what Charlotte was thinking. But, as he was scrolling through the messages, he came upon the heading "My *capitán*, my *capitán*." These words, recalled from the lecture, led him to open the letter.

Dear Professor Gross,

Your influence reaches as far as Brazil. I have read your books and articles and you are now my idol. You cross the continents, transit every system of law. Your word can become the new dogma of the law. This is why you are my *capitán*.

I really admire your personal friend Francisco Muñoz Conde, who cites you frequently, and mainly his book about Edmund Metzger's role in the Third Reich. His criticism of Günther Jakobs' theory also is admired. Well, I would like to know your position about Jakobs. My *capitán*, I had trouble getting your books and articles when I was in my small town in Brazil; that is why I am so fortunate to be here at your feet. So, my *capitán*, one more time I would like to demonstrate the admiration with your person and with your words. It's a great pleasure for me, a Brazilian, 21-year-old guy, to keep in contact with the idol. I only have to thank you for your kindness with my person.

Best regards, from Brazil,

Rodrigo

Adam's reaction was a mixture of laughter and unease. He was unsettled that a gay student would express his attachment to his professor in this way. If he received the same letter from a female student, he would assume that it was a sexual proposition.

Adam decided on the spur to hit the reply button and answer Rodrigo right away. He wrote, "Thank you for your interest in my work, but please do not call me your captain. I will hold office hours and you discuss your interests with me then. AG."

He was having second thoughts about whether getting to know his students personally was a good idea. There was virtue in the anonymous class, he thought. Everyone was but a voice, a disembodied post of reason and argument. No names, no personal confrontations. But Adam could not seem to avoid the drama of stewing up personal interactions. He convinced himself that if the drama was played out at the personal level as well as at the level of ideas, the class would be more meaningful for the students.

At this stage, however, his mind was torn in so many directions that he had doubts whether he could handle strong personalities like Rodrigo and Chen—and *Gott im Himmel*, he recalled, there is Mueller too. With his computer humming, he could not resist. He opened Charlotte's email.

Dear Professor,

First, I want to apologize to you for seeming very direct in class. I am not sure of the proper protocol in the USA. When I was taught in Canada, I was used to the French method of didactic lecturing. I find our spontaneous interaction much more amusing.

One thing you should know about me is that I have some experience that will influence our discussion of issues like abortion. When I was a student in France I fell under the spell of a professor who totally enchanted me with his mellifluous voice and the power of his ideas. He invited me to dinner, one thing led to another and we had an affair. I became pregnant. This was a major crisis in my life because in fact I wanted to keep the child but he was married and for him it was an impossible situation. I agreed very reluctantly to an abortion, but with enormous bitterness. At the time I could not express why I was so angry. Later, when I was in Canada, I came in touch with many feminist scholars and we shared my story in one of our consciousness-raising groups. They helped me realize that my bitterness was about my lack of power in the relationship with the professor. I really had had no choice but to have the abortion. I read Catharine MacKinnon, who convinced me that abortion primarily serves the interests of irresponsible men. If I had chosen it freely myself, I would not have been so bitter, but in light of his power and mine, I turned out to be the victim of his lust.

One of the reasons I have come here to Regina is that the feminist scholars here are very powerful. I want to learn from them, and of course, I am open to learning from you.

The air-conditioning was blowing full blast. Nonetheless, Adam felt the drops of sweat on his brow. Should he respond to this letter or not? It's clear, he thought, that she teases as well as she does because she wants to re-enact the drama with the French professor. Or at least she wants to demonstrate her power over men. A word in Hungarian came back to him, one that he often heard from his mother: *Vigyaz!* Watch out, take care. Charlotte seemed to be a dangerous woman— much more, he thought, than Chen Horowitz.

He needed a break, so he turned to one of the great pleasures in his modest apartment. A few years earlier Adam had remodeled and converted a large bathroom into a spa. He had taken out the tub and installed a six-foot by four-foot steam shower, a place where he could lie down on teak benches in the steam and reflect on the events of the day. It was a stroke of luck that the remodeling had ended up so well. He had been trying to do it on the cheap, without an architect, without a general contractor, and became bogged down with workmen who were stalling and making mistakes right and left. He appealed to a colleague in the law school, Hans Richter, a Dutch immigrant who taught international arbitration. Hans was not much of a scholar; he was too busy making real estate deals and taking arbitration cases, though he was rumored to have made a fortune in his extra-curricular wheeling and dealing. He spent a lot of time on law school politics, however, and played a role in most of the major decisions of the school. He was not hard to get along with provided you did not slip and call him "Haans" instead of "Hahns." He said that he did not respond to the bleating of sheep. Adam ran into him one day in the halls and boldly addressed him. "Hahns, I understand you know a lot about bathrooms."

"Of course," responded the ebullient maker of deals. "I have remodeled 16 of them. First you put in the roughing, and then work on the walls. It is not hard. Let me tell you about tiles I found that were really cheap..."

"Maybe you can help me more than that—I'm totally screwed up in my project. Will you come over and look at it?"

Hans Richter had, and he had helped Adam get the job done. The steam shower actually worked, and it had become a kind of bond between Hans and Adam. It gave Adam a lot of pleasure, as well as providing a constant subject of conversation with his Dutch colleague. He could rave about Hans' skill at interior design. After 15 years of passing each other by in the hallway, they had finally had an experience to bring them closer together.

The steam shower made Adam's flat a home almost as much as having a woman waiting for him there. The first thing Adam did when he came home at the end of the day was to enter the vast tiled inner space and press the button to turn on the steam. It took about five minutes to warm up. Then he would undress, enter the sauna and situate himself on the moveable teak benches. He could arrange them so that he lay diagonally along the space, or he could sit under one of the three shower heads. All these physical gestures gave him a sense of reconnecting with his habitat. He knew he was at home: he made contact with a responsive steam valve that he knew would bring him pleasure.

On this occasion, he had been too eager to read the email responses of the students, and he regretted not entering the steam shower right away, as was his routine. Now he turned on the steam and stretched out on the two benches. He felt safe—as though ensconced in a womb, protected against the outside world.

After cooling himself down in a cold shower, he put on his blue nightshirt and returned, fully relaxed, to his computer. I'll check out Jaime Sullivan and then call it a night, he thought. He's my last hope for leading the class in the field of religious sensibility.

Dear Professor,

I am a refugee from the Church but not from religion. I was born in Honduras of American parents and grew up there. This explains my Spanish Christian name and yet why I speak English fluently. After high school I went to Paris to study, and there I fell in with a group of Benedictine monks who were also taking courses at the Sorbonne. They took me to lunch from time to time in their monastery. Initially I was stunned by the beauty of their surroundings, their chapels, the quiet of their rooms and their tendencies toward deep and serious thought. My friends said I was carried away less with their ideas than with their flowing white smocks and the way they carried themselves— controlled and complete in themselves. They may have been right. In any event, I began to think of my life as a work of art, and the life of the monk as the most beautiful possible. I became a novitiate in the Order. My initial mission was to study archeology and to provide language lessons at the Ecole Biblique in Jerusalem. The students there are usually Francophone and need lessons in English.

I was very happy there, but at the same time I was exposed to the politics of the Middle East. The magnificent monastery of the Ecole is located on the main street in East Jerusalem, just a block from the Damascus Gate of the old city. I wandered freely around the Arab neighborhoods nearby. I sat with the merchants and the Palestinians hanging out in the cafés, we had coffee and talked about politics. In time I learned quite a bit of Arabic. I came to respect some of the Arab customs—their hospitality, their respect for the modesty of women. And then I began to notice the injustices of the Israeli occupation. I saw the humiliation in the streets, the long lines waiting at the checkpoints, the poverty of the third world Arab neighborhoods in contrast with the first world streets of West Jerusalem. My friends were suffering and I began to share their condition.

When it looked as if there might be another Intifada, I felt that if it came to action I would have to be on the side of the Palestinians. My superiors looked askance at all this... I started looking into the history of liberation theology in my home country. This was a branch of the Church I found I could fully identify with. These Churchmen accentuated Christ as the redeemer of the poor, which led them to take political action on behalf of the poor. I discovered that Pope John Paul II had done everything possible to suppress the movement. When Archbishop Oscar Romero visited him in order to explain why the priests in Latin America were engaged in social action, the Pope kept him waiting 36 hours for an audience. After the archbishop returned, without encouragement, to San Salvador, he was assassinated. No one knows the extent to which the Vatican implicitly encouraged the elimination of the archbishop, but there is little doubt in my mind that the Pope's shunning encouraged his enemies. Recently, when the Pope died and the press was full of eulogies for his excellence, for his leadership and great contributions to the world as a whole, no one mentioned the killing of the archbishop. No one suggested that perhaps the Polish-grown Pope had suffered from an obsessive anti-Communism that made him unduly suspicious of liberation theology.

My seniors in the monastery were becoming very impatient with me. I think I expressed my opinions too freely. When it came time to take my final vows we had a frank conversation. And we all decided that it would be better for everyone if I did not take those vows.

I felt very sad about leaving, but I am hopeful now that I can rebuild my life as a merger of faith and justice. I am thrilled by the possibility that we can talk about the role of religion in the law.

Adam was moved by Jaime's story. He identified with the struggle against the Church. It reminded him of his own anti-authoritarian impulses, which made it difficult for him conform to the expectations of his colleagues. He realized that this was part of his reason for giving a daring exam that his colleagues said flirted with perversity. He began to think of Jaime Sullivan as a purer version of himself. They shared a willingness to speak what they thought to be truth against what they perceived as power, but he thought of the failed novitiate as more admirable. He has a real cause, he pondered. I'm not sure what mine is.

In the wake of all these stories, Adam Gross felt tired and humble. He noticed that there were some more potentially interesting messages—one from a Romanian judge named Ilona Romanescu and the other from a Senegalese called Mohammad An'im—but he was too exhausted to read further. He lay back in bed and imagined a dance in the round. Marga was holding hands with Jiong—no, Holly

Chen, who was joined to Joerg, who gripped Chen Horowitz about the waist, and she was elbow to elbow with Gad, who was joined with Rodrigo and Charlotte, and she with Jaime, who closed the circle by reaching out for Marga. Around and around they danced, sometimes slowly, sometimes faster, kicking toward the center. With a vision of world in harmony, Adam slowly fell asleep.

8

Holy Books

ADAM'S MOOD of humility stayed with him next day as he prepared for his Thursday morning class and then entered the theater of students. He loved standing in the pit, at the base of the semi-circle of tiered seats. Sometimes he felt as though he were a gladiator about to perform for the crowd, other times as he imagined Emile Zola would have been, had he delivered his famous letter "J'accuse" as a speech to the French senate. This morning he felt like neither. He was simply eager to repay the students for their honesty of the night before by giving them the most stimulating lecture he could. He looked up at the students as if to thank all of them for the exposure and vulnerability of those who had offered insights into themselves beyond the routine steps of their professional lives.

His plan for the class was to present the American Constitution and the necessary background for delving into the First Amendment and freedom of religion in the USA. He began boldly.

"In the law we all have holy books. Some of you take the *Code civil*, the Napoleonic Code of 1804, to be holy. Others invest the same sanctity in the BGB, the German Civil Code of 1900. Or you might have local variations of these codes in your home country. In any case, you hold closely to your code as a symbol of national continuity. The French code has been through five republics, and it continues in force as the foundation of the legal system. The German code has outlived Bismarck's Reich, the Weimar Republic, Hitler's tyranny and the drive toward a united Europe. The Communists adopted a version of it in the East, but, with the fall of the Wall a decade ago, that too has given way to the old liberal ideas of the BGB."

Chen Horowitz was sitting next to Holly Chen. They were amused by the similarities of their names. Holly jabbed Chen and whispered,

"What does he mean by liberal? How can he use the word 'holy' to describe the law? I am shocked."

"So am I," replied the Israeli.

Overhearing, Marga pressed her finger to her lips. "You have no idea how important this is."

The professor noticed these interactions and, although he did not hear the words, he read their gestures as a continuation of the messages he'd read the night before.

"Now my question." Adam paused. "What is the sacred document for Americans? We have no national civil code, no national criminal law. What do we hold sacred in our national legal culture?"

Dead silence. "My answer is unconventional," persevered the professor. "Our national code is the Constitution, drafted in 1787, ratified in 1788, effective as of 1789, and amended by the Bill of Rights in 1791. Take note of these dates. They should become important to you, just as important as 1804 for the *Code civil* or 1900 for the BGB."

Both Chens' heads were swimming. For them both, the key year of history was 1949. Chen Horowitz was proud of her state's declaration of independence in May 1948 and the military armistice securing the state the year following. And Holly Chen knew little about history except the dynasties and the victory of Mao Tse-tung over Chiang Kai-shek in the same year. For Americans this was a low point of history. It was the beginning of the McCarthy era of accusation and recrimination.

"Sorry, Professor," Holly intervened, "these dates—1787, etcetera—are not my dates. 1949 is more important to me." And, echoing something from her lessons in Marxist-Leninism, she added, "I think in different categories."

"To tell you the truth," agreed Adam, "1949 is a critical year in the history I learned in school too. That was the year Juan Perón consolidated his dictatorship by writing a new constitution for Argentina. He seized the leading newspaper and began to suppress public gatherings. This meant that there was no place to dance tango."

Adam smiled to himself at bringing tango to the level of world politics, but the students looked puzzled.

"Maybe this is more than you want to know about Argentine history. But we all come from different histories, and here, as students of the common law, we acquire a new history. New dates become important to us. 1949 is not important here, I am sorry to say. 1789 *is* important."

"Yes," Joerg interjected, "but they do not become important by your saying so. We have to feel it."

"You're right," replied the professor. "How does Ruth, the first convert in the Bible, declare her loyalty to her mother-in-law Naomi? As I recall, she says, '*Your people shall be my people, and your God my God.*' Maybe she should have added, 'Your history shall be my history.'"

Joerg bristled at this argument. "You cannot change peoples and histories just by wanting to do so. One needs experience."

"Welcome to the experience," responded Adam. "I admit that this course is intended as a vehicle of conversion. I am trying to persuade you into a new way of thinking. You start with one holy book—perhaps it's *The Sayings of Chairman Mao* or perhaps it the *Code Civil*—and now you are learning to think of another sacred text, the American Constitution."

Holly Chen did not know whether to be more offended by the reference to Chairman Mao or by the metaphor of religious conversion. Was hers not a real conversion? Should it be compared to the trivial adoption of a new legal code? But on the other side of the room, Jaime Sullivan radiated a warm internal smile. He knew that his religion of liberation was supple enough to accommodate these new ideas, and he was curious to see where Professor Gross was going.

"By a holy text," Adam continued, "I mean two things. The legal text provides a symbol of historical continuity, a focal point for national identity. The *Code civil* does this for the French, the BGB for the Germans. The Constitution fulfills this function for Americans. We have no Crown, no royalty; the only symbol of our unity as a nation is the Constitution.

"Further, for the text to have this value, its language must take on liturgical value. Lawyers, citizens and schoolchildren must learn to recite its passages as though it were the national creed."

Charlotte de la Porte des Vaux was back in an ebullient mood, as though she felt relieved by her confession the night before. She pressed her way into Adam's presentation. "You know the story about Stendhal, the great French writer, author of *Le Rouge et le Noir*?"

"Yes," added Adam, "*The Red and the Black*, a great novel about the Church and the military.'

"The Church again," Chen Horowitz huffed.

"So," Charlotte forged on. "Do you know the legend that Stendhal wrote down ten provisions from the *Code civil* every night in an effort to allow his style to be influenced by the classical patterns of the code? And do you know how seriously the Québécois take the *Code civil*? It is one of the pillars of their distinctive culture, their claim to be a separate nation."

"Their language, their history, and their *Code civil*." Adam pronounced the last word in an exaggerated French accent, with a flourish of the hand. He continued over the giggles. "Some of the phrases coined in the French Civil Code are priceless. I particularly like the way the code expresses the relationship of a contract to the statutory law. It says that contracts properly made '*tiennent lieu de la loi*'—they 'take the place' of the statutory law. This is the ultimate liberal idea. People are left alone to regulate their own private lives."

Joerg became agitated at the mention of the liberal idea of contract. "Yes, this was the view of the BGB too, in 1900. But since then we have become concerned about protecting the weak. This is the socialist idea. The community must watch out for its weaker members. We cannot pretend that the weakest among us are free to choose the contracts they make." He looked pleased when his argument garnered nods from Jaime, Rodrigo and several other members of the class.

"I know," Adam agreed. "'The rich and poor are equally free to sleep under the bridges of Paris.'" This famous line by Anatole France was always useful. "But we should transport ourselves back into the original mindset of the nineteenth century. The idea of self-regulation influenced the American Constitution as well. The states and citizens chose to enter into a voluntary association to create, as the Preamble says, 'a more perfect Union.' The legitimacy of the Constitution depended on their power to think rationally and to make a choice that would bind not only them but their descendants."

"So a constitution," Gad Menachem spoke up, "is something like the covenant of the Jewish people at Mount Sinai. They entered into a compact with God not only for themselves but for their descendants as well."

Chen could stand no more of this. "Does that make any sense? How can I be bound by Moses at Sinai? Women could not even negotiate. The men prepared for their meeting with God by telling them to stay away from women for three days!" Secular Israelis like Chen were tough adversaries on these issues, Adam noted. Reared in the spirit of the Labor Zionists, they studied the Bible as their historical legacy. They knew the text better than most religious American Jews, probably better than did Professor Gross himself.

"Well, I must admit," replied Adam softly and pensively, "the Constitution was drafted by a group of élite white property-owning Christian men. Blacks, then called Africans or worse, were obviously not represented in the drafting of a constitution. It would have been odd for them to endorse slavery. Take a look at Article I, section 2, clause 3. It prescribes representation in Congress according to the number of 'free persons, including those bound to Service for a Term of Years, and excluding Indians not taxed, three fifths of all other Persons.' This is the infamous three-fifths compromise. Basically, it treated 'all other persons'—namely black people—as three-fifths of a human being."

Mohammed An'im from Senegal had been quiet in class so far, but the inherent racism of the Constitution provoked him to burst out, "Is this still true?"

"Obviously not," Adam reassured him quickly. "As we shall see, the Civil War changed everything. But the amazing thing is that your copy of the Constitution still contains this language. Every printed Constitution includes all the language that has been repealed. Once a word or phrase is part of the Constitution, it stays in the printed text forever. What does this show?"

"Well," Jaime Sullivan mused, "this is what you mean by the liturgical role of language. This is republished and recited simply because it once was part of the Constitution. In the Church we read the dietary laws of Leviticus even though we do not follow them. They are part of the holy text even if they are superseded by later law."

The professor responded, "True: the Prophets change the orientation of the Bible but they do not repeal the earlier text. The same is true about the New Testament when it supplements the Old, and the Book of Mormon when it adds to the New Testament, but none of these subsequent revelations changes the original text of the old law."

Out of the corner of his eye, he noticed Aschkin Yilmaz sitting at the back of the room. What was she doing there? His internal pause seemed to last for minutes.

He adjusted the direction of his lecture. "And of course the Koran supplements the Old and New Testaments and builds on them without changing their content.. This is the way the ten Amendments to the Constitution that comprise the Bill of Rights, and the further 17 Amendments following it, function—something like a series of new revelations."

Aschkin seemed keenly interested in this interplay of ideas.

Joerg was flicking through his papers. "This is shocking!" he blurted out. "I see it right here in my copy of the Constitution. It does not say black people but it refers to determining something by taking the whole number of free persons, excluding Indians not taxed, and 'three-fifths of all other persons.' What if the new German Constitution read in the same way? Let's say it excluded Gypsies not taxed, and counted three-fifths of all non-Aryans?"

"Well, I suppose during the Nazi regime you had even worse legislation. And certainly more brutal practices."

"Yes, of course, but we try to forget them. We do not republish all of our racial legislation punishing marriage to Jews."

"You will notice in your copy of the Constitution that are brackets around the three-fifths clause. In other places too. Look at Article I, Section 3, Clause 1, prescribing the election of senators by state senates."

"Yes," said Joerg, "I see the brackets. What does that mean?"

"It means that the language has been repealed. The Seventeenth Amendment says that we now elect senators by popular vote."

"This all seems very silly to me, and insulting besides. There are some things better forgotten."

"Or reserved for special parts of the library," Adam threw in with a touch of malice.

Joerg responded with an air of betrayal. He opened his computer pointedly, as if to demonstrate that this was a reference to his "private" email to the professor.

"Look at it another way," chimed in Charlotte. "It is holistic. You accept responsibility for your past by republishing even the passages about slavery."

"Also, on a more humble note," added Adam, "it says something important about codification. In order to understand how the senators are elected today, you have to read the whole document including the 27 amendments. They could have deleted the part about the senate electing them and printed the part about popular election right there, but they don't. They reprint the old law with brackets around it and then reveal the truth much later when you get to the Seventeenth Amendment."

Jaime looked very reflective. Adam tried to help him formulate his thoughts. "And, Mr. Sullivan, do you think of the Constitution as something like a collection of religious revelations in the Judeo-Christian tradition: always adding, never subtracting?"

"Perhaps," Jaime mused. "There is something special about constitutional moments. The drafter can speak across history and bind future generations. They are the men at Sinai."

"That's it!" exploded Chen. "I cannot stand it—the men at Sinai, the men who were told not to go near women for three days."

Aschkin looked as though she wanted to intervene. She glanced over at Chen to try to calm her down. Would I dare call on her? Adam asked himself, and his mind drifted to T.S. Eliot's poem, "The Love Song of J. Alfred Prufrock': "*And indeed there will be time/To wonder, 'Do I dare?' and, 'Do I dare?'/Time to turn back and descend the stair/With a bald spot in the middle of my hair.*" He put his hand to the top of his head, then quickly put it down again, thinking he was calling attention to himself. No, there is no time; I must act now, now...

"The constitutional framers were not prophets," he said. "God did not speak to them as to Moses or Mohammed." He paused, wondering whether Aschkin would think him too ingratiating. "The people actually involved in adopting and following the Constitution must have believed that there was something sacred about the moment of time that enabled their national leaders to speak across time. Of course, we borrow the word 'sacred' here from people who take it much more seriously."

This was one of those days when Adam felt he had no natural allies in the classroom. The religious were always puzzled and skeptical because they had never heard secular law discussed with so much respect. The orthodox Jews thought of secular law as *schmatte*— "rag"—law, implying that it was all worthless politics. Left-wingers tended to agree. Even the not-so-left, like Chen, got upset about the sexism and racism of most legal institutions prior to the Civil War. I need Lincoln and the Civil War, and I need them now, he thought. The words of Eliot came to mind again: "*And when I am formulated, sprawling on a pin,/When I am pinned and wriggling on the wall,/Then how should I begin...?*" And how I love to take myself seriously! Adam cherished his little confession.

He knew that by the end of the hour he must unveil his theory about the radical changes brought by the Civil War and the post-war amendments to the Constitution. I must hold fast to my method, he thought as he posed the next question to the class.

"Look at the first ten amendments to the Constitution, the Bill of Rights. How do you read them? Do they favor liberty or equality?"

There were no black Americans in the class so Adam hoped that one of the African students would respond. Mohammad was eager to get more involved, Adam could see it in his eyes. "There is a lot of talk about freedom and about rights but none about equality," said the Senegalese student. "How can you have a constitution without a statement about everyone being equal under the law?"

"Exactly," said Adam. "How could they claim equality as a principle when the Constitution itself says that slaves count as only three-fifths of a free person?"

Chen broadened the point. "You know, Israel does not have a written constitution and the reason, most people say, is that the Orthodox leaders do not want a clause on equality. They are worried about equality for Palestinians—but even more about equality for women. Yet under our Chief Justice, Aaron Barak, the Court has cultivated the idea of human dignity as a substitute. We adopted this idea from the German Basic Law of 1949."

Joerg looked over at her and smiled approvingly, almost as though he was inviting her to be friends.

Aschkin put up her hand. Adam noticed the time. 11.46. He waited. The clock moved. Then it was 11.47. For Adam it seemed like ten minutes. He called on her.

"May I speak to the question of gender?" she began. "The Turks have a commitment to the equal treatment of men and women, but I would be surprised if any other Islamic country did. Putting down women seems to be the job of every religion. Sorry, but I am afraid it is true."

Chen reached out her hands, as if symbolically to hug her.

Adam took a second to thank Professor Yilmaz. He wanted time to think his way out of what seemed a sticky position. Two themes had collided in the class's thinking: religion in the law, and the equal rights of women. He had not been planning to find himself in this corner. The subject of women and their proper treatment seemed to be his fate; he could never escape the problem.

Now he could either drop the subject of religion or he could, hypothetically, try to make an apology for role differentiations in the major religions of the world. He did not want to do either. But there was no easy way to get back on track and encourage the students to appreciate the close and valuable association between legal and religious thinking. Fortunately for him, he saw the large hand on the clock approach the number "10." The 50-minute session had come to an end. "This is enough for now," he said. He packed his books while murmuring the lines from T.S. Eliot: *"There will be time, there will be time..."*

Aschkin and Chen immediately struck up a conversation, but Aschkin shook herself loose and joined the small group around the podium. Marga and Jaime were chatting in Spanish, and Adam added a word here and there. Aschkin held out her hand to Adam and congratulated him. "It was fascinating. Do you mind if I come again?"

"Not at all," said Adam, wondering whether her husband, the dean, had sent her as a spy.

9

Messages from the Past

ADAM FELT NERVOUS and unsatisfied as he left the classroom. The discussion had ended with a whimper rather than a bang. He was a little miffed that Aschkin Yilmaz had intervened in his class, complicated his argument and forced him to retreat. But he struggled to get a grip on himself, trying not to resent her, but to focus on the subject.

He left the building and entered one of the side streets connecting the campus to the Hudson River. He felt soothed by the proximity of large bodies of water—he had heard that they generated associations with the womb. But as he walked along the bank of the Hudson he realized that there was something else that nurtured him in this particular waterside boulevard.

Riverside Drive was studded with statues of historical figures, mostly military heroes, and mostly drawn from the great wars of the nineteenth century. They were German, Hungarian, American. They stood for a consensus of liberal politicians who had fought, in their time, to resolve the kinds of conflicts that were troubling Adam in class at that very moment.

Adam was attracted to two statues of European heroes known for passionate defenses of freedom, particularly freedom of speech and freedom of religion. But could they offer him wisdom on his particular problem, namely the relationship between freedom of religion and the equal treatment of women? They had both made names for themselves by fighting in the wave of liberal revolution that had swept Europe in 1848. One was German, the other Hungarian. At 106th Street the German-American Franz Sigel, astride his horse, faced out toward the river. And seven blocks to the north there was Adam's favorite: the statue of the Hungarian liberal and revolutionary Lajos

Kossuth, standing tall and reaching a hand down to the peasants crouched at his feet. Adam felt he needed a conversation with these figures from the past.

As he walked toward 106th Street he recalled Martin Buber's philosophy as expressed in *I and Thou*. The statues were things and therefore one might suppose they were inert, incapable of communication. The only kind of relationship possible with a piece of bronze—according to conventional thinking—would be an "I/it" relationship—that was, to approach it as a dead object in the external world. But Buber discussed the possibility of communication with a tree, communication in an "I/thou" relationship, as if the tree were capable of responding to another human being. Adam pondered this question and concluded that if an "I/thou" relationship was possible with a tree, it should also be possible with a statue incorporating a heroic figure from the past.

He approached the statue of Franz Sigel, and, with his back to the Hudson River, looked up at the stately rider on horseback. This was a dignified pose that, in Europe, would be allowed only to celebrate the memory of kings and aristocrats. The man was rarely mentioned in history books in the USA, but Adam had done some research and therefore knew the basics about him. Sigel had been born in a small town in Baden, Germany, with a Romantic heart that had led him to engage in the military conflicts of his time. The ideas of freedom and democracy had spread across Europe in what was now known at the liberal revolution of 1848. Sigel had enlisted in the military when he was in his late teens and served six years, and then had several mishaps in his career, including a conviction for treason. He had experienced a military failure on 29 March 1849 when a small band of rebels—mostly professors and teachers—drafted a new democratic "imperial constitution" and demanded that rulers of the German states accept the new order based on freedom and democracy. This did not quite happen. The Grand Duke Leopold had fled his castle in Karlsruhe, but the Hessians in Frankfurt had called in Prussian troops to protect his authority. There had been much doubt whether liberals like Sigel could succeed in Germany.

Sigel had decided to try the English-speaking world. He spent the critical year of 1851 in London, where he came into contact with the grand figures of radical politics—Karl Marx, Friedrich Engels, and the more moderate Carl Schurz, who was later to become a distinguished figure in the American Republican Party. Eventually they found their way to the United States on the eve of civil war. When hostilities broke out in Charleston Harbor, Sigel was teaching in a German college in Missouri, a slave state. He immediately joined the side of the Union and raised a local army of 10,000 volunteers, including many immigrants like himself. They marched south to Arkansas and won a major battle at Pea Ridge. This impressed Lincoln, who promoted Sigel to major general. According to his loyal followers who erected the statue, he was a man most comfortable on horseback.

Adam looked up at Sigel as he rehearsed these facts in his head. I am an immigrant like you, he thought; I too was exposed to danger from the authorities. I feel a unity with you and your struggle. I understand you? I know you? The bronze statue glistened in the sun but Adam heard no reply. He stood there meditating. A few minutes went by. Then the words "freedom and democracy" began circulating in his mind. Yes, he said to himself, I thought the Americans had discovered these ideas, but perhaps they had to be tested in Europe and then brought home again.

"Freedom and democracy." The phrase rang in his mind as he walked slowly and pensively toward 113th Street and the statue of Lajos Kossuth, another "forty-eighter," as the European revolutionaries were called in the USA. The events in Paris and Germany had had repercussions in Vienna and then in Budapest. In the heady days of March 1848, as Sigel was riding around in the Black Forest with his troops, Austrian students met in a lecture hall and drew up a list of democratic demands on the Austrian Metternich government, primarily demanding a written constitution including the recognition of freedom of religion. The turbulence continued for several days. Metternich resigned, and various high officials nominally consented to the demands of the students, joined by some workers. Within a short time, however, the reform movement in Vienna fizzled out.

Yet Kossuth had persisted with revolutionary reforms in Budapest. He had an unusual way of mobilizing the Parliament with his oratory. His first speech to the Hungarian Parliament on March 3 triggered the passions of both the Austrian and the Hungarians, but March 15 became the critical day for the Hungarians. The leader on that day was neither a military figure nor a politician but a poet named Sándor Petőfi. He had walked through the city and read his nationalist poems coupled with a twelve-point political plan for bringing freedom, democracy and independence to Hungary. The key constitutional demand was a "national government responsible to an elected parliament." Like Jesus walking through Galilee, Petöfi picked up followers wherever he went. After a crowd had formed, they crossed the bridges to Buda and mounted the hill, demanding the release of political prisoners. The stage was set for the politicians to establish a counter-government to Vienna.

This might have been the only time in history that a poet could read words from his heart and find a deep resonance in common people willing to take up arms. To this day, Adam knew, Hungarians celebrated 15 March as a national holiday, and in New York dozens of patriots (mostly from New Jersey) would come to the Kossuth statue to pay their respects and perhaps to read one of Petöfi's poems.

Adam had visions of marching into class reading poems that would solve all his controversies about the role of women in religion. The students would line up and follow him, as they had Petöfi, and all issues would be resolved by a Romantic attachment to some twentieth-century vision of national liberation.

But Petöfi had failed. Kossuth held out for a while longer but eventually foreign troops attacked from all sides and the intellectual dreams of 1848 were soon smashed. Kossuth followed roughly the same path as the other failed intellectuals of the time, moving first to England and then to the United States.

Adam was beginning to feel that, without the infusion of failed intellectuals, Americans would not have accomplished anything in the intellectual wars of the mid-nineteenth century. Kossuth's impact had been enormous. Though he'd spent only six months in the country, he had traveled to 60 cities and given 300 speeches. The remarkable thing about these speeches was their range. He did not repeat himself but spoke originally, in apparently very good English, on every occasion. He trod lightly on the question of slavery but took on every other important issue vibrant in nineteenth-century American society. The highlight of his tour was his celebrated speech at Fanueil Hall in Boston, an important symbol of the American revolution.

Adam joined the people milling about at the base of the statue. It revealed the posture of an orator, he thought. Kossuth was in uniform but displayed no hint of force, no dramatic military posture: he was reaching down to the peasants and soldiers who were looking up to him. Adam looked up along with them, hoping for some illumination on the relationship between religion and equality. His class was going to start in an hour, and he was still yearning for communication from these figures he admired.

He laughed at himself as he thought that, if he used a few words of Hungarian, he might induce a response from Kossuth. But the secret of the "I/thou" relationship was not to demand a response but to stand quietly in the presence of the other and allow the atoms to flow from one to the other. He was not praying, he was not pleading. He was waiting.

Eventually a thought came to him: *Read my speeches. Internalize my work.* Eureka! Adam thought. Kossuth lives in his recorded work.

He headed quickly back to his office and searched the internet for Kossuth's addresses to his American audiences, a body of material that had been largely ignored. Most of Kossuth's thinking had focused on the freedom of the press and the critical importance of Hungarian independence, but Adam found one speech dedicated entirely to the freedom of religion. He spliced a paragraph from it into his class notes. He would wait for the right time to use it.

As he sat quietly in his office, eating a sandwich and drinking coffee, his eye fell on several books on his shelf by Francis Lieber, another long-time intellectual hero of his. There was no statue in *his* honor, in New York or elsewhere. Though he too was a forty-eighter, and also a German immigrant, no community had felt the need to organize, raise money and negotiate with the city to build a statue of him. His monuments were his books, and there were plenty of them. Adam walked over to the shelf and ran his hand across the chipped bindings. Great writers never die, he thought, but with time their bond with us begins to decay.

Lieber was a generation older than Sigel and a couple of years older than Kossuth. He had come of age in times even more Romantic than 1848. At the age of six, in 1806, he had seen Napoleon's troops march into Berlin. Thus was born his felt need to bear arms for the sake of his nation. As a youth he had enlisted, fought and been wounded at Waterloo. Then he returned to study in Prussia, but he was already in trouble with the authorities for his liberal ideas—the common denominator, thought Adam, of all the European figures that were at the center of his attention this lunchtime. To study,

Lieber left Prussia for Jena, where he came under the influence of the Jahnian school which represented a curious combination of Kantian philosophy and gymnastics. The discipline of the Jahnists shaped his intellectual life and his Romantic aspirations. It was natural for Lieber—like Lord Byron—to venture off to Greece to fight in the war of independence against the Turks. But, because his papers were not in order, he got stuck in Rome and then decided to leave for the United States.

He adapted very quickly to the northeast and established himself as a leading intellectual of the period. He edited the *Encyclopedia Americana*, the first reference work of its kind in English. Then he started teaching political science at a small college in Charleston, South Carolina, which eventually became the primary university of the state. Like Tocqueville, he was very interested in the prison system and wrote about it; the two carried on an active correspondence and became friends. But Lieber's main contributions were on the general theory of liberty and political institutions. He was particularly interested in the conflict between liberty and equality. He could see the problem all around him. If men were free to own slaves, there was no hope of equality under the law.

According to the legend, Lieber was lecturing in Charleston in 1848 when a student burst in the room and told him the revolution was under way in Germany. He wept on the spot and resolved to cross the ocean right away. He did, but apparently he did not arrive until the fighting was over. Adam identified totally with this event in Lieber's life. He too had the feeling that he wanted to fight, he wanted to *be there*, but he was always too late or too early.

Lieber's great break in life had come with the Civil War. First, when he was 60 years old, and the fighting was about to break out, he had received an appointment teaching political science at Columbia University in New York. More significantly, he'd had three sons fighting in the war, and one of them was injured in the battle for Fort Donaldson in Tennessee. When he went to visit the wounded young man, he met another father visiting a son in the hospital. The other man turned out to be Henry Halleck, the chief of staff of Union forces. The two men struck up a congenial relationship, which led soon after to Halleck's asking Lieber to draft a code governing the proper conduct of hostilities in warfare. Lieber brought to bear his Kantian training and produced an impressive code, which

Lincoln promulgated in 1863 and which was now revered as the first significant codification in the law of war.

As Adam concluded this two-hour investigation into the past, he felt both bonded with his predecessors and envious of their ability to enter into the inner circles of American society. They were all immigrants like me, he thought, but they had friends in the highest circles. They did things that changed the course of American history. Who in Washington is paying any attention to what I am saying?

No, this was not the point, he quickly corrected himself. Perhaps all these figures of the past lived in envy of someone else. All I can do is address the issues that present themselves to me. Perhaps, if I am ready and clever, events will present themselves in my life that will enable me as a lawyer to seize the moment and invoke ideas in the same grand manner that we see in the lives of Franz Sigel, Lajos Kossuth and Francis Lieber.

He did not know that, thousands of miles away, in Pakistan and Afghanistan, events were already percolating that a few years hence would confront the United States with its first major crisis of the millennium, and which would call on the talents of many lawyers to defend the civil liberties of thousands of Muslim followers of Osama bin Laden.

But Adam's quandaries occurred in a time of innocence. He was not called upon to act on the great stage of history but on the small side-stage of a law school in which students were puzzled by the meaning of equality and he—as professor—was in the midst of a brewing conflict about a criminal law exam. He wanted to feel challenged by history, but he cursed himself that the most he could muster was a few antagonistic feminists and an unknown criminal law exam. A far cry, he thought, from the crowd's demand to Metternich for a new constitution!

Even in his small and limited world, however, Adam could salvage one message from Sigel, Kossuth, and Lieber. They had been immigrants who had become critical figures in a new country because they were willing to risk everything. They happened to have won, but they might have lost. This was the message he brought home with him from his midday walk. As risks presented themselves in his life, he would take them. Perhaps he didn't have to ride a horse, perhaps he didn't have to make orations to stir peasants to rise up in revolt, perhaps he didn't have to fight in a civil war—but he would take risks.

He had no inkling yet that, in his personal case, one of the risks might turn out to be that of losing one's heart, not in a battle of fire, but in a love affair on the edge.

10

Freedom and Equality

A S HE STOOD before the students at the beginning of the afternoon class, Adam felt calm but enthusiastic about his spiritual journey back to 1848. He wanted to share his feelings with the students, but he had a plan for this class and he was going to stick to it.

"We are going back to the topic raised at the end of the previous hour," he began. "There is undoubtedly a tension between religion and equality, and indeed there is a great tension, as I will show you, between freedom of religion and equality under the law. This tension is part of the general conflict between freedom and equality. The more freedom, the less equality; the more equality, the less freedom. Can anyone think of a good example?"

"Yes," said Charlotte. "If you give men the freedom to control their wives, to have sex when they want, to have them cook and clean house for them, you have freedom for men but no equality."

"You're right. And if you are free to accumulate as much wealth as you can, you can bet there will not be an equal distribution of property. So can anyone think of reason why the Constitution of 1789 is all about freedom; why it never mentions the principle of equality?"

Chen Horowitz's hand shot into the air. "Because of the slavery of blacks—and I think women were equivalent to slaves."

Adam knew that she was trying to provoke him. How best to defuse this challenge? "One question," he ventured. "Did women at the time describe their condition as slavery?"

"No, they were slaves without knowing it."

"I hate to say this," said Adam provocatively, "but this is an insult both to women and the black slaves. Take the case of Muslims wearing the veil today. Are they slaves without knowing it?"

Out of the corner of his eye he saw Aschkin nodding yes, but Chen backed down. "We are not as extreme on this issue as the Turks, who do not permit the wearing of the veil in public spaces. In Israel we allow women to choose whether they wish to be traditional or not."

Charlotte, today wearing a miniskirt, was squirming in her seat. "This is a big argument in France as well. Neither the right nor the left wants to let Muslim girls wear the veil in school. In my opinion, women should uncover themselves when they want to do so, not at the command of the state." As though she was not thinking about what she was doing, Charlotte gently kicked off her sandals and perched her forefeet on the tips of her toes, walking them around them slightly like a ballerina. Her toenails were short and painted pink. Adam tried not to look, but they were very pretty feet, he thought. The room was tiered in a way that no one behind Charlotte could see them; her toe dance was carried on beneath an overlay of conversation about eroticism and modesty.

Mohammad struck the right chord. "Have you ever seen a woman's knee for the first time when she chooses to show it to you?" Most of the women in the class instinctively moved their sweaters over the knees or tugged down their skirts. Unmoved, Charlotte left her toes bare.

"Well," conceded Adam, "so much for trying to shift the conversion away from women. I see that the subject has a certain *je ne sais quoi*."

Ilona Romanescu, the Romanian judge, laughed out loud and called out, "Well, let's talk about men instead."

"All right," agreed Adam, spotting an opening. "Let's talk about men. Why did people in the past always say 'men' when they apparently meant to refer to all persons? We see this, for example, in the French Declaration of the Rights of Man—the *Déclaration des droits de l'homme*. Does this mean that women were not included?

"Of course women were included," replied Charlotte. "That was just a way of speaking, *une façon de parler*." Other women in the class were shaking their heads.

Adam said, "We had the same 'fashion of speaking' in the Declaration of Independence, which preceded the Constitution and the Declaration of the Rights of Man by 11 years. The colonists wanted to explain to the world why they were rebelling against King George III of Great Britain. Thomas Jefferson wrote the Declaration, and it contains some of the most inspiring language ever penned in

English. At the start of the document, the leaders of the rebellion committed themselves to these unforgettable words: '*We hold these truths to be self-evident, that all men are created equal, that they are endowed by their Creator with certain unalienable Rights, that among these are Life, Liberty, and the pursuit of Happiness.*'"

Adam was aware that he was waxing patriotic about "unforgettable words" that this group had probably never heard of. "So in 1776 the leaders of the new American republic wrote that they believed that 'all men are created equal.' Eleven years later, in the Constitution, they seemed to suppress their commitment to equality. What did they mean in 1776 when they pledged their sacred honor?"

Jaime Sullivan jumped into the thick of it. "There are more problems here than just gender—men as opposed to women," he said. "One issue of the time was slavery. Another was justifying the anti-colonial revolt against the English Crown: what right did they have to leave the legal system that gave birth to them?"

"Exactly right, Mr. Sullivan: the American ambivalence about the nature of this war against the English is interesting. Sometimes it is called a revolution, sometimes a war of independence. The revolutionary part is signaled, I think, in the lines that follow the passage I just quoted. They go like this: '*That to secure these rights*'—namely, equality, life, liberty and the pursuit of happiness—'*governments are instituted among Men, deriving their just powers from the consent of the governed, —That whenever any Form of Government becomes destructive of these ends, it is the Right of the People to alter or abolish it.*'"

Adam identified strongly with this impulse based on the right of the people as a collective. He sensed that Lieber and Kossuth would have thought that way too. "There you have it," he said. "A call to revolution based on John Locke's theory of the social contract. The People have the right to give their consent and to withdraw their consent—not arbitrarily, but when government no longer accepts their basic rights."

At the lectern he sensed a stirring in the Latin quarter, as if the scent of gunpowder was racing through their collective imagination. "We too can do it," cried Carlos, a Mexican student who had not yet spoken in public. The class rustled with approval.

"There will be time for revolutionary fervor later in our discussions," said Adam, smiling, "but for the time being I want to concentrate on the results of the Americans' gaining independence from England.

They could have remained distinct colonies or states. Virginia and New York could have turned out like Paraguay and Bolivia: separate nations emancipated from colonialism. But something brought the 13 states together, first in the Articles of Confederation and then in the stronger Union expressed in the Constitution of 1789. The party supporting the stronger Union was called the Federalists. Anti-Federalists were concerned that the Union would become too strong and encroach on their newly won freedoms—their 'unalienable rights' for which they had fought the war against England. To insure their rights, the anti-Federalists insisted on a Bill of Rights, which was added to the Constitution as the first ten Amendments."

He glanced around the room to check that the students were following. "We are interested primarily in the First Amendment," he went on, "which guarantees the basic freedoms of speech, including of the press, religion, and assembly. What does the First Amendment tell us about freedom of religion?"

Gad Menachem, who had been exposed to some of this material in his Jewish grade school, answered, "The first thing the Amendment tells us is that '*Congress shall make no law respecting an establishment of religion.*'"

"Very good," said Adam. "This is a uniquely American provision. What it means is that the federal government may not declare that the official religion of the United States is Calvinism or Lutherism or Catholicism or any other religion. Now, the government was obviously reacting against something here. What was it?"

"Well," said Jaime, "England had an established Church, the Anglican Church. Many states in Europe are committed to particular religions as their official religions."

"In Latin America, too," added Adam, "Until recently, the president of Argentina had to be a Catholic. That seems to me a way of establishing a religion."

Chen looked puzzled. "Does Israel have an established religion? It is called a Jewish state, but does that mean that the Jewish religion is any way obligatory? We think of Jews as an ethnic group, analogous to Germans or French or Italians."

"Yes," intervened Jaime, "but you require Jewish storekeepers to close their shops on Saturday."

"True," she responded, "but this doesn't apply to Arab merchants in the Old City. They do terrific business on the Sabbath."

"We have experience with Sunday closing laws as well," said Adam. "It's one of those issues that tests the meaning of the anti-establishment clause of the First Amendment. The big question," he continued, "is whether it prohibits the establishment of religion in the abstract, or the establishment of a particular religion."

"What would it mean to 'prohibit the establishment of religion in the abstract'?" queried Chen.

"Well, according to the recent decisions of the Supreme Court, public schools are not entitled to do anything that smacks of religion. They are not allowed to read the Bible; they are not to post the Ten Commandments in the classroom. It goes without saying that they are not allowed to pray in class; even a moment of reverential silence is prohibited."

Chen reminded Adam of her comment in her email. "Yes, but you are allowed to write 'In God We Trust' on your money. Don't you think that is a little outrageous?"

"Yes, and so are other little inconsistencies, such as opening Congress with a prayer and swearing in the president with his hand on a Bible."

Jaime found this enormously amusing. "I guess this is a little like the Catholic Church. You believe in hypocrisy as a virtue."

"I'm not sure it's so simple. First we have to try to understand what the establishment clause was originally about. Note that it refers to Congress alone. What follows for the states?"

Grigor Krysztal answered by analogy to the 1949 German Basic Law. "Well, I assume that the Constitution pervades all of society, not true? It must regulate the states as well."

"I'm glad you said that. It's wrong, but it's a natural mistake. The fact is that Congress originally meant just Congress. The states were exempt, and in fact many of them did have established churches, for example the Congregational Church in Connecticut. The purpose of the establishment clause was to keep the federal government neutral among the established Protestant sects in the states."

"In Israel," offered Chen, "the state runs secular schools and religious schools. Both study the Bible, but in different ways. Is that possible here?"

"Absolutely not—for reasons of this clause in the First Amendment. The states are now totally bound by the same principle of neutrality toward religion. Later we will talk about how this change came about, so that the Bill of Rights now applies in the states. Private religious schools can still teach religion, but they do not receive a penny from state. The public schools cannot do anything that comes even close to prayer or affirmation of religion. They're lucky if they can have a Christmas program, now usually called a Christmas/Chanukah program. If there were a Muslim holiday in December, they would probably include it in the catch-all idea of a Holiday program."

Aschkin took this comment as a slight against Islam. She spoke her thoughts out loud. "Not a penny from the state? Totally neutral? All these religious institutions receive tax exemptions. Some pigs are more equal than others."

Chen loved this quote from *Animal Farm*, George Orwell's satire on Communism. "And the ones who eat pigs seem to get the best deal of all," she added, with a certain air of triumph.

Adam was taken aback. "I yield to the brilliant arguments from the delegations from Turkey and Israel." He tried smiling at Aschkin, but his lips did not quite curl into a natural pose. He had no choice but to continue. "True, we tell ourselves that the state is neutral about religion. This is the official policy. It is also true that many people in the USA are very religious, even if the élites are not. They say that the Indians in Asia are the most religious people in the world, and the Swedes the least given to believing in God. The United States sometimes looks like a bunch of Indians ruled by a bunch of Swedes."

This gained him snickers around the room. Adam explained, "The secular 'Swedes' who run the country are smart. They pretend that the state is entirely neutral. They do not force the Bible down the throats of the naturally religious Asian Indians. If they tried, many people would resist. Sometimes the most effective teaching requires doing nothing—or at least pretending to do nothing."

Joerg whispered to the Japanese student next to him with a wink, "Maybe that is why he does not teach us the dogmas. He is waiting for us to discover them."

"I must admit that the clause more relevant to our discussion of freedom and equality," the professor said, taking a didactic tack, "is further on in the First Amendment. It says that 'Congress shall make no law respecting an establishment of religion, *or prohibiting the free exercise thereof.'* What does the 'free exercise' clause mean? Do you get a special exemption from the criminal law because you are religious? Can you smoke grass if your religion requires it? Can Mormons have two wives and Muslims four, even if the law of bigamy applies to everyone else?"

Holly Chen from China felt too much pressure. "I think you are ridiculing religion. This is the kind of talk I used to hear at home." Several other Chinese students turned around and stared at her.

"Maybe I am just trying to provoke you," suggested Adam gently. "You decide. I am just asking questions, pretending to say nothing."

"All I know is that in Romania," Ilona jumped in, "freedom of religion means that the police do not harass Jews on the way to synagogue or Protestants in their churches. Everybody is allowed to pray as he or she pleases."

"Yes," countered the professor, "but religious obligations include more than prayer—a religious society may wish to follow other rules also, according to the dictates of their faith. In a very famous case, in the 1970s, the Supreme Court decided that the Amish in Wisconsin were allowed to keep their children out of school after grade school even though the truancy law required all children to go to high school. Of course the Amish could have established their own school, but they wanted their children to adopt a rural way of life and to work on their farms. Also they were afraid that their teenagers would be corrupted by contact with secular children. They claimed a religious obligation to remain apart, and appealed as well to the danger of assimilation and the destruction of their community."

"Wow!" exclaimed Chen. "This is the argument the religious make in Israel. They deprive girls of education so that they remain faithful and obedient."

"Not only that," Joerg added, "but you are violating the principle of equal application of the laws. In Germany we do not believe in granting special exceptions for religious people. The same law for everyone."

"Yes," Adam countered, "I have heard that the circumcision of males is illegal in Germany. Is that right?"

"Well, mutilation of the body is forbidden. It is a crime, but there is a clause called 'social adequacy' for religions that have this custom."

"Yes, this affects the millions of Muslims—and the few thousand remaining Jews in Germany." There was an edge in Adam's voice. He could not get past his impression of Joerg's fascist tendencies in his email. His including of Muslims in his appeal had the hidden purpose of winning back Aschkin's sympathy.

Joerg defended himself. "There is no constitutional right to circumcision, if that is what you mean."

"Why not? Is there no freedom of religion in Germany?"

"Of course, according to law. There are no laws expressly discriminating against religious groups. But we don't grant exceptions either."

"I gather this is the general attitude in Europe. This is what the European Convention on Human Rights implies when it says that the free exercise of religion shall 'be subject only to such limitations as are prescribed by law,' and then goes to say that the law has to be, among other things, 'for the protection of public order, health, or morals.' This means the law has to have a legitimate purpose. It cannot be targeted against religion simply because the government does not like the religion."

"That's right," said Joerg.

"And it follows that a law could easily prohibit many of the practices that Mormons, Muslims and Jews think are necessary for the way of life. Some countries even prohibit the kosher slaughter of animals."

"Well," said Chen, "I think that is right. The protection of animal rights should prevail over quaint and outmoded ideas of killing animals according to the superstitious ways of the Bible."

Several students looked at her, aghast. This was too anti-religious even for them.

"I'm afraid we're missing the point here," countered Adam. "We have to transport ourselves into the mindset of the late eighteenth century. Note that freedom of religion is the most important right mentioned in the Bill of Rights, even ahead of free speech, which is 'sacred' for Americans. Now, why have they favored a Constitution that seems to exempt religious believers from certain laws of the state?"

"I'm not sure what you are getting at," offered Gad Menachem, "but even if the state I lived in prohibited kosher slaughtering or male circumcision, I would do it anyway. I would engage in civil disobedience. The state cannot legislate in areas where my religion tells me to do the contrary."

"OK," responded Adam supportively, "and can you think of a Biblical verse that would support your view?"

"There is something in the Christian Bible about Caesar, but I don't remember exactly."

Holly came to the rescue. "It's *'Render unto Caesar the things which are Caesar's, and unto God the things that are God's.'* This is said in the book of Matthew and other places."

"Yes," Jaime intervened, "but the context is different. The Pharisees were testing Jesus about whether he should pay taxes. Did the state have any authority to legislate over him at all? He answered that, at least as far as the coins had Caesar's head on them, they could be paid to the state. Now you are turning it around, but I like the argument anyway."

Adam replied, "The problem might be same. How can people live under the state's law and God's law at the same time, especially when they conflict? Can't you read the First Amendment to mean 'Render unto God the things that are God's and, afterwards, render unto Caesar the things that are his'?"

"So," Jaime pressed the matter, "suppose a newly elected president in Latin America believes that it is his Christian duty to expropriate the oil fields or the United Fruit Company or any other American business. He does this in imitation of Jesus's commitment to the poor, literally to allow the meek to inherit the earth?"

"OK, you lawyers out there—what do you think?"

"No," said Joerg. "If you were to take an extreme approach to putting conscience ahead of the law, you would have to formulate a theory for deciding what a real religious obligation was. And you would have to decide whether all religions were included, even those that sacrificed animals in the worship of God."

Aschkin was growing restless. She could understand the full implications of this conflict for her home country. If conscience prevailed over the policies of the government, women would be able to wear their headscarves everywhere—in the Parliament, in the university, everywhere. This idea disturbed her.

Adam sought to mediate. "I think there are two basic approaches here. One is to say that conscience matters but that it must be balanced against the harm that the religious act might cause to others. This is the most popular approach in the United States as well as Europe. Those who take this approach would overrule the Latin American expropriation on grounds of public order. The other approach would be to take religious obligations as absolute: to agree that as a matter of conscience they admit of no compromise. Of course, as Mr. Mueller says, if you take the second approach you have to define your notion of religious obligation very carefully. Not everything can count: expropriation to help the poor would still not qualify, in my opinion, since it is not a Christian duty shared by all believers.

"Let me ask for a show of hands. How many of you support the balancing approach?"

Ninety per cent of the hands went up.

"And how many the view that those who feel bound by God's law should be exempt from secular law?"

Here he got a handful—Holly, Jaime, Gad, Marga and Mohammed.

"Let me say," responded Adam, "I favor the absolutist approach. I don't think it makes sense to consider religion at all—any more than we consider astrology—unless we recognize the conflict of conscience for those who are believers. Take the case of conscientious objectors to military service. If their objection is grounded in religious beliefs, then we should recognize them."

"But it is not so simple," said Chen. "In Israel we have Jews who say that as a matter of conscience they will not fight in the territories to suppress Palestinians, and others who say, equally as a matter of conscience, that they will not help the army in evacuating Jewish settlers. They all have the same religion but they come out on opposite sides."

"These are very touchy questions," responded Adam, "but I would be willing to allow those whose conscience is on the line in either way to have an exemption from military service."

"I hope this is not one of the dogmas of American law?" queried Joerg.

The time to use the quote scribbled down in front of Adam's computer at lunchtime had finally arrived. "Revolutionaries are always absolutist in their commitments," he began. "Let me tell you about some of the revolutionary thinkers who like most of you were immigrants and visitors to the United States. If you walk to the corner of 113th Street and Riverside Drive, you will encounter a statue in honor of Lajos Kossuth. Kossuth was one of the heroes of the Revolution of 1848—a liberal revolution that promoted the basic values endorsed in the First Amendment in the leading states of Europe. At the forefront of the revolutionary cause were freedom of speech and freedom of religion. After the Revolution failed in Hungary, Kossuth left for a lecture tour to the United States. He was a journalist and a lawyer and detested any form of censorship. But he felt just as strongly about freedom of religion. Here is what he said: *'My principles are, that the Church shall not meddle with politics, and Government will not meddle with religion. In every society there are political and civil concerns on one side, and on the other social concerns; for the first, civil authority must be established—in political and civil respects everyone has to acknowledge the power of its jurisdiction. But, in respect to social interests, it is quite the contrary. Religion is not an institution—it is a matter of conscience.'"*

Aschkin could not hold back any longer. "But you—and your Hungarian friend—" she added softly, "your enthroning the conscience of the individual undermines the authority of the state. If you allow this to happen, our Muslim believers in Turkey could soon take over the state. You forget you are dealing here with laid-back, Protestant people. But the Muslims are an institution and they want power; they want to take over Turkey as they have taken over Iran, Saudi Arabia and other countries."

"Does that mean you have to prohibit all public displays of religion?"

"They can wear what they like in the mosque and at home, but not in the public space. The public space belongs to all the people—the republic."

"Didn't Napoleon believe the same thing?" intervened Charlotte. "The Jews could be Jews at home, provided they were French in public."

"But that was a form of emancipation for the Jews, who until that time had been restricted to ghettos. As for the general problem," Adam mused, "a lot depends on whether you are afraid that a minority group will take over the whole society. This is true about freedom both of speech and of religion. Americans are not afraid. We let a thousand flowers bloom. No one of them will dominate the garden."

"But our history is different," objected Aschkin. "We have reason to fear." Many students around the room nodded in agreement.

"Yes, our histories are different." Adam wondered why he had allowed a division between "us" and "them", between "I" and "thou", to enter into his interactions with Aschkin. He himself felt on the fence. The Argentines, after all, had plenty of reason to fear. In the years before he'd emigrated, there had been constant threats from all points on the political spectrum. Yet now he identified with American sensibilities. He was not afraid of freedom—even of too much freedom. His course was designed to induce a conversion to this idea among the students. He realized that he himself had once undergone the same change of loyalties.

"I want to leave you with one big idea," he said. "Freedom of religion in the First Amendment symbolizes the entire Constitution. Let us call it the 'Freedom Constitution.' This implies that there was another big idea that was totally absent. What was that?"

"I was thinking about this," said Mohammed. "You have a constitution that recognizes slavery. It glorifies freedom. Whatever happened to 'all men are created equal'?"

"Very good. We have a conflict between the Declaration of Independence and the Constitution. You have the principle of equality declared in 1776, but not in 1789. The Constitution is totally silent on the principle of equality before the law. And, as we know, the more freedom, the less equality."

"Of course," said Joerg. "If you grant special exemptions to religious people, they have more rights than others. This is not equality under the law."

"We have to leave it at that. Tomorrow we will talk about how the principle of equality made a dramatic comeback in American history." Adam summed up the lecture with a sense of satisfaction. Glancing at Aschkin, he closed his books, and slowly left the room.

* * * * *

This was the end of the second day of the intensive short course before the beginning of regular classes. There was time now to relax a bit, to enjoy pizza and beer on the terrace of the law school—time to socialize and to get to know each other.

At five o'clock about a hundred students gathered on the terrace and gratefully filled their glasses with cheap red wine or simply grabbed bottles of beer. The pizza was served with no plates, just napkins. All of this contributed to the informality of the occasion. The students mingled, shook hands, talked to people they had never addressed before. At the beginning they were caught up with freedom of religion, and rather intense comments passed between the free-exercisers, on the one side, and the law-enforcers, on the other. As the afternoon sun bore down on them, the intensity of the discussions waned and many of the guys wearing ties were prompted to pull them off and unbutton the top buttons of their shirts.

Scenting the odor of men stripping away their professional façades, Charlotte and Chen drifted toward a group of the more vocal students in class. "Are you guys talking about where you're going to find your next date?"

"I wish I knew," said one. "Two days of law school and I'm beginning to feel like a monk."

Jaime overheard this line and started laughing. "You have no idea what it what it's like to pray five times a day in a monastery."

"I bet Professor Gross would like that," said Chen sharply. "Maybe they'd let him talk about the law between prayers."

At the moment, however, Adam was engaged with a group of Latinos imitating dance steps behind Carlos from Mexico. Each had a bottle of beer in hand and was following his commands. Feet together, now shift your weight to the right, then step to the left, bring your feet together, weight on your left, now step forward with your right, but slightly to the left side, then forward and together with the left. Adam recognized the instruction as the *paso básico* of the Argentine tango. He joined in, forgetting for a moment to consider whether this was appropriate for an instructor. The students loved it.

Aschkin came on to the terrace. "Come join us in the tango," Adam called across the crowd. She slithered, seductively (at least in Adam's eyes), across the space between them. By now, most of the students had shared the gossip that she was a professor who taught tax law and happened to be the dean's wife; opinions differed on why she had come to Professor Gross's class with them.

"Here, let me show you," Adam said. He assumed the ballroom dance pose with his left arm extended and his right prepared to embrace Aschkin around the waist. She entered the pose with the style of an experienced dancer. "I love the tango," she said.

"If you don't know how, I will teach you," Adam said.

"Don't worry, I can dance well enough to impress this group."

Someone put on a CD of Carlos di Sarli, one of the composers of the classical period; it had a clear, regular beat. Adam held Aschkin in the formal pose and shifted weight with the beat from the right to the left foot, the left foot to the right. Aschkin went with him as though dance was a natural part of her life. Then he stepped broadly to the left and Aschkin followed with a long, graceful move of her right thigh, fixing her position firmly on her right toes and then bringing herself erect in front of him. Adam paused and then, having shifted his weight to his left side, he stepped with the right foot toward the left and outside, which signaled to Aschkin that on the next step she should move into the *cruzada*, the cross-step with the right foot on top snuggling the left. Then Adam opened his embrace, and shifted his chest to the left. Aschkin understood *la marca*—the lead—and went gracefully into a forward *ocho*, a figure-eight to the front—one of the basic and yet most graceful of steps in the tango. She lifted her right foot, paused in mid-air and extended broadly to her left, and then pivoted, precisely—no slipping or wobbling—on the right foot, turning to face Adam, who remained motionless as *el hombre*, the anchor for *la mujer*. "The beauty is in the pauses," Adam whispered. "In the waiting."

"Yes," said Aschkin, "sometimes the man does his best when he does nothing."

"Or at least pretends to," smiled Adam .

As Aschkin continued her execution of the *ocho adelante* by extending her left leg, returning to her position directly in front of Adam, he almost swooned. He remained motionless, as good tango dancers sometimes did. "Ah, I can feel your legs as they move gracefully across the floor." This was a bit too "friendly" for the occasion. The tango was very much like the sauna. From a certain point of view it all seemed like a prelude to sex, but if you were in it, you were not supposed to look at or respond sexually to your partner. Physical evidence of arousal in either place would get you thrown out.

Adam's mind drifted back to all the glorious nights he had spent dancing tango in the clubs of San Telmo, and later in New York on a barge moored in the Hudson River. For him the tango was freedom. He had been consumed with passion for Sara when he'd first been learning the dance, and the tango clubs had offered him asylum, a pause in the constant press of sexual energy: even when he'd danced in close embrace with Sara, the sexual gymnastics had been replaced by an impersonal, stylized form of sensuality that was devoid of personal attachment.

But the dance was not impersonal in the eyes of the students. The entire party was transfixed, gazing, stunned, at the couple dancing in the middle of their circle.

Aschkin and Adam were emboldened to try a series of more advanced steps. They went into the backwards *ocho* and then Adam blocked Aschkin's left foot with his right and sandwiched her foot by placing his left on the other side. It was though his two feet were her thighs grabbing him in a horizontal embrace. He stepped back with his right foot and then Aschkin pivoted, rubbed her right shoe against Adam's pant leg and then lifted it slowly over the leg, the entire time with a look of studied passion on her face. The students went wild. Even Chen was applauding. They had never seen two professors engaged in a ritual act of seduction.

"I was a little fresh, but you didn't complain," said Adam to Aschkin as the dance came to an end.

"No, I did not complain. I wish my husband could dance like this."

"I wish we were as harmonious in class as we are on the dance floor."

"Harmony is not necessarily good. I enjoy a good argument."

"Well, let me comply. How about lunch tomorrow?"

Aschkin shook his hand and said OK. "Tomorrow, 12.30, at the Eatery."

As Adam left, shaking hands with everybody, the student festivities were in full swing. National boundaries were breaking down. People he had never seen talking to one another were trying to dance a few steps of tango. Aschkin danced with Joerg and a few others eager to take center stage. Adam was reluctant to leave, but he had a vague sense that the spotlight was too much on him.

As he made his way to the front door of the building, he ran into Charlie Fairfield, carrying a bundle of files and papers. "Hello, Professor," greeted the young reporter cheerfully, and added—Adam thought slightly challengingly—"The next issue of the paper is going fine."

All of a sudden, Professor Gross felt at the center of great historical currents.

11

New Beginnings

ADAM AWOKE EARLY on Friday morning with the tango on his mind. The dance with Aschkin had brought back memories of many summer evenings of chance meetings on the dance floor. Yet he had never met anyone with whom he could dance regularly. He yearned for a woman who could appeal to him both on the dance floor and in dinner conversation. He smiled as the French expression crossed his mind: "*Tout est bien à table et au lit*"—"All is well at the table and in bed." The dance floor was at least as important to Adam as bed. If the rhythm was right in the first, it would right in the second. Aschkin seemed like the kind of woman he had always looked for. She could hold her own in an intellectual conversation but yield readily to his lead on the dance floor.

The tango was associated in his mind with the barge tied to the Hudson River at 23rd Street. The best summer dancing in New York was always on the barge. It was at the end of a half-hour bike trip south along the new bike path hugging the riverbank. Originally used by the Lackawanna Railroad to ferry railroad cars back and forth to New Jersey, the barge now stood alone—with occasional visitors with a refined taste for the romantic and the forlorn. The dancers felt fortunate when the barge was opened to them for an evening.

He rose, dressed and descended in semi-automatic gestures from his twelfth-floor apartment and retrieved his mountain bike from the utility room. As the day was dawning, Adam glided down Riverside Drive toward the bike path. At 79th Street he cut down to the boat basin and surveyed the houseboats and mini-yachts moored in the slips off the river. He always wondered what it would be like to live in one of these boats, confined in a narrow space but sleeping to the rhythm of the tides in his little escape from the quotidian of the city.

As he pedaled further south, he felt as though he was sailing down toward the Statue of Liberty. He paused in front of the "works of art" as the locals called them—the rotting structures left in the shallow water crouching like many-legged spiders, decaying buildings imitating giant insects; there were threats to tear down the skeletal structures, but the Hudson-lovers had banded together to save their favored strip of New York from becoming too yuppified. Soon the path arrived at the giant luxury liners moored at 59th Street, which came from all over the world to get a glimpse of the city.

Past the houseboats, the giant cruise ships, the sailing rigs fit for racing, Adam pedaled south. Had he kept going, he would have come to the twin towers of the World Trade Center, pointing up at the sky from an array of modern office buildings. But he chose to stop at the Chelsea piers and veer off the path toward the water. There he entered a secret world defined by the four corners of the Lackawanna barge, tied in deceptive permanency to the riverbank. An old railroad car, installed permanently on the barge, served as the master's office. Perhaps the name was just hype, likewise the master who worked around the barge pretending to be the owner. No one quite knew where the barge fitted into the scheme of conventional property rights and management hierarchies. It was simply there, and once in a while, in the evening, the cognoscenti came to dance under the stars. It existed in time, but out of space and beyond the order of urban life.

Every time Adam rode to the edge of the barge and peered into the water, he was overcome by a sense of gratitude that this little place was not as orderly as the world of rights and duties, rules and exceptions, that dominated his classroom. The Romantic poets pulled at him, the sense of the ineffable and inexhaustible, the frisson of love burning to a climax in a momentary flame.

He dismounted his bike and held it in the formal pose of the tango, his right hand on the seat, his left on the handlebar, imagining Aschkin rising up in the space between the seat and the rubber-tipped bars. Holding the bike and imagining her hand in his left and the small of her back in his right, he hummed the melody of Di Sarli and began to shift his weight from the left to the right, the right to the left. Then he took a broad step to the left. The bike glided with him. Though alone, as abandoned as the railroad cars that once trafficked the river, he sensed a third eye taking him in. The eye winked at him and he began laughing in return. Overwhelmed by the absurdity of dancing with his bicycle, he broke out in yelps and then guffaws. His body convulsed with waves, racking to the side and then off balance. The bike fell to the floor and he tumbled into a fetal position on the threadbare couch that the barge regulars used as their makeshift living room. His mind flooded with lines from Keats and Blake. He swung himself back onto the ripped cushions and blurted out the words, "The poetry of earth is never dead," as a surrogate for the prayer that his lips could not form.

Death, like sex, was always close to his mind, but now he felt suspended in life, as though he had discovered the secret of the permanently unfulfilled priapic state. Could it have been better for Byron, he thought, as he waited—perhaps on a barge near the water in the port of Missolonghi—for his chance to fight in the Greek War of Independence? He meditated on Keats' yearning to be among the greats, the cultivation of genius among the Romantics. Would he, Adam Gross, be among the greats? What did it mean to be "great" in the humble craft of European jurisprudence?

Sigel, Kossuth and Lieber were all among the greats, he thought. What do we have in common? Is there any hope that I could become like them? I wonder whether they consciously imitated the poets in England and Germany, who had lived and written a generation or two before them. The truth is, he concluded, they probably didn't think about their greatness. Perhaps they thought the issues they faced were no more important than a criminal law exam. Maybe their secret was that they weren't concerned about whether they would be remembered by history.

And do I have a cause that will be remembered? Is resisting the feminists on an issue of academic freedom worthy of being called a cause? Adam still had no sense of the extent to which falling in love would loom larger than any political cause he could imagine.

Time, the greater reminder of the rational world, closed in on his moment. His meditations on Romantic struggle would have to wait. With the day's first lecture set to begin in an hour, he remounted and started pedaling up-wind to regain the Upper West Side. A few moderate hills required down-gearing and heavy pumping. A quick shower, a hastily chosen tie, then out of the door and a ten-minute walk to lecture hall 104. The students were already gathering in anticipation. Adam entered, headed for the front of the room and stood fast, waiting for the top of the hour.

* * * * *

Aschkin awoke thinking and feeling that she might be bearing life within her body, but she knew it was not true: the final stages of the *in vitro* fertilization had not yet taken place. She had an appointment that morning, as every morning, in Dr. Bluestone's office. This time they had asked her to bring along another sample of Peter's sperm. She snuggled up next to her husband and felt the warmth of his firm chest, then glided her hands over his body as though she was discovering it anew. She enjoyed his firm build and the hardness of the organ that was going to provide her the magic serum she would transport surreptitiously to the hospital. As Peter, still asleep, was about to come to a climax, she reached for the flask from her collection of exotic bottles that she had carefully prepared by sterilising the night before. She picked a round bottle with a hole in the center, enclosed in a leather case, the kind of canteen Hungarian cowboys carried on the Puszta. Peter started to wake up and, still half-asleep, he said, "Ah, I was dreaming about being with you in the sauna." Aschkin inconspicuously sealed the bottle and placed it in her briefcase.

As they were dressing, the phone rang. Peter answered. "Yes, Charlie, I'm familiar with Adam's exam. Several faculty members came to me to complain about it. You need a quote from me? Let me think about it. I'll call you from the office in an hour or so."

"What was that about?"

"That was a kid from the law school working on the *Report*. They're doing a story on Gross's exam last year. Say they need a comment from me. Have you heard about the brewing scandal?

"Actually I haven't, but I'm going to his class now, the one for graduate students, and I love it."

"I had no idea you were sitting in. Does he mind? Some faculty do, you know."

"No, he seems to appreciate my being there. He even gets me to participate. He seems to flourish with an international audience."

"Well, he didn't do so well with last year's first-year students, particularly the feminists."

"Do you think that is his fault or theirs?" she challenged.

Peter resented Aschkin's taking Adam's side without knowing more about the details of the exam. "I have to be going," he said abruptly. "I'll send you a copy of the exam and you can decide for yourself."

Half an hour later Aschkin was walking briskly across Central Park, with her little secret contained in its round flask in her briefcase. It occurred to her that she had acted unilaterally. Why was I secretive with Peter? she asked herself. Maybe I am trying to tell myself something: this is my thing, my thing only.

When she arrived at the clinic within the hour's deadline, she relaxed and handed the nurse the elegantly decorated flask. "It's in there."

The nurse was bit befuddled by the leather case and the unusual shape of the flask. "I hope it was sterile," she said.

"Yes, I was very careful."

The nurse shook her head as she took it. What can you expect, she muttered under her breath, from one those Regina professors?

As Aschkin was waiting her turn for her shot, she looked at the available selection of current magazines and medical literature. Her eye fell on a brochure about IVF. She picked it up and started reading.

The first stage of the IVF is to provide hormone stimulation of the ovaries to produce more than one egg in each menstrual cycle. Either the doctor or nurse will administer a shot of FSH (follicular stimulating hormone) every morning until the desired number of eggs is ready to be released. This is likely to be several weeks from the beginning of treatment. Under good conditions women can generate between three and 40 eggs. The eggs are then fertilized with the husband's or donor's sperm and within 24 hours the fertilized eggs form a blastocyst, which we examine closely for growth and development for five days. During this period we can also test the potential fetuses for gender. On the fifth day we will give healthy blastocysts an opportunity to implant themselves by inserting them with a catheter into the mother's uterus. Whether they take and develop soundly thereafter depends on the general conditions of age and health that affect every pregnancy. In view of the risk that some will not mature to the point of a heartbeat, we encourage the implantation of up to six or eight blastocysts. If there are others remaining they may be frozen and used at a later date.

Aschkin's eye paused in several places. When she saw the word "donor," she began to wonder. Would that make any sense for me? What if it turns out that this doesn't work with Peter's sperm? I don't really care whether the sperm comes from Peter or from some other "donor." My name is not Yilmaz for nothing. I am going to succeed at this. And then, as she read on, she was taken aback by the prospect of implanting six or eight embryos. How was this possible? They were thinking of not bringing all of them to term? I have to talk to the doctor about this, she thought urgently.

It was usually the nurse who administered the injections, but this time Aschkin insisted on waiting and talking to Roger Bluestone. "How can you possibly implant six or eight embryos?" she demanded as soon as she was in his office.

"Well, it is not really an 'embryo' as such until it implants itself in the uterus," the gynecologist said. "If there are more than two or three successful implants and they look as if they are going to reach a heartbeat after three months, then we can engage in selective reduction."

"You mean abortion?"

"Well, I wouldn't put it that way, I think of it more as saving the few who will live rather than killing those who might not make it anyway."

"But if you only implant one or two in the first place?"

"That's possible, but it lessens the chances of success, so it means you might have to repeat the process."

Aschkin only had to think for a moment. "I think I might prefer to take the risk. Would it possible to do that on this cycle?"

"Well, I wouldn't ordinarily do it so fast, but if it's really important to you we could try with just one or two eggs."

"It would be more practical to get pregnant in this cycle because I could have the child just before next summer and have time to take care of it." Like many professional women in the United States, Aschkin had a keen sense of timing.

"OK," said Roger Bluestone. "We can try for a fertilization on this round."

Aschkin felt relieved that there would be a lesser risk of killing implanted embryos simply for the sake of convenience. As she left the office and made her way back to Regina to attend Adam's 11 a.m. class, she was appalled by the science-can-do-anything mentality of the clinic. She still thought of having a child as the highest possible spiritual encounter with the world. The miracle of birth reduced to a test tube. And "selective reduction"—"Newspeak" for abortion—all this made her very uncomfortable. Why did the world of medicine have to be so this-worldly? Perhaps it was because of women like her, women who felt compelled to have a child.

As she arrived and took her place amid the buzzing of the students, she looked over appreciatively at Holly and Marga and Jaime and thought to herself, I am in a haven here from the godless world of modern science. Maybe I will even tell Adam how I feel when I see him for lunch.

* * * * *

"Ah, freedom," Adam began. "We all yearn for freedom. Freedom of speech, freedom of religion, freedom to own property, the freedom to invest and to get rich as a capitalist." There were some funny looks from the European quarter. "Well, I admit capitalism is not mentioned in the Constitution, but the right to private property is relatively clear. The Fifth Amendment secures everyone against the deprivation of 'life, liberty, or property, without due process of law.' There is nothing similar in the European Convention on Human Rights."

Grigor suddenly became animated. "Finally, someone understands this. I am a student of Friedrich Hayek. I regard private property and the free market as the foundation of all individual rights. But all we get in the German Constitution is '*Eigentum verpflichtet*'—'Property entails duties.'"

Adam sought some balance in the analysis. "Remember the conflict between the Declaration of Independence and the Constitution. In 1776 the Declaration of Independence declares that 'all men are created equal.' In 1789 the Constitution endorses slavery and remains deafeningly silent about equality. This contradiction could not endure forever. The problem came to the head in a critical case called *Dred Scott v Sanford*, decided in 1857. The real issue in the case was whether former slaves could be citizens of the United States. The Court decided, shamelessly, that people of African descent could never become citizens. For Chief Justice Taney, who wrote the opinion in the case, the only problem was whether the Constitution prevailed over the Declaration of Independence. He concluded—not irrationally, by the way—that the latter in time was superior in right: the conflict should be resolved in favor of the Constitution and its endorsement of slavery."

Several students were disturbed. Jaime provoked the class by saying, "Is the situation much different in Israel today? The law of return allows all Jews to become citizens, but not Arabs."

"Whoa!" Chen yelled out. "There are over a million Arab resident citizens of Israel."

Before Adam could respond, Mohammad pressed forward on a different tack. With some distance from the racial issue, and thinking like a lawyer, he observed, "The logic is not compelling to me. Even if slavery is legitimate in some states, if it is possible for a slave to be emancipated by being taken to a free state, why should it follow that emancipated slaves could never become citizens?"

"You're right," said Adam. "The Court was overreaching—in a way that can only be described as racist. The Court went even further and argued that the Missouri Compromise of 1820 was unconstitutional because it forbade slavery in some of the newly acquired territories. Lincoln was furious about this decision. In large measure, the constitutional entrenchment of slavery—in the name of freedom and the right to property, mind you—made the Civil War inevitable."

"It could not have been just one decision by the Court that generated the Civil War," protested Grigor, with Joerg nodding in agreement.

"No," replied Adam. "In fact, the entire decade of the 1850s was about the politics of slavery. The overriding question was whether slavery would be tolerated in the territories. Can you imagine why the Southern slave states were so concerned about this issue?"

"Yes, we learned this in school," replied Carlos. "It is part of the story leading up to the invasion of Mexico in the 1840s. The United States was constantly expanding. They talked about '*manifest destiny from coast to coast.*' The new territories would become states and they would be able to vote to amend the Constitution. If there were new free states, three-quarters of them might vote to abolish slavery in the entire country."

Adam decided not to challenge the Mexican view of history. "Most of the politics of the first half of the nineteenth century were about slavery, one way or the other. It was the obsession of the country. When Lincoln ran for president in 1860, the level of political engagement was so high that over 80 per cent of the eligible voters—all white men—went to the polls."

Charlotte articulated her pain. "Ugh, I can see what is coming. Race will become the dominant obsession of the country. There will be war. Black men and white men will march side by side. After the war, black men will get the right to vote. But women will be still locked in the kitchen."

"Perspicacious," Adam said. "War did come. As soon as Lincoln was elected, seven states seceded from the Union. Shortly thereafter, on 12 April 1861, South Carolina bombarded Fort Sumpter, a federal fortress in the middle of Charleston Harbor. Lincoln immediately blockaded the Southern ports. Skirmishes and full-scale battles followed in the succeeding months."

Mueller sat up straight with his hand jutting forward in way in a way that Adam did not enjoy witnessing. "Permission to speak, sir?"

Adam nodded and added, "To repeat, this isn't the military, Mr. Mueller."

"Sorry, sir. But I am concerned about the breakdown of authority. You see, revolution breeds revolution, secession breeds secession. The mistake was failing to respect the supreme authority of the Union. Once it starts, it never ends."

Charlotte shot back, with a hiss, "You sound like Edmund Burke arguing against the French Revolution. Sometimes the people must revolt. They must kill the king."

Adam rode the wave. "Ms. de la Porte des Vaux has a point. The secession was in the spirit of the Declaration of Independence. This time Lincoln was the king. When the war ended four years later, they in fact *had* killed the king. A Confederate sympathizer assassinated him in April 1865, just as the war was coming to an end. Lincoln was dead, but the Union survived."

The students sat spellbound. For most, this was a new saga. They were becoming absorbed in the American national epic—the ongoing story of racial justice in the United States.

"And why did it happen? The best explanation, I believe, is Lincoln's own. In the middle of the war he was elected to a second term. That there was an election as the blue and grey were killing each other—that is an amazing story in itself. And when he gave his second inaugural address he reflected on the war and why it came: *'Both read the same Bible and pray to the same God, and each invokes His aid against the other. It may seem strange that any men should dare to ask a just God's assistance in wringing their bread from the sweat of other men's faces, but let us not judge, that we be not judged. The prayers of both could not be answered. That of neither has been answered fully. The Almighty has His own purposes. "Woe unto the world because of offenses; for it must needs be that offenses come, but woe to that man by whom the offense cometh."'*

Adam paused. "Lincoln doesn't explain how religious fervor drove both sides of the conflict, but it is fairly easy to reconstruct. The abolitionists took seriously the claims of Genesis, chapter one, about the creation of all human beings in the image of God. The slave-holders drew on a different passage in Genesis, Noah's curse of Canaan. As you will recall, Ham, one of the three sons of Noah, saw him sleeping naked, told his two brothers and the brothers went into their father's tent backwards and covered him. It is not clear what Ham's great crime was, but when Noah awoke he discovered the wrong and cursed someone who was not even present, namely the fourth son of Ham, called Canaan. In the Middle Ages people began to read Ham and Canaan to refer to the dark people who lived south of Suez, those who lived in the land of Cush, the people we now think of as Africans. So some people read the Bible to support the equality of all of humanity; others read it to support the inferiority of blacks and thus to justify slavery."

"Ah, my *capitán*, my *capitán*," swooned Rodrigo, barely audible.

Chen Horowitz made a note on her pad—"*Interesting stuff, why did I complain to the dean?*" Then she looked up and asked, "But is invoking the Bible a legal argument? What could Lincoln argue to refute the South's claim that they were the heirs to the American Revolution?"

Adam replied, "In fact neither he nor his radical Republican supporters had much to say. Sometimes they claimed that the Union was engaged in guaranteeing the states of the Confederacy a 'republican form of government.' OK, this is required by the Constitution, but I think it was a weak argument. In contrast to France, we never had much of an idea about what a 'republican form of government' was supposed to mean in practice."

"Here is an argument," added Jaime. "The state cannot be a republic—a *res publica*—it cannot belong to all the people, if half the population are slaves. I could say something about the plight of the Palestinians, but not now."

"Good point," conceded Adam, overlooking the comment about the Palestinians, "but you have to keep in mind that in the beginning Lincoln did not go to war for the sake of the slaves. He needed an argument against secession to overcome the image of South as the heirs of the revolution."

"How about the line 'all men are created equal'?"

"This would be fine—it would turn the Declaration to his favor—but how does he argue that the Declaration is superior to the Constitution? Interestingly, there is a connection between his religious sensibilities and his argument for the Declaration. I will prove this to you in the next session, when we turn to Lincoln's Gettysburg Address."

The students were on the verge of applause. The excitement that day had been more intense than the first two days. Yet, for different reasons, both professor and students were pleased that the time for lunch had arrived.

12

Lunch

ASCHKIN WAS LOST in thought as she left the class and walked automatically to her mailbox to retrieve the day's campus mail. After distractedly fumbling with the lock, she pulled out a batch of single-sheet announcements. On the top of the pile was a memo from the dean's office.

> MEMO: *To the Faculty*
>
> FROM: *Dean Peter Levenger*
>
> RE: *Professor Adam Gross's Exam in Criminal Law*
>
> A number of students and faculty have complained to me about Professor Gross's exam in criminal law given last spring. Their claim is that this examination portrays women as conspiratorial lesbians, as criminals, and as perverse victims who desire the harm that occurs to them. In one example, one woman suffers a malicious abortion by an aggressor on the street and then tells her doctor that she wants to send a thank-you note to her attacker. Many women have claimed that this scenario excessively embarrassed or disturbed them and made it difficult for them to concentrate on the exam. This may constitute an unlawful form of discrimination against women. I am asking university counsel to study the matter further and to keep me informed. Copies of the exam are available in my office. While these procedures are pending, I would advise against visiting Professor Gross's classes.

Aschkin could not decide whether to fume or to cry. Peter's behavior was absurd, but there must have been ample support in the faculty or he would not have done it. To get it out so fast, she thought, he must have had the memo ready when he got the call this morning from Charlie Fairfield. He had added the sentence about not visiting Adam's class as a specific message to her.

Fat chance, she thought to herself, and then wondered how she would say that in Turkish. She smiled at the combination of fat and probability. There was no translation for any of this, she thought as she walked toward the Eatery.

Adam had arrived first and picked out a booth on the far side of the restaurant—a spot good for talking, with some privacy by New York standards. As he sat and waited, he imagined himself in one of the private dining rooms where Russian princes would meet their mistresses behind closed doors.

The fantasy appealed to him. A surreptitious meeting with a married woman, an Anna Karenina, would enable him to play the prince. The image fed his fantasy of noble descent on his father's side. His grandfather had been a rich landowner in rural Hungary and had received privileged status in the liberal period of the Austrian-Hungarian empire at the end of the nineteenth century. Once, when he'd traveled in Hungary and mentioned that his grandfather had been a *földbirtakos*—a major landowner—he had found people deferring to him in the most unusual ways.

His father Miklós had taken this culture with him when he emigrated to Argentina. He had held on to his keen sense of courtly honor almost as though he were still in the service of Franz Josef. A breach of manners—for example, parting company without saying goodbye—was taken as personal insult. This transplanted chivalry was actually well suited to Argentine culture. The militaristic ethic and the instinctive respect for anything European had served Miklós well. Adam knew that his American friends now regarded honor as akin to the dueling ethic, fit for the nineteenth-century dustbin. For the last generation, the buzzword had become "human dignity." Peter Levenger and others in the human rights crowd spoke endlessly about this intangible value shared by all human beings, however miserable and ignorant. They delighted in leveling down, in bringing everyone to the same status as the common or even the most lowly man or woman. Honor was available only to the privileged few. The poor and the disenfranchised had inherent dignity, but they had no honor to lose.

Adam's 1848 heroes—Sigel, Kossuth, and Lieber—had all had a keen sense of honor. They were in his father's camp, but more adventurous. Their honor required political commitment, a willingness to risk their lives. They were in the camp of those who had signed the Declaration of Independence, who knew they were committing treason and ended with the words "We pledge to each other our lives, our Fortunes, and our sacred Honor."

Honor, for Adam, had the humble meaning of taking pride in his profession. If he was not a soldier in a revolutionary cause, at least he could be a warrior of the law. He had been a professor and scholar his entire adult life, but in recent years he had come to feel that he must take on cases of indigents on death row, or of others without funds claiming civil rights abuses. He took some cases with his old friend Bill Goodman who worked for the Center of Constitutional Rights. He advised them on the phone about theoretical aspects of their cases and occasionally had the opportunity to work on a brief, laying out an argument for the Supreme Court or one of the Circuit Courts of the Appeal. He was hoping for a case that would require him to argue for freedom of religion, particularly of Islam, but one had not yet come his way.

Adam associated honor with an upper class ethic but he realized that he could not compete with real aristocrats in their moral aloofness. He could not share their contempt for bourgeois morality. He cared about the way his sexual conduct appeared to others. Once when he was traveling in Germany he had spent the night at a B&B and shared his room for a few nights with a female traveling companion. Nothing sexual, just sharing the room. The day after she left, he met a German woman in a café and revealed to her his fantasies about noble descent. When the time came to search for a trysting place she inquired about his room. He said they could not go there because he had just been sharing his room with a woman. What would the lady of the house think when he brought home another? She broke out in a gusty roar, "This what you call aristocratic contempt for bourgeois morality?"

As Adam was recalling the pain of that put-down, Aschkin arrived. He stood to greet her and waited for her to extend her hand. He knew that a gentleman should never extend his hand to a lady first, though he had never met another American who "knew" this. She did hold out her fingers with her palm down. He took her fingertips in his grasp as though he were about to click his heels and say "*Küss die Hand, Madame*," but then he felt slightly foppish and said simply, "I don't know whether I'm happier to see you here or in class."

"I feel the same way," she replied. No foreplay in this conversation. Adam sensed immediately that she quickened his senses. He must be prepared for challenging questions and witty ripostes. He liked the feeling.

"So why are you doing me this great honor?"

"Here or in class?"

"Colleagues meet for lunch, it's no big deal, but coming to my class is extraordinary. No one on the Regina faculty has ever been to any of my classes."

"I had heard that you were discussing the relationship of law and religion and I became curious about what it would be like to think about law in this way. Ever since I left Turkey in my late twenties I have been cut off from my religious life. Even then I did not have much to do with the imams and the mosque, but the sentiments of Islam were everywhere. We lived in a constant dialectic with the Koran. My tradition no longer speaks to me, and without it I feel alone. Something is missing in my life, so I took a chance that perhaps your approach might satisfy me."

Adam could not but think of the sexual innuendo. He knew that Peter was a totally assimilated Jew. Was Aschkin's comment about being alone and searching for satisfaction some kind of reference to her private life?

"You know, I'm not sure why the subject of religion intrigues me so much," he said, hoping to pursue the theme. "If everyone were doing this I would probably gravitate toward something else. How about tax theory? I wouldn't imagine you and your colleagues talk too much about God and income brackets."

"Economists have no gods except incentives and individual self-interest. It gets a little tedious."

Adam could have explored the theme of the poverty of economic thought, but why ruin a good lunch? Better to turn the discussion toward Aschkin. "Tell me," he said leaning closer, "do you feel the way I do...? Are we both contrarians too? We don't say the same things that other people say?"

"Totally," she said, with a slight lilt that made her accent, a mixture of German and Turkish, so unusual. "I want to explore the religious life without others forcing me to wear the veil. I hate the militant Turkish secularists, but I am still part of them. I am what you would call...a liberal atheist?"

Adam smiled and relaxed. "You want to be different from the masses and yet not alone?"

"*Evet.*" She lapsed into her native language. "How paradoxical!"

"Welcome to the party where nobody is celebrating."

"Well, at least we are dancing," she said.

There was a long pause and then Adam mused, "Do you realize that we both come from empires that no longer exist? Well, at least my parents are from the Austrian-Hungarian empire, which is no more, and the great Ottoman empire is reduced to a fraction of its former territory."

"And you know," jibed Aschkin, "we defeated the Hungarians in the famous Battle of Mohács in 1526."

"I know," said Adam. "That moment is a source of great shame for my father." They both chuckled. And Paul Keskemeny had the nerve, he recalled, not to recognize him as member of the Magyar tribe.

"What about our personal empires?" Aschkin asked. "I don't know anything about the women in your life."

Adam was taken aback by the directness of the question. He paused.

"Sorry, I didn't mean to pry."

"No, it's OK. I was married once to a woman, also from Latin America, from Mexico, She became a fierce Zionist and left me to go and live with a settler on the West Bank. She met one of these right-wing gurus in New York and that was it. Now she keeps the Sabbath strictly, covers her hair, and marches against the Oslo Peace Process."

"Sounds like a radical way to leave a lover. Did you see it coming?" Could she herself do something similar? Aschkin wondered.

"To tell you the truth, if it had not been that guy, something else would have broken us up. I don't miss her, but I haven't seen my daughter for the last couple of years."

Aschkin sat up straighter. "Oh, I didn't know you had a child. What is her name? How old?" Her voice was carefully casual.

"Abigail. Now she is 12. She used to come and stay with me and sleep on an air mattress on the floor of my apartment. We had a lot of fun. But in the last couple of years she has adopted the simplistic religion that she hears from people around her on the settlement. It causes me pain, but I hope that some day she will grow up and find her way back to me."

Aschkin did not know what to say to comfort Adam. "I guess this is unfinished business."

"I have been dwelling lately on lost children. I think you missed the second class when I talked about abortion. These issues penetrate me like the hot jets in my steam shower."

"I think about these issues too, though I don't know anything about steam showers," said Aschkin with an air of innocence. "Anyway, as long as they are alive, there is hope." She reached out and gently took Adam's hand. Adam found it hard to respond. He passively enjoyed the touch.

At that moment the waiter arrived. Aschkin quickly withdrew her hand and grasped the menu. She ordered the vegetarian special. Adam went straight for the super-sized hamburger with chips. He felt robust and aggressive.

"You are very *aimable*, Aschkin. I guess that means 'nice,' but I hate the word 'nice.' My colleagues—the Americans—are nice."

"I know you are a bit of a loner. I think you're just flattered that I'm coming to your class."

"Of course I'm flattered, but it also means that we have a similar quest."

"Yes, it has something to do with religion and its proper place in the law and in our lives. So what is it to be a Jew? Is it a religion or a nationality?"

"Liberal Jews insist that Judaism is a religion, not a nationality. But that reminds me of the Jewish child who goes to Trinity or one of these other élitist Christian schools in New York City. He comes and starts praising the Father, the Son, and the Holy Ghost. Finally, the atheist father can't stand it any longer. He bangs his fist on the table and says, 'You know God is one—do you hear, one!— and we do not believe in Him.'"

She laughed. "So are you more Jewish or Argentine?"

"It depends on who you ask, If you ask the masses of Argentines—not the intellectuals—I am Jewish. If you ask me, I am Argentine—with an unfulfilled desire to be like my father, a displaced Hungarian atheist and a wannabe aristocrat."

"All that? And Israel? Is that an additional twist on your identity?" she probed. "You know that Ben-Gurion, Israel's first president, studied law in Istanbul, and Turkey is still one of Israel's strongest supporters against a common enemy to the East. So what is it? Are we enemies or friends?"

"I have an instinctive bond with Israel. I was able to visit there from time to time in the past, but now emotionally I can't go. I feel too conflicted about being so close to Abigail and not being able to see her. This will have to resolve itself some day."

There was a moment of silence. Adam noticed that the table was not set properly. His spoon was missing. "There is an old Yiddish anecdote," he said. "A Jew sits down at the restaurant. The waiter serves the soup but the Jew finds that his soup spoon is missing. He complains to the waiter that the soup is too salty; he should come over and taste it. The waiter agrees and looks for the soup spoon in order to taste the soup. 'Hey, wait, you don't have a soup spoon!' 'Ah, how clever of you,' responds the Jew."

Aschkin thought for a second and then got it with a seductive purr. "Why did he not ask for the spoon directly?" she asked sensibly.

"This is Jewish logic," Adam said. "It is like the story of the two Jewish merchants who meet on the train in White Russia. One asks the other where he is going. 'Minsk,' the man replies. 'Why are you lying?' the first man then says. 'If you were really going to Minsk, you would tell me you are going to Pinsk.'"

Aschkin seemed delighted. "How wonderful! The line between reasoning and humor disappears." She could never have talked about these things with Peter, who she had noted, to her distress, was reluctant even to mention the word "Jew."

"Is humor a way of expressing your connection to God?" she pondered.

"Maybe it is. I'm constantly looking for my connection to God. Humor would be a good way of achieving it. Why? God is basically absurd. He or she creates human beings and then makes them suffer, makes them search without revealing himself in any way that we understand in modern science."

"But if the voice of God suddenly came to you and told you to sacrifice your daughter, you would not believe it anyway. You would think it was a trick."

"Obviously, but maybe not if he told me to sacrifice my ex-wife..."

Aschkin could not but help laughing this time. "Humor is also very human," she reflected. "A computer cannot understand it. I often find that economists cannot understand it." As Adam was laughing, she repeated to herself her complaint that Peter had no sense of humor. "You know, we have a serious, humorless marriage—I mean, profession." She hoped Adam had not noticed the slip.

"It is horrible." Adam added, "But have you ever met Sydney Morgenbesser? He's the funniest person I know."

"I've heard about him. Very Jewish humor."

"Absolutely. He's an alternative type. In yuppified, goal-oriented New York, a rare commodity. Humor, romanticism, religion, sex— these are all part of an alternative existence—a way of escaping *la vida cotidiana*. Because humor takes us out of ourselves in a very human way, we become more open to each other's erotic selves and to a higher order of reality."

Hmm, thought Aschkin, interesting that he added sex to the list. I am not about to disagree with him.

"For us, in Turkish culture," she said, "we often drift into alternative reality—in poetry, for example. We indulge in abstractions that have nothing to do with the facts on the ground. '*Istanbul'u dinliyorum, gözlerim kapalı.*' 'I am listening to Istanbul, my eyes closed.'"

As she said these words in Turkish and English, she seemed to drift back across the years. The sound of the plates on the wooden table brought her back to their booth, with her eyes fixed on Adam. She recalled the sorry facts of Adam's political situation. She considered whether to mention Peter's memo, and how much of it she should disclose. Adam would discover it, in any event, within a few hours.

"I think I have to tell you something, Adam. I hope you have some clue about it already. You know that some of our colleagues have objected to your criminal law exam last term and they have worked up a group of students to go along with them?"

"Yes, and there has been talk about an article in the newspaper. It *is* just the feminists, right?"

"Well, I think you should prepare for a fight. Peter seems to have caved in to Ann O'Sullivan and her crowd."

"Frankly, I'm not surprised. I didn't think he had the courage to stand up to a minority with conviction and a righteous cause. And I haven't paid enough attention to lining people up on my side."

"I am worried for you," Aschkin said, and she extended her hand for the second time to touch him gently on the forearm.

"Well, this means I have one friend on the faculty."

"I am your friend, and I'm afraid that this is going to be messy."

"As Ted Kennedy once said, we'll cross that bridge when we come to it. Right now I have a class to think about. Are you going to eat the rest of your salad?"

"No, I'm ready to go and I wouldn't miss your class. But don't we have time for a short walk? I'm enjoying this time with you." She knew there would be an argument at home later, but there was no way that Peter, either as dean or as husband, could tell her not to sit in on Adam's class.

"Great idea. Let me show you the statues of some heroes on Riverside Drive." Adam nonchalantly left a twenty and a ten on the table. He assumed this would cover the check and tip and show his disdain for paperwork. They walked slowly toward the Kossuth statue. Aschkin looked at the inspirational figure and laughed. "Where was this guy when you needed him in Mohács?"

"Well, actually, he was more of a political leader and intellectual than a fighter. Speaking of poetry, however, you know I think that the Hungarians are only the people to start fighting after having listened to the words of a poet? Petőfi walked around Budapest in March 1848 reading his poetry and the Magyars then took up arms. Romanticism at its best."

"Tell me, have the Hungarians ever won a war?"

"I don't think so, but that reminds me of a joke." They started walking slowly back toward campus as Adam recited the story. "The Hungarian government declared war against the Americans in 1944. Roosevelt turned to one of his advisors and asked, 'Who are these Hungarians?' 'They are a kingdom in Middle Europe.' 'So what is the name of their king?' 'They don't have a king, they have a regent and his name is Admiral Horthy.' 'An admiral, very good—so they have a navy, a strong one?' 'No, not exactly; they used to have a navy but they lost all their ports on the Adriatic in the Treaty of Trianon after the First World War.' 'So why are they declaring war against us?' After an appropriate pause. 'Actually, they would prefer to declare war against Romania, but the Germans won't let them.'"

Aschkin smiled, though she did not completely get the particular Hungarian disdain for Romanians. Probably it is the same way Turks think about the Kurds, she thought to herself. She slipped her hand into Adam's and said softly, "Are we going to be able to preserve our honor, Professor Gross?" What is she talking about? Adam asked himself—the exam? Maybe us? "In class you are my Romantic warrior," she whispered as they entered the lecture hall 104.

13

The Gettysburg Address

ROMANCE WAS ON Adam's mind, but of a different kind. The great American love affair with death, the one that had cost more American lives than all the others put together, the constantly re-enacted war, the battle sites that had become national shrines—yes, the Civil War, the War between the States, the War to Free the Slaves, the War to Preserve the Union. That was going to be the subject of the afternoon lecture.

Tom Lehrer used to get a laugh singing the ditty, "I hate war and so does Eleanor." Perhaps Eleanor Roosevelt did hate war, but these attitudes changed every generation. After Hiroshima, Americans had become disgusted with violence. But within a few years they had joined the UN's peacekeeping force in Korea. Half a decade later, when there was a chance to help the Hungarians fight off the Soviet tanks, they had hated war again. Then Vietnam seared the nation's soul. Never again, thought many, but then, in the 1990s, the media began to cultivate the legend of the "Greatest Generation." War meant brotherhood and social progress. The compelling line was that the Civil War had given black people their freedom, the First World War had brought women the right to vote, and the Second World War had led to Hubert Humphrey's epochal speech in the 1948 calling for an end to segregation in American life.

Adam reached the podium before the room filled up. He was lost in dreams of brotherhood in arms. He thought of Henry V's great speech before the battle of Agincourt: *"We few, we happy few, we band of brothers;/For he to-day that sheds his blood with me/ Shall be my brother."* Could he speak these Shakespearean words to get his colleagues or students to join him in the exam fight? He doubted it. This was not the early sixteenth century. And he was not fighting the French. The ecstasy of battle cannot be transferred from time and conflict—I am not Henry V, he mooned. I am not even Lazarus returned from the dead, he lamented, his love for T.S. Eliot percolating again.

As the students trickled in, he tried to identify those who might have had some direct experience with war, and think what their attitudes might be. Of course, there were the Israelis, but they were probably weary of military service, not likely to be receptive to the exhilaration of brothers joining together in the last flame of life. The few Serbs and Croats had recently known war. They were likely also to be sick of bombing and ethnic cleansing. This was a generation of intellectuals that, all in all, would not understand why the Romantic poets had felt most alive as they drew nearer to death in warfare. If he had had any Palestinians who as teenagers had participated in the Intifada it might be different, but that year Regina had not been successful in attracting students from any of the Arab countries.

He began the hour from an unexpected place in his psyche. "The world is—or should be—a rational place." The students were puzzled by the sudden, ungrounded declaration.

"This classroom," he continued, "is an emblem, a symbol, for the rational discourse that should be possible in all human affairs. And what is the opposite of rational discourse? The possibilities range from war, at one extreme, to love at the other. I am constantly torn between the flights of imagination offered by the irrational side of our personalities and the order and regularity offered by the law." As he said this he glanced over at Aschkin, sauna-style, in the hope that she did not catch his eye. "The law centers us on the rational and the pragmatic, on the necessity of living with others. But it leaves little room for some of the greatest moments of life—for poetry, for religious faith, for love, and, yes, for committing one's life to fighting for an ideal. The law, I hate to tell you, is not all there is to life." That line at least brought on a few giggles. Adam laughed too, and relaxed and embraced the moment.

Charlotte could not resist blurting out, "I hear you Americans say that all is fair in love and war."

"Since Nuremberg, the world has tried to bring the rule of law to the breakdown of civilization called war."

Joerg recalled the teachings of Hans-Heinrich Jescheck and other ex-members of the National Socialist Party who had opposed the

Nuremberg trials. Despite his love for his grandfather, he had come to the conclusion that the trials were the right way to differentiate between the good and evil leaders of that generation.

"We enacted the Geneva Conventions in 1949 and they have led to the idea of 'war crimes'—crimes that will eventually be punished in an International Criminal Court. But Ms. de la Porte des Vaux," Adam continued, turning to Charlotte, "we have yet to negotiate an international convention on love crimes." A good line, he said to himself as she nodded. He was beginning to feel light on his feet.

"We are not here to fall in love" —an audible "ahhh" was heard from the back of the room—"or to engage in war, but we should try, at least, to understand the other side of our personalities. Some people call this other side the right brain, the non-linear side, the Romantic impulse." Aschkin smiled to herself as she mused about the meaning of her name Aschkin: "thy love." The tension of which Adam was speaking was built into her name. The alternative meaning was "transcendental," the highest form of rational thought.

"I am sure—or I hope—you know something about love," Adam pressed on, "but how about war? How many of you have seen war up close?" The Israelis raised their hands, plus a few others whom Adam identified as coming from the former Yugoslavia and the disputed border territory between India and Pakistan; and one unexpected volunteer explained that she was a Greek from Cyprus. Aschkin watched all this with rapt attention. Growing up in Turkey, she had come close to armed hostilities both with the Greeks and the Kurds.

"You all hate war, I am sure," Adam said. Nods were evident around the room. "Since the 1960s," he continued, "Americans too have said that they hate war. The film *Dr. Strangelove* brought home to everyone that the arms race of mutual nuclear deterrence against the Soviet Union was slightly mad. The disaster in Vietnam left us burned and disillusioned."

Jaime raised his hand. "Yes, but we could not allow Saddam Hussein to invade and occupy Kuwait, and we could not tolerate ethnic cleansing in Bosnia and Kosovo. We must fight against racism and the colonial occupation of third world countries. War is a necessary means of seeking justice in the modern world."

Adam felt the pulse of the class quickening. He was not sure what would happen. "Can we talk rationally about war?" he asked. "I'm not sure we can. It's like trying to talk rationally about friendship and matters of the heart. There are some human drives, some irrational impulses, that we do not completely understand.

"I find it very hard to understand, for example, why Americans went to war in the 1860s and generated one of the most merciless campaigns of bloodletting known in our history. In those days we were very much under the influence of the German Romantics. Ralph Waldo Emerson wrote under the banner of 'transcendentalism.'" Adam was not aware that he was invoking the alternative meaning of Aschkin's name. Her colleague and tango partner was gaining steam. "When war came in 1861, the South fought for its honor. They were greatly outnumbered but they were defending their homeland." Adam had escaped the conventional education about the war in Northern schools. When he had begun to study the conflict he had felt a surprising degree of empathy with the Confederacy. "The South's two top generals, Robert E. Lee and Stonewall Jackson, were more daring than the men who led the North, at least in the early stages of the war. In the first two years of fighting, the Union army made hardly a dent in the Southern line of defense in Northern Virginia. The killing fields remained close to the White House and not far from Lee's family estate across the Potomac River in Arlington, Virginia.

"Having won a series of battles in the South, Lee made the mistake of taking the war to the North. He led his troops across the Potomac River into Pennsylvania and after minor skirmishes he met the Union troops in the fields outside a little town that every American schoolchild knows about: Gettysburg, Pennsylvania. This was in the beginning of July 1863. The opposing infantry and cavalry fought hard, with little change, for the first two days. Then the Confederate leadership made a bold decision to attack. General George Pickett led his 15,000 troops across an open field toward one of the elevated spots called Cemetery Ridge. The Union men holding the hill were running out of ammunition. As the Confederates approached in 'Pickett's charge,' the Union men in blue mounted their bayonets and charged down the hill fighting hand to hand. In less than an hour, 10,000 Southerners fell, dead or wounded."

The class was transfixed. Is our history becoming their history? Adam wondered.

"At the end of the fighting, on the fateful day of July 4, 1863, Lee ordered a retreat and, although both sides lost massive numbers of men, the retreat was interpreted as a victory for the North. In retrospect this is seen as the turning point in the war, but the fighting would last another two years before Lee, in April 1865, handed General Ulysses S. Grant his sword and the other Southern generals eventually joined in the decision to surrender.

"Gettysburg has become much more than a battle, largely because of what happened there five months later in November 1863. Can you imagine the work involved in clearing and burying nearly 50,000 bodies, not to mention 5,000 dead horses? Think of the logistical problems. Do you bury them all together? Or do you have separate burial grounds? Did they die as Americans, or as soldiers in opposing armies? Each side had its own cemetery. If Lincoln had had his choice, however, he would have done everything possible, in death as in life, to emphasize the common ground between the two sides.

"The founders of the Union cemetery planned a dedication. They invited a famous orator from Harvard, Edward Everett, to give the keynote speech. In 1860 Everett had run for the vice-presidency and lost. Almost as an afterthought, they invited the man who won the election and who was commander-in-chief of the Union forces. The day before the ceremony, on November 18, Lincoln took the train up from Washington to participate.

"Everett spoke for at least two hours. Then Lincoln mounted the podium and spoke for about two minutes. His 268-word address became a defining moment of American history. This was his first sentence: '*Four score and seven years ago our fathers brought forth upon this continent a new nation, conceived in Liberty, and dedicated to the proposition that all men are created equal.*'

"Let's think about these 30 words, phrase by phrase. Four score and seven years ago. You may not know that a score is 20, which means that he is referring to a time 87 years earlier. What happened then?"

Several hands went up. "We know," said Marga and Gad in unison. "He is thinking about the Constitution."

"Do the math," countered the professor. "What year did he have in mind? 1863. Subtract 87. Ah, the result is not 1787, when the Constitution was drafted in Philadelphia, but something else that happened in that famous city."

"The Declaration of Independence," was the mass response.

"Yes, 1776—the Declaration of Independence. It's just amazing. In Lincoln's view the American nation was born, not with the Constitution, but in an act of defiance against a colonial power."

Jaime looked pleased that Adam had defined the American experience as rebellion against colonial powers.

"In fact, in my view," Adam continued, "Lincoln never cared much for the Constitution. He said that he never had a political thought that did not emanate from the Declaration of Independence."

"'Four score and seven years ago our fathers brought forth upon this continent...'" Adam repeated the words slowly. "What does this language remind you of?" He guessed that Gad Menachem might get the association.

Menachem responded as though he was in tune with Adam's mind, the first violinist in the professor's orchestra. "Here the language reminds me of the Bible. This is the pattern in the Book of Exodus when God reminds the people of Israel that he is the God of their fathers—Abraham, Isaac, and Jacob. Lincoln reminds the Americans of the link between their country and their fathers."

"I agree," added Adam. He could hear a muffled groan coming from the back row, where Chen was writing furiously.

"And what about Lincoln's mentioning of 'this continent'?"

Aschkin appeared puzzled. Perhaps she was missing something because she had grown up unexposed to the defining myths of American history.

"Remember the Puritans thought of America as their promised land. So what is it that our fathers bring forth upon this continent?"

"'A new nation, conceived in Liberty,'" answered Gad.

"Note the birth images," Adam said. "First our fathers 'bring forth,' and then the nation is 'conceived.' The central idea is a nation born in the course of history. In the Constitution the emphasis is not on the nation but on 'we the people' who come together in a voluntary contract to form a new and better government. The element of history is lost. In the here and now of 1789 the people made a choice: they created the Union. And the Union became the rallying cry for the North. As a famous orator Daniel Webster invoked the idea in 1830: 'Liberty and Union, now and forever, one and inseparable.'

"Lincoln was a genius," Adam continued, "at finding the right words to avoid the image of division and civil war. He was dedicating a Union cemetery but never once mentioned the Union or the division of the dead, some buried here, some there. The focus was now on the entire nation, implicitly including the South. This was the birth of a new rhetoric. The term 'nation' appears five times in the Gettysburg Address—five times in only 268 words."

Holly Chen was beginning to see why they studied the Gettysburg Address at home, and she volunteered, "Yes, I get it. We study Lincoln to justify our claim that Taiwan is part of the Chinese nation. *Taiwan da Pangyo*," she could not help adding. "It means 'our Taiwanese friends'—really our brothers. We do not want to let Taiwan go, any more than Lincoln could tolerate losing a part of his new nation."

Adam responded, "You've put your finger on the issue. The rhetoric of national unity provides an argument against secession—against the way in which the South could invoke the Declaration of Independence. We cannot let our brothers go. Do you have any doubts about this argument?"

Aschkin raised her hand. "Do you mind if I add a word? Empires collapse all the time. Before I was born, the Ottoman empire fell part. The Americans separated from the English. This century we have seen the same secessionist demands in the Soviet Union and Yugoslavia. Why should the South not be able to separate from the North?"

Adam felt stirred and excited by the challenge. "Thank you, Professor Yilmaz. This is the precisely the concern we should have. Lincoln must have meant to guard against this argument by insisting on a single American nation. The Civil War can be seen, not as a war of secession, but as a campaign for unity, a new solidarity among those whose history was already defined by regional identities."

"I see it," intervened Joerg. "It resembles the campaign for national unity under Bismarck in Germany. This was only a few years after the American Civil War. So the Americans were fighting a war *for* national unity and not a war to resist division?"

Adam was pleased. "In Italy too, under Garibaldi. The mid-nineteenth century was a time for national consolidation. In all these cases, strong national leaders were able to conquer regional sources of self-definition. Do not forget that all Americans spoke the same language, were mostly Protestants and shared a history of revolt against the British—all these factors made it easier for Lincoln to impose a new idea of unbreakable ties on the American people. These ties were real, but they were also a product of imagination."

"Imagined communities," Charlotte noted on her pad. The author Benedict Anderson had become a minor celebrity, and the idea that national bonds required feats of imagination had seeped into the law schools too.

Bringing the class back to the text of Lincoln's address, Adam said, "And let us recall how the first sentence ends: 'conceived in Liberty, and dedicated to the proposition that all men are created equal.' This is remarkable. The great promise of 1776 now returns to correct the moral blindness of a Constitution that accepted slavery. With Lincoln's address in November 1863 there was no longer any doubt about the aims of the war. By taking the moral high ground against slavery, the Americans convinced both the French and the English to stay out of the war. European powers might have intervened in a war of secession, particularly in the light of their economic interest in the South's cotton, but they were not going to spill blood for the sake of the outdated institution of slavery."

"True," Jaime offered, "Lincoln asserted the equality of all human beings, but the day after the victory in Gettysburg, race riots against the draft broke out in New York City. The Irish tried to burn down the black neighborhoods."

"In this country," Adam conceded, "you can never forget the issue of race. It almost an obsession. Lincoln at Gettysburg was one of our better moments. We have had many disastrous racial confrontations since then." He paused. "In the next sentence of the address, Lincoln makes it clear that the purpose of the war was to determine whether *that nation, or any nation, so conceived and so dedicated, can long endure.* In other words, the commitment to liberty and equality was inherent in the very idea of the American nation. Lincoln was clear that this was not a celebration of a mythical tribal origin or of *Blut und Boden*—blood and soil—as the German nationalists argued. We were held together by a commitment to values, not by a shared set of genes."

"Ah," commented Aschkin, "you are thinking about your heroes of 1848. The liberals who fought and lost in the old world could finally win on the new continent."

"Indeed," said Adam, savoring the solidarity with Aschkin.

"What are you trying to say?" interrupted Charlotte. "The French Republic and nation are committed to the idea of secular rational discourse. This is our legacy from the eighteenth-century *philosophes.*

The American nation seems similarly to be committed to the values of liberty and equality."

"Great," responded Adam. "I don't think I can be more precise than that."

"Yes, but we have to be careful here," said Joerg. The Romantic German reaction to the French faith in rational discourse—it has its negative side too. The Germans got their ideas of nationalism from somewhere."

Adam acknowledged the point with a nod, but continued on the entrancing subject of the Gettysburg Address. "The next portion of the speech is preoccupied with the themes of death and rebirth. Lincoln describes the cemetery he was dedicating as '*a final resting place for those who here gave their lives that that nation might live.*' And he resolves that '*these dead shall not have died in vain.*' Then, approaching the end, he used a phrase that has remained at the center of controversy: '*that this nation, under God, shall have a new birth of freedom.*'

"What intrigues me," continued Adam, "is how the idea of 'the nation' fits into all of this. Why should thoughts of death and rebirth lead Lincoln to say that the nation, and not the people, not the Union, should enjoy a new birth of freedom?"

"That's easy," commented Jaime, who had studied Latin in seminary. "The word 'nation' comes from *nasci*, which means 'to be born.'"

"Yes," Adam sought to sharpen the puzzle, "but why the phrase 'nation under God'?" There seems to be a natural linkage between these ideas. We hear it today in the Pledge of Allegiance: 'one nation, under God, indivisible with liberty and justice for all.'" It sounds almost like an adaptation of the Gettysburg Address."

Chen got agitated. This violated every secular sensibility of her Israeli youth. "How can you talk about a nation under God? That should be considered an 'establishment of religion' under the First Amendment."

"Now you are arguing like an American lawyer," glowed an avuncular Adam. Most American teachers would have pronounced this compliment with complete enthusiasm. For Adam the praise was mixed with some regret about the gradual Americanization of his students. This, of course, was his purpose, but his ambivalence about his own identity extended to his mission in the classroom. "But does the phrase 'nation under God' make any sense? What joins these three words together?"

The Talmudist Gad intervened, puzzled. "Well, this is the way the Bible speaks about the Jewish people. Could Lincoln really have meant the same for Americans? That would strike me as sacrilegious, if not downright idolatrous."

"Paradoxically," responded Adam, "there is a long Protestant tradition of envying and imitating the Jews as a nation. This was a source of the inspiration for the early German Romantics like Johann Georg Hamann, who was obsessed by the story of the Jews as a particular people different from all others."

Joerg glowed and dropped his pen. For the first time, he understood the love/hate relationship between Germans and Jews. It was two sides of the same coin. "I must search for the love that great Germans like Hamann felt for the Jews," he muttered under his breath.

"Following the Puritans who thought they had come to the promised land," Adam continued, "Lincoln once described Americans as 'His almost chosen people.' The pronoun 'His' obviously refers to God."

Gad almost fell off his bench. Chen looked stunned.

"Don't take it so seriously." Trying to lighten the atmosphere, he added, "During the Civil War just about everyone thought of himself as Moses leading his people out of slavery. Have you heard the black gospel song, 'Go down Moses to Egyptland/Let my people go'?" Adam tried to sing the melody but the off-key ramble made Aschkin giggle. She quickly put her hand over her mouth. Several students caught the impulse to levity, and when they noticed that she covered her mouth, they imitated her in mock-embarrassment. Aschkin thought that this too was funny and laughed even louder. The mood was infectious.

Adam enjoyed the playful mood that swept over the class. The students' right brains were on full power. He thought he would try to go with the moment. "I am glad that you see that the law is not all reason and logic. We sustain ourselves on the drama of war and of revolution, of birth and of death. These are events to make us cry and sometimes laugh."

Caught again between the left and right sides of his brain, he recalled his conversation with Peter Levenger and Ann O'Sullivan. They couldn't understand him, but he seemed to be in perfect harmony with these students. They could flow with him between the rational and the irrational. After a pause, Adam continued, "Well, do we have a problem talking about the nation under God or not?"

Chen was sure there was a problem. "However much you talk about the separation of Church and State in this country, you have never worked it out. In Israel it would be unthinkable to have 'God' written on our money, however *meshuggenah* our religious people are." Adam enjoyed the sudden introduction of Sydney's favorite word. Most people got the point from the context.

"Well, there are some mysteries about the American tradition, I concede. The linkage of nationhood and religion is not an accident, and yet we really do not know what it is supposed to mean.

"But we can be sure of one thing." Adam began to sum up. "Every age has its yearnings that dominate all others. In the mid-nineteenth century the theme was national consolidation: the solidarity of people thought to be brothers was considered worth fighting for. This was true in Italy, in Germany, and in the United States.

"I am not sure why it was so important for Lincoln to speak of a 'nation under God.' But it is worth noting that Lincoln's religion was an Old Testament religion. He did not speak about Jesus but simply about God. His language overflows with references to the Psalms, not the Gospels. His language always confirmed the unity and the equality of the American people, North and South, black and white, men and women. As we shall see when we reconvene next week, national consolidation in the United States entailed the victory of equality over freedom. Next week we will explore that theme in great detail. Take advantage of your two days to enjoy the city and perhaps to catch a glimpse of the great heroes on Riverside Drive. Thank you."

Adam felt an electric response from all corners of the room. But he could sense some differences. The students had become individuals, each with a distinctive take on the experience. Most notably, on the one side there was Joerg Mueller, for whom any mention of Jews and their national experience was always a charged moment, leaving him pensive and distracted. Both he and Adam knew that eventually they would have to have a conversation about his background, about his grandfather's role as a National Socialist scholar.

And then there was Aschkin, who seemed so engaged, even thrilled, as though she were just starting law school and discovering the beauties of the subject for the first time. Adam was becoming more and more curious about her. What was she thinking about when speaking about love and war, death and life? What did it mean to her, in her soul? Adam mused.

He had taken the first steps into the realm of the irrational, into the world where love and war came closer than in the ordinary imagination. And Aschkin was already there waiting for him.

As he was leaving class, the two encountered each other in the hallway.

"What do you think?" he asked.

"Two good classes today, but are you really irrational, or do you only talk that way?"

"Shall I ask you to taste the soup? Was there a spoon missing? "

"I think the class is wonderful, and you are wonderful. You are a little crazy. But it's not so terrible. You have helped me reach a side of myself that is uncalled for when I'm teaching tax law."

"Aren't you afraid that the students will hear us?"

"What did I say?"

"You said you wanted to meet me tonight."

"I did? Where?"

"Will this constitute harassment?"

"Of whom? By whom?"

Adam paused and realized he was being flippant. He needed to designate a spot. "I have an idea. Have you ever been to Friday night services? There's an event ten blocks from here that you'll love. It is a cross between Jewish ritual and Sufi dervishes."

"I've heard about a place on 88th Street. Is that what you mean? Peter and I were planning an evening at home, but I will find some way to get out of the house. What time?"

This was it. She was in; he could not back out. "Let's say 7.30 on 88th Street, between Broadway and West End. Look for a Moorish-style building in the middle of the block. I will be out front."

Adam knew that Aschkin's first deception would be the most difficult. They were crossing a line. He felt like Pickett charging up the hill in Gettysburg. Would that my fate be better, he offered in silent prayer.

14

God at Home

WHEN ASCHKIN CAME home and opened the door to greet Peter, she heard music playing on the stereo. At first she could not believe her ears. The room was filled with the classic strains of Astor Piazzolla. "What's this?" she inquired as she gave Peter a kiss on the cheek. "Since when have you been interested in tango?"

"Since yesterday afternoon. I heard that you gave a terrific demonstration with Adam Gross. The students raved about it."

"It was great fun."

"Including the part about dancing cheek to cheek?"

"That is the way you dance Argentine tango. You can't do it at a distance. The Americans hold each other far apart as though they were afraid of touching. It is considered phony. Did any students complain about that?"

"No, but I heard about it."

They both remained calm. Peter and Aschkin had a professional way of talking about their problems. They never allowed themselves to have tantrums or to scream—behavior that he, and also she, associated with less educated people. Peter knew about Aschkin's having attended Adam's class for the last two days, but he decided not to push the issue at the moment. Perhaps she had not seen his memo. Perhaps he wanted a sign that she was on his, Peter's, side in the dispute. Aschkin meanwhile wondered, What is he waiting for? For his colleagues to tell him it's all right to try to lay down the law at home?

She was encountering one of the paradoxes of modern American life. There had been a time when families had been hierarchical and all workers had banded together and sought equality on the job. Now people insisted on equality at home but tolerated hierarchy in the workplace. Aschkin and Peter shared the household work, but at the law school he was still her dean.

Aschkin felt a sudden yearning for a male presence. She wanted to smell anger on his skin, as she might have expected—but also hated—from a Turkish man. She wanted to hear the word *izzat* as she heard it on the streets in Istanbul—some appeal to a standard of honor, some threat of violence toward women that would trigger her pride and resistance. Let him just try to lay down the law. The thought of it quickened her breath. If he only would, she thought, I could complain about his lack of virility, his inability to produce a child.

But Peter would not take the bait. There was only one kind of dominance he understood, and that he had learned on the job. So he played his strong card. "You know that a lot of students and faculty are upset about Adam's criminal law exam."

"Yes, but I don't see what the big deal is."

"As dean I have to make sure that everyone is treated properly, and I'm afraid that Regina is not doing right by its female students."

She fell silent. "OK, I've seen the exam. Let's talk about it," she suggested. "What is so terrible?"

"Didn't you read the part when the woman is taken to the hospital and then she wants to write a thank-you note to the man who attacked her? Isn't that over-the-top?"

"I don't know. I would have thought that something like that would be covered by academic freedom. Would you be so upset if someone else, like Julien Wright, had written that exam?"

"Julien would not have written that language. He was trained at Oxford, for God's sake. He has a proper sense of tone. And Adam indulges in all sorts of romantic nonsense. I have a whole file on him. Years ago he used to sleep with students. Once he got angry at a female secretary and said, 'When the fuck are you going to finish the job?' You have to read this exam in the context of his history with women in the law school."

"I don't think so. Have you ever heard of New Criticism? You read a book as a statement within its four corners. You do not pay attention to the personal history of the author. When you read *Marbury v Madison*, do you look at the personal history of John Marshall?"

Peter suspected that he could demolish Aschkin in this argument, but what he really wanted from her was greater subservience at home, not in the arena of legal debate. He grumbled to himself about Scalia and textualism as he retreated to the kitchen and started to prepare their early dinner.

Aschkin was burning inside. She was seeing Dr. Bluestone and taking hormone shots. She had a kind of private relationship—an intimate one at that—in the doctor's office. She was beginning to feel a bond to her yet unconceived child. She yearned for intimate bonds other than with Peter.

Perhaps the fight brewing over Adam's exam would give her a chance to catch Peter out in his moral ambiguities. There is quite a dance about to begin at Regina, she thought, and it is one that might give me what I want. I will improvise on Adam's lead. In the tango the female can add flourishes from the *cruzada* position, her *ochos* or *ganchos*. Maybe, she thought, I will let him lead and I will follow until there is a political explosion at the law school. Then I will do my thing: my *ochos*, my figure-eights. She smiled in the mirror as she washed for dinner, Piazzolla still playing in the background.

She did not exactly want a fight with Peter that evening, but she needed a good reason for leaving the house. She did not have one, so she said she was going for a walk to clear her head. It was after 7 p.m. when she started walked walking down West End toward the mosque-like synagogue in eager anticipation of meeting Adam. She noticed all the families dressed in their Sabbath finest, walking to services together. She was envious, first of the children, secondly of the common pursuit of some meaning higher than their careers and their worldly comfort. She turned left and looked for a Moorish structure. She saw Adam standing next to the main entrance. "Hurry," he said. "They have already begun *L'cha Dodi*."

"What's that?"

"I will explain later."

When they entered the main hall of the synagogue, Aschkin gasped. The building reminded her of the old mosque she had visited often in Istanbul. The walls were decorated with abstract designs set against a tiled background, almost as though the design purposely imitated the great Islamic principle of avoiding human representation.

The congregants, mostly students with a sprinkling of over-forties Upper West Siders, were all standing and singing to the rhythms of two musicians—a guitarist and a drummer—sitting in front, slightly to the left of the two people wearing shawls. "Those are the rabbis," whispered Adam. "They are wearing *talitot*—prayer shawls." The rabbis, a man and woman, stood on the podium facing the crowd as though they were about to deliver a lecture. Aschkin was immediately transported by the enthusiasm in the room. The singing was in Hebrew, which she did not understand, but she sensed an energy that indeed made the group seem like whirling dervishes temporarily at rest.

Adam and Aschkin took positions at the back of the room and leaned against what appeared to be a standing desk pushed off to the side of the room. "They usually read the Torah from this lectern," whispered Adam in Aschkin's ear. Aschkin stood as close as she could to Adam without embracing him. Adam, concerned about propriety as he had been when they'd danced in front of the students, asked whether they should be standing so close to each other. "Perhaps the students here will think that we are having an affair?"

"I hate to tell you this," replied Aschkin, "but we already are."

Adam blushed and tried to find the right place for his limbs. Where should he put his hands and arms? An arm on Aschkin? Should his feet be crossed or straight? Then there was that other part of his body, stirring to Aschkin's warmth. How could he control it?

Suddenly the rhythm changed. The musicians shifted key, from minor to major, and started to play a faster, less mournful melody. First one student and then another left their place and came out to the aisles. They joined hands and began dancing down the aisle, a simple dance modeled after the Israeli *Horah*. First the left forward and then right behind, then a little hop and the right forward with the left behind. Soon there was a whole line of congregants snaking around the room in versions of the same dance. No one seemed to care whether the steps were right or wrong, only that you were out there with the group celebrating the Sabbath. Young and old, male and female, foreigner and Jew, they imitated the steps and raised their arms up and down, grabbing people on the sidelines as they went.

"It is not exactly the tango," whispered Adam.

"I love it," Aschkin said. "It reminds me of the Sufis—but much more communal." Suddenly, as the line came around to them, they noticed the short, stocky frame of Joerg Mueller being dragged along by the train of enthusiasts. He was struggling to get his feet into the proper rhythm. They gasped and tried to pretend there was a lectern they could hide behind, but there was none. They were naked in the garden.

As they were adjusting the inevitability of Joerg's seeing them, they noticed a tall, familiar figure approaching just a few steps behind. She danced in perfect form and in fact was leading and trying to coordinate many of the novices in front and behind her. It was Chen Horowitz.

A few moments later, Joerg and Chen broke from the line and came over to them. They extended their slightly perspiring hands to the two professors. For an instant, no one knew what to say. "*Shabbat Shalom*, y'all," Adam volunteered, and they all laughed. The passing snake line beckoned and the students rejoined it.. The music changed again and the congregation drifted back into positions of prayer, turning to face the back of the room for the final verse of *L'cha Dodi*. Out of the corner of his eye, Adam saw that Chen and Joerg were sitting together.

"What do those words mean, *L'cha Dodi*?" asked Aschkin.

"They mean 'Come, my beloved.'"

"Thank you," Aschkin said. "This is similar to the meaning of my name."

"Aschkin, Aschkin," he said, "God is welcoming the Sabbath as his bride. Originally the words are used by lovers in the Song of Songs. If you hear them that way, you are in touch."

"I am definitely in touch," Aschkin said, smiling. Surprised by her own audacity, she brushed her hand against the back of Adam's leg,

After the central prayer called the *Schmah Israel*, the silent standing prayer and some additional singing, the services came to an end. It was a few minutes after 8.30 p.m. "I think we should linger and talk," Adam said. "You know, damage control... Let's pretend that we're more shocked to see them together than they us." Aschkin agreed, and they stood outside until Joerg and Chen emerged and, seeing their professors waiting, tried to mask their surprised and censorious looks.

The two students stood out in the crowd. Chen, tall and erect, with a long twisted braid hanging below her shoulders, looked feminine and yet proud. Adam could envision her in a military uniform and found her both intimidating and seductive. Joerg, short, packed with emotion, looked cowed but relieved. Their body language was mutually sympathetic. Adam could not tell whether they had come together or not, but now they would be taken for a couple. The collective harmony of the service and the enthusiastic singing of others had given them a sense that, despite their differences, they could encounter one another in a spiritual world. They glowed at the discovery of a side of themselves little cherished in their university studies.

Aschkin imagined that she and Adam probably looked the same way.

"I know a great Turkish place a few blocks from here," Aschkin said. "Let's go there and have some tea." The four of them started walking north on Broadway. It was not easy to find the right topic of conversation. Adam wanted to ask the students what they were doing there. They wanted to ask their teachers the same thing. For the time both sides held off from potentially embarrassing questions.

When they sat down in the Turkish restaurant, nestled comfortably on cushions around a low table, Chen decided to open the bidding with her own confession. "You are probably surprised to find me at Friday night services. The truth is, I miss the connection with Jewish culture. I love the singing, particularly in Hebrew. I would never go in Israel because it would be a political statement, one that I do not want to make."

"In Germany," said Joerg following her lead, "I could not go either. It would look strange, as though I were one of those philo-Semitic freaks. But I have always been curious."

At that moment, an old man dressed in Turkish garb appeared above them and Joerg fell silent. The waiter began with the greeting in Arabic, "*Ahalan w-Sahalan*"—my tent is your tent. Aschkin responded with a Muslim greeting, "*Salaam Aleicum*", and then switched to Turkish, which delighted the waiter. She ordered *chai*—tea—for all four.

Adam said, "OK, I could have ordered at lunch in Spanish, now you can order in Turkish. It's only fair." Chen and Joerg tried to avoid noticing this revealing remark. It was as though they were all sitting in a German sauna together, trying not to look too closely at one another. They felt free to talk as though there would be no memory of the words passed when the conversation became official again on Monday.

Adam picked up on Joerg's thoughts. "I guess the Jewish-German theme has been coming up a lot in class."

"Yes," said Joerg. "I have wanted to discuss this with you for a while. It is obviously a charged theme for me—supercharged. I have a family background. I feel proud and ashamed of being German at the same time."

Chen volunteered, "This is a sign that you are a strong person: you do not lie to yourself about who you are." Joerg looked at her as though he wanted to kiss her.

Aschkin felt that it was her turn to speak. "I think my reaction to the service was more spiritual than all of yours. I felt moved by the approach to God. Abstract, joyful, life-affirming. Muslims should have nothing to object to in this service, except perhaps the men and women sitting together."

"Ugh," said Chen. "Don't remind me of why I hate religion. In Israel men and women always sit apart."

"I understand," said Adam. "I thought you complained to the dean about our discussing religion too much in class." At that moment, everyone was indifferent or oblivious to Aschkin's tie to the dean. She lowered her eyes.

"I did complain to him, but he told me to go away. Academic freedom and all that."

"Good for him," said Adam, now realizing the *faux pas* of introducing a fifth wheel. Peter is a good man, Aschkin was thinking, at least in the abstract—not joyful, not life-affirming, but a good man.

As that moment the waiter brought the tea in beautiful glasses with ornate silver decoration, together with unsolicited ceramic dishes holding baklava. Both Adam and Joerg murmured, barely audibly, "Thank God, it is not paper." They paused and looked at each other. "We share one kind of religion," said Adam as he extended his hand to Joerg.

"And now between us, tell us, Chen," Adam asked, "we do not agree about religion. But how serious is the problem in class?"

Chen was touched that he would even ask. "At times I have thought it was serious, for me," she said, "but I have to learn to argue with you and enjoy it."

All four drank their tea and relaxed on their cushions. They were the fortunate ones, Adam reflected, fully alive, on the verge of romance. They were emancipating themselves from their demons: Joerg from his obsession about being German, Chen from her secular Israeli bias, Aschkin from her fear of expressing her spiritual self— and me, Adam thought, I want to liberate myself too, but it is not so easy.

Perhaps his mentioning of Peter had not been an accident. One of the few rules he had adopted in his pursuit of women over the last several decades was that he would not sleep with a married woman. Why was it, he thought, that I took this rule about married women so seriously? He knew that the Jewish sources—the Bible and the Talmud—tolerated male adultery but severely castigated women who had affairs. They were considered whores and, if they had a child by another man, the child was called a *mamzer*, a bastard, and was tainted for life, excluded from the Jewish community. The men, however, could have children out of wedlock, who were fully accepted into the community.

There was proof in the book of Genesis, Adam thought, for treating the ban of adultery as one of the most fundamental principles of Jewish life. The story was told three times of a patriarch, Abraham or Isaac, going down to Egypt with his wife, and lying to the local potentate about his wife being his sister, thus suggesting that she would be sexually available without the need to kill her husband. The local men would take the supposed sister as a wife and some disaster would befall them. Thus they would realize that in fact she was married and that they were committing a sin. Adam inferred from these stories that it was a violation of natural law to attack the household of another man.

Chen and Joerg rose to leave. They thanked the professors effusively. As they walked out of the door together, Chen put her arm around Joerg's shoulder.

"Ah, youth, said Adam. "They have no moral inhibitions about sex."

"What kind of inhibitions are you talking about?" asked Aschkin, "Sex is always on people's minds when they attend religious services.

How could it not be—the separation of men and women in the mosque, the ecstatic appeal to higher powers. Did you notice the way some of the boys in the temple tonight were swaying back and forth when they were praying?"

"That is called 'davening.' The Orthodox do it, and some of them drift into what you might call 'hip service.'"

Aschkin smiled at the pun. "Don't you think it is a little homoerotic—all these men standing up and swaying back and forth as if they were copulating with each other?"

Adam thought this amusing and suggestive. "Yes, I agree; I too feel an awakening of my physical self just being in the room with those praying. Perhaps that's why men are supposed to make love with their wives on the Sabbath. And it helps to answer the question left over from lunch: why religions get obsessed about sex. They awaken it, and therefore they have to control it."

"Absolutely, for me too." Were women supposed to make love on the Sabbath too? Do as the Romans do, she recalled Peter saying, banally, when introducing her to the sauna. Love now as the real Jews do, Aschkin thought—that is more original.

Adam was about to drift off into reflections about Jewish law and the rights of the woman to sexual satisfaction as well as food and clothing. Bringing him back to the moment, Aschkin put her hand on his arm.

"I have a present for you," Adam said, retreating to familiar ground. He took out a little wrapped box and placed it on the table in front of her. She took his hand and pressed it firmly against hers. The ritual of opening the box held great meaning for her. She was opening herself up to Adam, and the gift was about to become part of her.

It was a necklace, designed in the shape of small silver crescents hung together in several layers around the neck. As she put it on, she glimmered like an eighth moon, full of sensual promise.

"I bought this a few years ago. Now I realize I bought it for you—anticipating you," he said. "It was made by a Jewish artisan in Jaffa, an Arab community, and it conveys an Islamic symbol." It was a good line, and Aschkin felt no need to question its logic. In fact, on his last trip to Israel, Adam had bought three necklaces with the intention of giving them to women he dated. He had already given away the other two necklaces, though each time the gift had brought almost immediate doom to the relationship. When he asked a buddy of his, a psychiatrist, why this happened, he was amused by the wordless answer. The shrink put his hand to his neck and started choking himself.

But Adam now felt free of the curse that surrounded the necklaces, or at least he thought he was. He felt drawn to Aschkin, and he considered the gift the first concrete expression of their closeness. He yearned to kiss her.

It was nearly midnight when they were ready to leave. As they got up from the table, Aschkin stood squarely in his way. Their lips met and their breath quickened. They sat back down on the cushions and continued to kiss in the semi-dark. The old Turkish waiter, standing near the exit, discreetly turned his back.

Adam's hand began to explore Aschkin's body. Her breasts felt firm and he wanted more, but he did not quite dare to undress her in public. He slid his hand up her jeans-clad inner thigh right to the top, and tried to feel the outlines of the tantalizing spaces below. She gripped his leg and then moved her hand upward to verify his male arousal. He began to moan and she put a finger gently on his lips. The zipper on her fly beckoned him and he slid it downward a little way and inserted his finger in the open space. Adam loved this version of high school necking. It took him back to the days when he could not look at a car seat without having erotic thoughts. He could feel the pleasures of an erection without having to perform, without taking responsibility for the woman's pleasure.

Aschkin thought of Voltaire's description in his novella *Candide*, the young hero and Cunégonde allowing their hands to roam freely as though they were searching for knowledge.

"I want to know you," said Adam, "as Adam knew Eve."

"And I want to incorporate," she whispered in Adam's ear. The word had been dancing in her head and she could not resist the pun.

Adam stopped moaning long enough to riff on the words. "Well, in which state should we incorporate?" he said, kissing her ear. "Where are the best tax advantages?"

"Maybe New Jersey," she said.

"All right, we will go down to Egyptland." They laughed, so loudly that the waiter brought them the check immediately. Adam adjusted his trousers to that he would not be embarrassed to stand up. He paid quickly in cash. Aschkin put an arm over his shoulder as they went through the door.

15

The Sabbath

PETER WAS ASLEEP when Aschkin entered their apartment. She let her hair down and went through the ritual of her evening toilette, as she always did, but this time she washed herself several times, unsure whether there might still be the scent of another man on her skin. She slid into bed next to her husband, but with an edge she feared he might feel. He slept on. Aschkin was not sure what she was going to tell him in the morning.

Adam returned to his solitary quarters. His apartment was beginning to take on the feel of a bachelor pad. He had not shared his two large rooms with a woman for many years and, almost as a defense against too much intimacy, he had reinstalled the loft bed that he had used as a graduate student. He knew that women hated climbing up and down the ladder but, sleeping there, he had the thrill of a little boy hiding out in a tree house. He placed a large potted Ficus between the bed and the window. When he lay in bed he could look through the leaves and see the river below.

As he lay in bed alone that night, he started repeating Aschkin's name over and over, like a mantra. He remembered doing something similar the first time he'd touched a female in a way that left an imprint on mind and body. When he was 14 he had used to go to one of the cafeteria ballrooms in Palermo for instruction in tango. The porteño tango required a cheek-to-cheek embrace, which was not all that easy for a 14-year-old pubescent male to handle. After dancing all evening with a slightly older girl named Gayle, he had lain in bed and whispered "Gayle, Gayle" to himself over and over. He knew then that he was afflicted with an aching Romantic heart and that he would probably suffer must of his life, calling out the names of women who would never come to him.

"Aschkin, Aschkin," was on his lips as he fell asleep.

* * * * *

Saturdays were always a slow time for Adam. He missed the routine of teaching and mingling with students, and sometimes with the birds from the Aviary—at least the European birds. Yet he nourished a lingering, abstract respect for the Sabbath. He recalled the time that Sara, though she was not Jewish, had joined him in observing the *Shabbat* in Buenos Aires. It had meant a lot to him that she'd embraced the rituals with enthusiasm. He sometimes imagined that they did this together in New York, and that they were joined by the child who had never been born.

When he could not observe the Sabbath—or there was no one close to observe it with—he mourned the loss. He yearned for the transformation from normal to holy time. In holy time—on the Sabbath—there was no spending of money, no cooking, no traveling, no housework. There were set times for people to get close to God and to the humans they loved. The afternoon nap was the time, as every Jewish man knew, that he was supposed to fulfill the commandment of bringing satisfaction to his *jedid nefesh*—the friend of his heart. The Jews knew how to awaken sexual desire and how to regulate it.

Alone for many years, he could not sustain the charged tranquility of the Sabbath on his own. But he retained the idea that work from sundown on Friday until a hour after sundown on Saturday was, or at least should be, taboo. He tried to read outside his field. He found friends to share the long stretches of time. Occasionally he would meet Nkwame Mavioglu, whose family was often abroad, for a meal, or he would encounter Ariel Colline at a museum and invite him on the spot for coffee to listen to Ariel's explanation of one school of art or another. On the whole, however, he found the down-time isolating and painful.

Sometimes he would ride his bike down to the barge, sit in the nearby café with a book, and look wistfully at the couples passing by. Adam was constantly at odds with himself about whether it was better to make compromises in order to be in or out of a relationship, that is. Being in provided a source of comfort; being out, he was distracted by his compulsive assessments of the women passing him by in life. Were they available? Should he try something? Would he dare to eat a peach? Now he felt that circumstances were drawing him in from the cold. He was already in the foyer but it was crowded—and the other occupant was the dean of his faculty, no less.

On this Saturday morning the café was bristling with cyclists. They came for their coffee, served of course in a proper mug with a nice slice of coffee cake on a plate. The setting and the service reminded Adam of the old European cafés in Buenos Aires. The coffee and cake were served as an art form, and the customers played their part by contributing to the environment of intellectual seriousness. Adam was a welcome guest because he often sat there with his laptop, writing. The staff liked him because he spoke Spanish with them, not to mention that he tipped well.

Adam ordered his usual—a decaf cappuccino and two biscotti, one chocolate and one almond. When the biscotti arrived, lying side by on the plate, Adam pondered them. He wondered why he had such strong taboos against love triangles, against allowing himself to yearn for the chocolate when the almond might feel neglected. In his self-absorption it did not occur to him that the real issue was Peter. How, as the book of Genesis taught, could he invade the realm of another man? Would he not stain the earth with guilt, as Isaac had when he'd convinced Abimelech that Rebecca was his sister and therefore available for marriage? His biblical learning was suspended in the breathless mantra of "Aschkin, Aschkin" that stayed with him from the night before.

He started to relive the moments of yesterday night, at the service and after. Was he discovering a new version of "holy time"? His reflections only made him feel more lonely. He called Ariel on his cellphone and made a date to meet him at the Metropolitan Museum for coffee in the early afternoon. "Ariel, Ariel," he murmured to himself as he rode up the Hudson, and then veered off toward Central Park and found his way to the back of the museum. The physical activity soothed him. It was his mantra of the body.

*****

When Aschkin awoke in the late morning, Peter was already ensconced in his study. He seemed not to have not noticed or cared that Aschkin had come home late. It could have been another long night at the library for all he cared. This irritated her. She had expected a confrontation that would force her to hone her skills at dissembling in preparation for a double life.

She volunteered, "While I was out on my walk I ran into a few students and we went for tea and talked until it got late."

"Which students were they?"

"A few grad students in Adam's class. They were just about to go into the local Turkish place and I joined them." It turned out that she was not too good at the lying game after all. She felt a compulsion to reveal as much of the truth as she possibly could.

Peter was a good enough lawyer to know when not to press his case. He gradually let Aschkin off the hook. He saw no need to skewer her for having disobeyed his instruction not to visit Adam's class. He could make no specific objection, either, against her talking to a few students outside of class.

"Did you talk about his class?"

"Actually I didn't probe them on those things." Here she was being very precise, for only Adam had pressed Chen about the context of the class.

"Was one of the students called Chen?"

Now Aschkin found her back to the wall. If she said yes, Peter might talk to Chen about the conversation; if she said no, he might catch her in a lie. She saw an opening in Peter's Americanized pronunciation of the Israeli name with a soft "ch" as in "church." She devised a Clintonesque reply. "Yes, there was a Chen there."

"Oh," Peter said, "You know, as an intellectual matter I have nothing against discussions of religion and the law. Chen"—again with a soft "ch"—"also got me interested in human rights in her country. She has a very strong commitment to the field. I like her."

"In case you were wondering," Aschkin said, trying to shift the focus from last night, "virtually all the students in Adam's class are learning well and admire him."

"Well, we'll see how loyal they are to him next week, when the student paper finally goes public about the exam."

"You're going to allow that happen?"

"Don't you believe in freedom of the press?"

* * * * *

Adam found Ariel at the Met, standing before an exhibit that had been the subject of controversy in the press. It was a statue of the Virgin Mary, with a look of ecstasy on her radiant face, holding the baby Jesus. Only on closer inspection did one notice that the baby boy was sprouting a miniature but unmistakable erection, and Mary was clearly masturbating with her free hand, under her cloak of numinous blue. The title read: *Happy Mother*. The author was the French avant-garde artist Pierre Brunau.

"Don't you think it's disgusting?" murmured Adam.

"Oh, don't be so conventional," Ariel snapped. "You sound like our mayor, who wants to censor art in the name of decency."

"Well, I'm not sure it should be censored. I'm just asking whether you think it's disgusting."

"What is disgusting anyway? Let's go *prendre un pot* and talk about it." Ariel loved to throw in French phrases in his conversation. They reminded other people and himself of his wonderful years in Paris, and distracted them from his Israeli accent in English.

They sat down in the café set aside in the corner of the huge museum dining room on the South Side. Adam felt comfortable. This was the only café north of 23rd Street that he was fond of frequenting. Ariel's salt-and-pepper mop was all over the place—something like his mind. He was eager to talk about *Happy Mother*. "You know, the artist is a friend of mine. I used to hang out with Brunau in my days in the Marais. He is not a disgusting person."

"I can go along with that."

"So tell me," pressed Ariel, "what does 'disgusting' mean? Let me give you some examples. How about eating fried human body parts?"

"Definitely."

"How about making designs with your *caca* on the bathroom floor?"

"For sure."

"How about homosexuals kissing on the bus in the best part of town?"

"I plead guilty."

"I am not sure what you are guilty about," replied Ariel, "but I know that ten years ago Joel Feinberg made this point about homosexuals in his book *The Moral Limits of the Criminal Law*. He actually argued that homosexuals kissing publicly in places where straights lived was so offensive that it could be penalized."

"Our attitudes have obviously changed."

"Well, for some people," said Ariel, "Maybe our mayor who believes in zero tolerance would still want to prosecute, if he had the laws to back him up."

"So what *does* it mean to say that something is disgusting?" asked Adam, intrigued.

"Well, think about it. Are all these things something you might crave to do—or as a child you craved to do—but which you have learned to repress?"

"I guess you're right. Incorporating the mother's breast, playing with shit—we all wanted to do that, didn't we? And it's also true that we have a repressed attraction to the same sex."

Before Adam got too pleased with himself, Ariel injected, "Well, not all of us repress the latter, *mon vieux.*"

"Tell me about that. Do you find it disgusting to see men kissing women?"

"Not at all, it just does not appeal to me. Well, kissing is all right, I kiss women too, but the rest of it leaves me cold."

"I understand, but it is not disgusting to you?"

"No. It is just not my thing."

"And how about a woman having sex with two men at the same time?"

"You mean one orally, the other vaginally?"

Adam threw his head back in mock revulsion. "That's hilarious. I meant one at a time, but in a *ménage à trois.*"

Ariel smirked with pride at his jab's hitting home. "As the great teacher Hillel said, we have these kinds and these kinds. I cannot get too excited about any of it."

"Well, tell me, if you have a *ménage à trois* among three gay guys, does one of them sometimes feel betrayed?"

"Yes, of course; gays have the same emotional lives as straights do. *Epater les bourgeois, tu comprends?*" Ariel leaned over the table and looked at Adam with studied intensity.

"I think so, but what about the morality of having two lovers at the same time?"

"What do you mean by morality?"

Adam got the point of the parry. "I think you basically believe in 'different strokes for different folks.'"

"How could I not believe it? My whole life I have been different, and people have preached their morality to me. Here they don't even let gays into the army. They call that morality. In Israel this was no problem."

Adam was feeling light, unburdened. He wished he could talk to others as easily as he connected with this man who thought of himself as different.

"Do you think I am the worst scholar in the world?" Ariel's tick suddenly intervened.

"No," grinned Adam, "I think Ann O'Sullivan is worse. But let's stick to art, shall we?"

"Have you had sex with *her*?"

"Like I say, let's stick to art. What about Bruneau's *objet d'art*? Do you think it is deliberately provocative?"

"Yes, of course it is. But art *should* be provocative. If you see *Happy Mother*, you will never forget it."

"Does that mean you think that it's good?"

"It's original. It forces us to pay attention. It forces us to think."

"You know," said Adam, "I gave an exam like that and now it is a major center of controversy."

"You are changing the subject. Is that because you think I am the worst art critic in the world?"

"No, I am the worst and I need your opinion about the aesthetics of my exam."

"I heard about your exam. A lot of fetus-killing, right?

"Yes."

"I think Bruneau might have liked that. But the gyno-Americans are shocked?"

"I did not write it in order to shock the students."

"So what is the worst part? The most gruesome possible episode in the most gruesome possible language?"

Adam thought for a second and then began, "A guy uses a steel bar to beat up a pregnant woman he finds on the street. He wants to kill the life growing in her womb. She secretly wants to have an abortion but the guy doesn't know that. When she's knocked out, he takes her to the ER at the closest hospital. They treat her properly and she suffers no serious injury besides loss of the pregnancy. When she's told that she has lost the fetus, she expresses relief and tells her doctor that she wants to send a thank-you note to her attacker."

"Great. I love it," enthused Ariel. "I can imagine what the gyno-warriors would say about that. Better than Bruneau. Do you think the thank-you note would be effective, or is the guy still guilty?"

"That's exactly what the students are supposed to think about. There is a precedent that you might read to get the guy off the hook. The case is called *Morgan*."

"Yes, I've heard about it. It is the kind of kinky stuff that only the Brits could dream up."

"Well, you know the facts. Morgan tells some RAF officers in a bar that his wife enjoys forced intercourse, even though she protests violently. The officers have a few drinks and then follow him home and gang-rape Mrs. Morgan. She protests and resists. They claim that they thought the resistance was simply part of the game. The UK House of Lords says that, if they acted in good faith and believed that the wife wanted violent sex, then they had an innocent frame of mind and they could not be guilty of rape. So, if good faith is enough to get you off the hook, then perhaps our assaulter with the steel bar has a case for exemption as well."

"Well, the difference," said Ariel, who was very clever when he started thinking like a lawyer, "is that Morgan's officers have an innocent frame of mind when they act. Here the assaulter has a guilty attitude when he acts and then afterwards the woman condones his actions. This does not cleanse him of evil purpose at the time he took the pipe to the woman's womb."

"Yes, that makes a huge difference. But there are some facts in the exam scenario that are more favorable for consent as a defense. In *Morgan*, the wife never consented; it was all a lie. Here she does not actually want to write a thank-you note, though, after the fact."

"Don't you think that the whole thing is a little weird? I would say 'queer,' but that word is already taken."

"Yes, most cases in criminal law are about very odd people. This is not corporate law."

"Do *you* have an answer to your provocative hypothetical?" probed Ariel.

"I really don't know. I lean in favor of conviction. Consent after the fact is troublesome, even if it coincided with her uncommunicated attitude before the beating. But I am open to argument. The purpose of the exam was to get the students to think about it and devise arguments. There is no orthodox answer."

"Yes, that is the hardest thing to get across about our business. People want nice questions and nice straightforward answers. They remind me of the guy downtown—the Italian. He wants clean, inspirational art—as if we should know exactly what every piece in the museum is supposed to mean."

"OK, I'll think of myself as the Bruneau of the law school," laughed Adam. "If I say that, will they lynch me?"

"The mayor and his friends might crucify Bruneau before this is all over. Then the headline might read 'Unhappy over Happy.'"

"I am not sure what headline Ann O'Sullivan will write for my eulogy."

"But I am tired of thinking about her. Can you help me line up some votes? Who are your best friends on the faculty?"

"Well," mused Ariel, "I have a chance with the blacks. You know, outsiders and all that. We have a common language. I will talk to Nkwame and to Pat. Then I think I have a special connection to Hans, and I am good friends with Paul."

"A good beginning." Adam rose and gave Ariel a hug as he was still sitting. "Time to go, *mon ami*." They set off in separate directions, with Ariel waving his long fingers gently as they parted.

16

And Then There Was Evening

SATURDAY EVENING, a balmy August dusk, was perfect for people-watching on Broadway. On evenings like this Adam often took a seat at one of the tables outside at one of the cafés, ordered a beer, and waited there to see who might pass by. If a hour passed without his encountering students or colleagues he would consider it a loss. Anders Andersson, an eccentric Swedish professor of anthropology, was one of several regular bar hounds in the area. He always had some intriguing observation about his local tribe under study—the Regina faculty. Then there was Steve Riley, a portly, humorous Mississippian, a graduate student in law, who would stride up with his two huge Great Danes in tow, tie them to the lamppost, and check in for a few beers. Many colleagues on the Regina law faculty would pass by too, but typically they were in a rush to get somewhere.

On that particular Saturday night a group of Adam's Asian students—the most reclusive in this class—were sitting together in the air-conditioned interior as Adam took up his watch at a table on the sidewalk. They nodded toward him as if to say "It is our honor," and then turned back to continue poring over their class notes. He returned a few words in Japanese and their jaws dropped. "*Sensei, Sensei,*" they repeated over and over again. "*Joozu desu,*" which meant, "You are really good."

Adam acknowledged the bow with a tip of the head then returned to his beer. These Japanese girls are so sexy, he thought. Wonderful to have in bed, reputedly good to live with—but I'm not thrilled about having them in class. They're too deferential. Jewish girls are just the opposite: terrible to live with but great to have in class. For the Jewish girls—and yes, he knew he was generalizing wildly—argument was a form of prayer. They validated themselves and the world by identifying the underlying conflicts God had built into the world. Perhaps it was an attempt to fill in the blanks of Eve's persuading Adam to eat of the fruit. There was not much of an argument in the Biblical text. Adam succumbed immediately. Eve—and all women since—were accused of having seductive wiles that took the place of reason. Women who argue, thought Adam, are writing the script that Eve never had. They are proving that women can persuade by reason as well as by sexual appeal. He thought how he adored having Chen Horowitz in class, but then realized that he had fewer Jewish students in class than he would have had in an undergraduate Regina class consisting of a good percentage of urban Americans.

He allowed his mind to drift to the other females in the class. He thought of the other Chen, Jiong known as Holly, as secretly courageous, and he could not but smile thinking of Charlotte and her evershifting hemline and her bare toes in class. Marga disarmed him with her effusive Colombian charm and fidelity to the Catholic orthodoxy. Why, he thought, did he have so much affection for these women, while he had such trouble with the feminists on the faculty?

At that moment he caught a glimpse of Ann O'Sullivan walking with Kathy Kong. Ann was in the lead and Kathy following, looking as though she wanted to take Ann's arm and parade down Broadway as Ann's partner. They made an effort to ignore Adam but he called them over. Who knew? Perhaps the balmy air of Saturday in a café on Broadway might soften them towards him. To his surprise, sitting down next to him, Ann looked more approachable than usual; she looked positively radiant. Flushed with the anticipation of battle? Adam wondered. Kathy sat up straight and aloof as though engaged in a Yoga exercise.

"How are your students doing?" Ann asked.

"Wonderful," he said.

"Are you encouraging romance in your class?"

"Not that I know of."

"Did you know that there are a few affairs going on in your class?" Ann adopted an interrogator's style.

"Wait a second—have you read me my Miranda rights?" This was an invitation to play. Would his "prosecutors" accept the bid?

"You are among friends, *chico*. There are no Miranda rights among friends." Ann had accepted.

"OK," said Adam, "let me think. I did see a German guy and an Israeli girl holding hands, but it was the Sabbath, so I think it was all right."

"Do you mean Mueller and Horowitz?" Ann always used last names, as though she were talking about felons. Adam wondered if she'd have been happier as a cop, like her grandfather. "Yes, they're definitely at it, but there are others too."

"'At it'?" blurted out Adam. "It sounds as if they are doing something illegal."

"You know about Sullivan and the other Chen, the Chinese girl?"

"I believe she is Chinese. And if they are 'at it' too, I'm happy for them. They actually have a lot in common and I'm fond of both of them. Why are you telling me these things?"

"We think you should know." He saw Kathy suppress a pleased little smile at the "we."

"Why?"

"Just in case you get any ideas."

"What ideas?"

"Well, we know that in the past you've seduced students, and if you do it this time you might find some guys trying to protect their turf."

"Ah, you mean I would be tampering with the natural order by having sex with a taken woman—something like Abimelech almost sleeping with Rebecca, or Pharaoh with Sarah?" Adam picked up the theme that had been troubling him in relation to Aschkin. "I don't believe in intruding on the turf of others."

Kathy looked totally perplexed at these references, but Ann would not let the allusion pass without a response. "Are you telling me that these women who took your fancy in the past were really your sisters?"

Adam was delighted that she would duel with him on biblical ground. "Touché, Ann. You know your Bible. But Abraham and Sarah were only half-siblings on their father's side. Anyway, think about it. If I am in the role of Abimelech, the all-powerful one, then they are the visitors to my kingdom and they are pretending in class that they are unattached—not owned by anyone, least of all by the other guys in the class."

"Yes," said Ann, "but when Abimelech looked out of the window and saw Isaac and Rebecca 'sporting' or 'necking' in the yard, he realized that they were not brother and sister."

"Yes, very profound: it is the first time we get a signal in the Bible that incest is taboo. But aren't you getting off track?"

Kathy Kong looked frustrated. "What the hell are you guys talking about?" In general she let Ann set the tone, but Ann seemed too playful now to handle. She took a deep breath and tried another tack. "Adam," she said, "tell me about discussing religion in class. Is there something I'm missing, particularly on the role of the Church in the repression of women?"

"No, I don't think you've been missing anything. The first thing that religious forces do is obsess about sex. Do you think you have anything in common with them?" Adam needled.

"Well, they do it," retorted Kathy, "in order to suppress women. The sexually free woman is a major threat to the male order. We raise these questions about sex in order to protect women and to liberate them."

"I'm not sure I see the difference," said Adam, ecstatic that the game was being played on Kathy's court and she was now down 30-love.

"But still," Kathy parried at the net, "sex with students is a serious thing."

"Do you mean 'by students' or 'against students'—if that is the right preposition?"

"Huh? I mean in and around students." Kathy swung wildly.

"No, you cannot mean that. There is nothing wrong with sex by students. They're adults. What you don't want is someone in authority taking advantage of them. Someone like Abimelech."

"Cut the Biblical crap," snapped Kathy. Ann threw back her head in pleasure, partly to hide her smirk. For all their sparring, she realized that she and Adam had a mode of communication that most people did not share.

"Do you play chess?" asked Ann.

"Yes."

"Well, Adam, if your chess game is as good as your knowledge of the Bible, you will hold your own in the coming endgame."

"But what is the game about? You're too smart to pretend it's really about my class now, nor about some exam given in the past."

"You said it." Ann looked pleased. "Of course your criminal law exam from last semester plays a role in all this, but between you and me the stakes are higher."

"Oh, really?"

"Well, let me put it this way. We are a community. We will resolve the controversy about the exam with due regard for everyone's interests, like a family."

"I feel like vomiting when I hear this talk about 'community' on the faculty. Why don't we work together on something serious, like the situation of convicted murderers on death row? I'm going to get a case like this soon. A Muslim accused of an honor killing. His sister went out on a date with a stranger. Do you want to help me?"

"Sorry, Adam, it's not our thing. Guys like that deserve to die," dismissed Ann. "Anyway, here within our community we do not operate like the courts. We prefer informal procedures. There's no need for the guarantees of due process if we're talking about the behavior of a member of the family."

"God save me from your community," responded Adam, suddenly cold and estranged.

"Adam, *amigo*," said Ann, sighing, "this is not really about you. Try to maintain a sense of humor. And don't forget the channels of communication, particularly with me." Kathy nodded too, and tried to appear as pleasant and supportive as possible. Ann added mysteriously, "If things work out the way they should, you will find out and it will not be so bad."

Adam wondered if Eve had a plan like that when she offered her Adam a bite of the apple. He got up, shook hands with Ann and Kathy, and wandered aimlessly down Broadway, looking for a few lighter-hearted souls.

* * * * *

Sunday mornings were always quiet in the law school. When he was a young scholar starting out, Adam had got in the habit of taking Saturdays off but going to his office to work on Sundays. The pattern, both the taking off and living, as it were, out of time on the Sabbath, and the returning to work when others were reading *The New York Times*, made him feel virtuous.

It was still early—there was a whole day of quiet and reflection ahead. He booted up his computer and, as the machine was going through its motions, he leaned back in his swivel chair. The chessboard in the corner beckoned him. He walked over to the board and stared at its neatly arrayed wooden pieces. He played the conventional opening moves on both sides and then moved his black bishop to the edge of the board. This was a move that could threaten the other side's queen, but it was not hard to defend against. It was also a dangerous position—to have the bishop out front, unprotected. He kept his fingers on the bishop and pondered whether it was good move.

"You like feeling vulnerable?" came Aschkin's voice from the still open door.

"I am vulnerable." He walked over and gave her a hug.

"What are you doing here on a Sunday?"

Avoiding a direct reply, she said, "There is old saying in German: *Renner am Rand, Denker im Sand.* When the bishop is on the edge, the thinker, meaning the player, is in the sand."

"Is that really an old expression in German?"

"No, actually, I just made it up. It suits you perfectly. You are my *Renner am Rand.* My runner on the edge. You love being on the edge."

"Yes, and you know Rand was my mother's name?"

"No, I didn't, but it suits you."

"And what are you doing, my security-loving, stay-at-home bourgeois wife, my Aschkin, my beloved one?" The verbal game titillated them, an easy surrogate for the clawing and biting they craved.

"Um—let me see: I had some work to do. How does that sound?"

"I think you wanted to see if I happened to be here."

"Guilty as charged."

"Is there anyone else in the building?" queried Adam, his mind racing.

"Yes, I'm afraid there is."

"Why afraid?"

"There's a lot of activity among students in the *Report* office. I passed them on the first floor. They're getting ready to release the new issue tomorrow."

"Have you seen it?"

"Yes, I got a copy. It's not pretty. She handed Adam a copy of the paper and gently touched his hand in the transfer.

He let it fall open and stared, transfixed, at the headline. "Professor Gross's Exam Stirs Controversy." The black border lent an air of mourning. Adam sat down and started to read:

A criminal law exam given by Professor Adam Gross last spring has sparked controversy on campus, with women and other students complaining that the exam question was offensive and prevented them from concentrating properly. Several student organizations, including the Lesbian Alliance, the Christian Student Association and the Feminist Phalanx, have protested to the law school dean, Peter Levenger. Professor Ann O'Sullivan, the adviser to the law review, has proposed to Dean Levenger that he improve the grade of every female student who received less than an A in the class. She has also urged the faculty to consider a resolution censuring Adam for "conduct unbecoming a professor."

The exam question asks students to evaluate a hypothetical situation involving a lesbian cult that worships a deity called "The Big Monkey" under the slogan "Motherhood is Death." The group persuades a follower named David to kill pregnant women on the street to protect the world against the wrath of the Big Monkey.

Critics say they were particularly offended by the part in which David beats up a pregnant woman with a steel pipe, killing her fetus. David takes the victim to the hospital, where it turns out that she had wanted all along to have an abortion. She tells her doctor that she would like to send a thank-you note to her assailant.

"This exam is over the top," said Professor Kathy Kong. Adrienne Fox, spokeswoman for the Lesbian Alliance, said that she found the exam "disgusting," particularly the slogan that "motherhood is death." Professor Julien Wright has challenged Professor Gross to a public debate about the propriety of the exam. Professor Gross has not yet responded and has been unavailable for comment.

As he read the last line, Adam exclaimed, "Unavailable, my ass! They never asked me. I'm going to sue the bitches. And a debate with Julien—I cannot wait."

"You might win the lawsuit and the debate," said Aschkin calmly, "but I think you should think first about which tactic will best save your ass."

"This must be a special occasion. You don't usually talk like that—I mean, in the language of the street."

"Right," she said, as she approached him and hugged him in way that was both motherly and inviting. She reached down and patted his rear, and then held it firmly as she felt the swelling close to her body.

Adam felt torn between his distress and his immediate arousal. He kissed Aschkin on the lips but then drew away. "I don't know whether we should talk or incorporate."

"Hmm," said Aschkin. "You know what I want to do, but maybe we should go somewhere and plan our strategy to save both your popo and your bishop. I am ready to snap up both of them."

"Do we have a car?"

"No," she said, "I don't drive."

"OK. Let me call Avis and I'll come by and pick you up in half an hour." Adam's hand was already on the phone. Aschkin took the black bishop and moved it back to the center of the board, and then stepped quietly out of the office.

With the car reserved Adam returned briefly to his computer. He had time to check his email. Not much came in over the weekend but he compulsively went through his junk mail and deleted the irrelevant items. He was thinking about leaving campus with Aschkin. What was he doing? Would he do it?

He jaunted by her office and invited her to join him with an extended bow and a deep wave of the right hand. She saw through the affected insouciance. "Sure," she said. "Let's take a drive and talk."

They took a cab down to the local Avis dealer, both looking around to see whether anyone might spot them. Their glances circled and then met, as though in a embrace. They laughed but refrained from touching each other in public. Adam was about to start complaining about how much better it was to rent a car in Europe: they always had a new model stick-shifts available and you could drive across the country with no drop-off fee. Aschkin saw it coming and gently touched his hand when she sensed his impatience brewing at the check-out desk where—as a reminder of the high crime rates before Giuliani—he had to negotiate everything through a two-inch space under protective glass sealing off the Avis employee from all possible foreign threats.

Adam took the wheel of the rented Chevy—with gas-wasting hydromatic, he thought—and started driving uptown, back toward the George Washington Bridge. As they crossed on the upper level, the grandeur of the bridge in the open air reminded Adam of the *faux* passage in the emblematic film of his youth, *The Graduate*, when Dustin Hoffman was driving east toward Oakland across the upper level of the Bay Bridge. It was an urgent drive. He had to get to the other side to prevent the marriage of his flame to the wrong guy. Everybody—all the students in California, at least—knew that the upper deck was for San Francisco-bound traffic only. Hoffman was breaking a taboo and the college kids all loved it. He broke a Talmudic taboo too, thought Adam, ever the scholar on these matters. He had sex with both daughter and mother. Why was this triangle so problematic for the rabbis? he pondered, pretending not to be troubled by his own drift toward a morally dubious triangle.

"You know that Julien claims there are two kinds of authority," he said. "Either you have to think someone else has better expertise to make a decision than you do, or that there is a coordination problem. Driving on the wrong side of the road is a coordination problem. There is no right or wrong but you need someone to regulate traffic to avoid collisions." Silently he continued to himself, So what is adultery? Does someone know better than we do whether we are doing the right thing? Or is this something like Dustin Hoffman's driving against the rules? Is there likely to be a big crash?

"It's good you are thinking about Julien's philosophy," said Aschkin, "since you will have to debate against him next week."

"I know. He is articulate, with that Oxford accent and all, and he speaks well, but I think I can play on his emotions."

"I hope so," said Aschkin, as Adam's mind drifted to another iconic movie in his constant sexual meditations, *Cousin, Cousine*. He remembered little about the film except one scene. A man and woman, who happened to be cousins, one or both married, spent a lot of time together in public. Finally, at the side of the pool where they both swam regularly, the man suggested, "You know, *cousine*, everybody thinks we are having an affair. If that is their opinion anyway, we might as well do it." Adam found this argument enormously titillating.

He turned to Aschkin. "Did you ever see *Cousin, Cousine*?"

"Yes, of course," she replied, "I forget the director but I remember the starring roles of Victor Lanoux and Marie—who was it?"

"Well, you know cinema better than I do," Adam said.

"Why do you ask? Do you see a parallel in our story?"

"Yes, I was just thinking about it."

"Ah, but," said Aschkin, "we are not cousins. More seriously, other people have no clue about us. I want to keep it that way."

"All true," replied Adam, "but I'm interested in the way the characters in the film take conventional opinion and turn it on its head. Since everyone thinks they're having an affair, they say, they might as well."

"I'm not convinced. If all the students think you are a sexist, does that mean you might as well become one?"

"Good point, *mi abogada favorita*."

She reflected a minute. "I'm not sure that we respond well to taboos. We are post-taboo, as it were. We think about self-interest. Even when we argue human rights, we are ultimately talking about our own long-range interests." The argument reminded her of Peter. For goodness' sake, she thought to herself, why am I making the kinds of arguments he would make?

"Is that what you've learned from the economists doing tax law?" Adam asked.

"Not exactly. Tell me something, Adam—have you ever loved anyone, I mean, with your entire being?"

"You mean, since Gayle when I was 14 in the tango club?"

"Yes."

"I think I loved Sara, my girlfriend in my college years, and then there's my daughter Abigail who left to live with her mother on the West Bank, but I don't see them any more. Since then I have had affairs, distractions."

"And why don't you see Abigail? You could fly down and stand at her door until she came out."

"Like stalking her? I think I prefer to cherish her in memory. I have broken with my life in Buenos Aires. But the memory of Abigail sustains me. I don't feel alone in the world. And you?"

"I think I loved Peter once, but our lives have gone different ways." She was full of resentment for the accumulated stresses of years of living together. He was part of her biography, part of her self, but she felt the need to break loose, to emancipate herself, to be Aschkin alone, undefined by parents, by any adult relationship. Adam's cool, his very inability to attach himself deeply, drew her in.

"Don't you think that your love of Abigail is the purest form of love? In general, I think the deepest human bond is with our children." She was asking and answering her own question.

"You think? Didn't Abraham show that he was willing to sacrifice both of his sons? He had already driven Ishmael out of the house and into the desert."

"Yes, I know. But did Abraham really think of sacrificing Isaac as killing him? Isn't it possible that he expected a resurrection? Maybe he wanted to be a father and to be alone with God at the same time."

"There may be something to that," responded Adam. "Perhaps it's the way I feel about Abigail. I'm afraid that parents sometimes want to get rid of their children. Take Laius in the Oedipus story. He believes the prophecy about the danger posed by his baby son Oedipus, so he puts him out to die. Maybe he just wants to return to his life alone with Jocasta. His actions show that he wants to be childless and have a son at the same time."

"Fatherhood, motherhood—it is all scary," said Aschkin. "Adam was alone with God before the birth of Eve. Maybe that is better."

"Better perhaps—but not very passionate. In the end he complains to God that he's lonely and needs a partner."

These words lingered in the air. *Passionate, lonely.* "Why are we drawn so much toward passion?" she asked. "The passions of Jesus, the passions of man and woman, they are all about suffering."

"The Romantics understood this better than—well, better than the lawyers, the people we are around all day. When we are passionate, we are alive." It sounded banal to Adam but he could not find better words.

"Just as we approach death," she said.

Adam was sure that at this point Ariel would have said something about *la petite mort*, that lovely French euphemism for sexual climax.

"To me it is interesting," continued Aschkin, "that about some things you seem to be careful—not getting too deeply involved with women, for example—but about other things you are the bishop on the edge of the board."

At that moment Adam pulled off the bridge and headed south on the two-lane roadway along the Hudson. They had a glorious view of Manhattan with the sun still high above the taller buildings. He drove into a parking lot abutting the river, and found an empty parking space set apart on a concrete slab built on pillars driven into the riverbank.

"The edge is for me," he said, nosing the bumper up to the railing that stopped them from dropping off into the river.

"I'm nervous," said Aschkin.

"I am too," he said as he reached over and nestled his cheek against hers.

"Do you remember the tango in front of the students?" she asked.

"I loved your scent."

Adam realized that this was the moment. He induced her to make the first move by sitting up straight and turning the key as if to start the engine. Suddenly she grabbed his head in her hands and kissed him firmly, driving her tongue into his mouth. He felt transformed into a flame, fuelling, consuming itself. He reached for her thigh, slipped his hand up to her crotch and held her firmly.

"*Leidenschaft, Leidenschaft*," she said.

Adam did not bother to ask for a translation. He knew what she wanted. A sense of agony filled the air...her breasts pressing hard against her blouse, his pants about to rip open, her jeans blocking her moist desire. He remembered the scene with the Turkish waiter standing nearby and picked up where he had left off, with her zipper half undone. This time he almost ripped the zipper open and forced his hand in; she began to pump against him so violently that the car began to rock. He pulled down her jeans and rushed to the scent that drove his blood to the center of his body. He kissed her and she spread her legs apart as far as she could in the confined space. She moaned something incomprehensible and his tongue danced on her longing clitoris. A minute and her short, taut screams vibrated against the car windows. Adam sat up and unzipped his trousers. She reached over and took his swelling organ in her mouth and passed back to him, in their moment at the edge between life and death, all that she had taken. His flame did not last long. They sat there in their fogged-over Chevy for two or three minutes, not moving, their bodies exhausted but still burning.

Finally she said, "It's time to go back."

"I don't think we can ever go back," he said as he drove in circles around the parking lot.

17

Good Taste

ON MONDAY MORNING, after a bike ride to the barge, Adam felt confident and decided to do the most difficult thing he could think of, namely confront Julien directly to find out what his grievance was. He was prepared to debate him in public, but first he wanted to find out what the the terms of the dispute were.

Julien was the most distinguished of the small group of Commonwealth scholars who were located politically somewhere between the Europeans (including the Latinos) and the straight Americans. He was a tall, gracious man of about 50, well respected as a legal philosopher, and with an interesting past. Adam knew he could use his support and, as he approached Julien's office, told himself to be more respectful and tolerant.

Julien was a serious Catholic, a British Catholic, slightly deviant from the norm. He prayed at the cathedral regularly and the word was that Ann would often go with him. He was not ashamed to discuss Christian faith in his work—much to the disdain of the professional philosophers at Regina and other élite schools. Julien was a maverick on the question of faith, and that was fine with Adam. Indeed, there had been times when the two had found themselves tossing Biblical references back and forth in faculty seminars. The others would look on and defer, as though the odd couple had found the wrong way out of their monastery.

Adam realized it might have been pure accident that Aschkin had decided to sit in on his class rather than Julien's. She could have renewed her connection to her religious past by pondering redemption on the cross. But maybe there was something in the Jewish tradition that attracted her. Jews and Muslims shared a love of abstraction and an aversion to concrete images. They also rejected the concept of original sin, an idea that was still fundamental in the Catechism. In many respects they were the same religion, Islam understood as a more abstract and universal version of Judaism.

When he knocked on Julien's door shortly after 10 a.m., a booming resonance—tinged with resignation about the disturbance—bade him enter. Adam enjoyed visiting Julien's office and inspecting the overflowing shelves for books on legal and political philosophy that he knew he should read. He usually felt humble in the presence of all these works he had not yet mastered. This time he noticed the short row of slim volumes of T.S. Eliot. Eliot was one of his favorite poets but he also knew that Eliot was an avid anti-Semite.

Julien stood to greet him.

But where was Adam to begin? Was there "*time yet for a hundred indecisions,/And for a hundred visions and revisions*?" What did Julien already know? Adam had not prepared his approach. So he simply asked, "Have you heard about the exam I gave last spring in criminal law?"

"Of course I have. I've challenged you to a debate, at least according to the local newspaper."

"I guess that's right. So you basically know what happens in the question. There is a cult that worships the Big Monkey and one of the members commits violent crimes for fear that said Big Monkey will wreak revenge on pregnant women."

"I've read it. The *Report* gave me a copy."

"I see. Well, do you think there is anything wrong with it?"

"Are you serious?" said Julien. "The question uses lurid descriptions of violence against pregnant women—steel pipes hitting swollen uteruses, people stomping on the stomachs of pregnant women, fetuses becoming hyperactive before dying, and so on. Of course this could upset the women in the class."

"Do you know that the exam question is based on three actual cases? For example, there's a very similar German case in which a cult worships the *Katzenkönig* or Cat King. One of its members feels intimidated into committing an attempted murder in order to avoid the wrath of the Cat King—"

"Spare me," Julien interrupted him. "There's really something perverse about your obsession with pregnancy and the death of fetuses."

"There is also a 1970s California case named *Lynch* about the malicious killing of a fetus," Adam persisted. "It's a very important precedent in the law of homicide."

Julien was not impressed. "Didn't it occur to you that there might be some pregnant women in the class, or women who had been pregnant in the past? Don't you think that the scenario would have disgusted them to the point of distraction? This exam was in extremely bad taste."

"Well, that's strong language for so early in the morning," Adam said. "I hope you didn't say that to the *Law School Report*."

"Look, I understand your problem," Julien said. "I was trained in the British academic system, where our exams are subject to review twice before being foisted on the students—first, by the head of department, and secondly by an external examiner who also reviews our grading. This provides two layers of reality check, which I suspect were sadly lacking in your case."

This point hit home. Adam felt—he also enjoyed recognizing the feeling—that he was caught mid-ocean, between the old world and the new. There was something very American about his assumption of total freedom to say and do what he wanted to do with the exam and, if that was the case, why did he expect to find support from his European colleagues? He didn't know how he was going to get past this contradiction. But he pressed on.

"So what would the British examiners have said about my 'bad taste'? If they had said, 'We don't like the language you use,' I would have asked them to tell me which words to change. Or would they have said, 'We don't like the issue raised by the question'?"

"If you had asked me," said Julien, "I would have advised you to set an entirely different question."

"So you mean I can't examine on a subject that is prominent in the case law and which raises rich theoretical issues?"

"What's so theoretical about blood and gore?" Julien was now sounding defiant.

"When I heard about this controversy I wrote a long memo laying out the issues for the students. If you like I will send it to you."

"Just give me an example," said Julien, sighing.

"Well, there are many, but the overriding question is whether the lead character, David, can justify or at least excuse his killing of fetuses on the basis of his fear that, if he did not, the Big Monkey would come down and kill a thousand pregnant women."

"Oh, come on. And I thought I was too academic in *my* class!"

"Actually I think it's a real and important question. What motivated the Unabomber? He thought he had to kill in order to avoid the wrath of technology. What about Yigal Amir, who thought he had to save the state of Israel?"

"Yes, but these guys were a little off. Should we have excused them for their wacky views?"

"Ultimately not, but they did sincerely believe they had to do what they did. So did David in my question."

"You could have raised that question without indulging in excessive descriptions of blood and gore."

Adam was nonplussed. He didn't know what to say at the level of legal theory, so he tried another tack. "Let me ask you one question, Julien. In the Catholic Church, you display images of Jesus with hands and feet nailed to the cross. He's bleeding profusely. When children see for this for the time, they are shocked and frightened."

"So?"

"Aren't you ashamed of the bad taste?"

As Julien glared at him, Adam held his gaze, rose slowly and unsmilingly backed his way out of the room.

"I guess we will have the debate after all. Let's say 11 a.m. on Wednesday; it can count as a class for my students—they will learn just as much from it as they would from a lecture. Daggers allowed."

As he closed the door behind him, Julien was already on the phone.

* * * * *

It was time for Adam to go back into the classroom. For the first time in all of his years of teaching, he thought of the familiar amphitheater as a refuge from a strange and hostile world. He was deeply fond of the dozen students he knew well, and comfortable with the others. As he entered and stood before them, he felt at home, at ease among his people. He caught Aschkin's eye and felt she was close to him.

He began, "We already know that in the history of American law, as well as in other legal systems, the great struggle is between freedom and equality. The first Constitution—in force until the Civil War—stood for freedom. The second Constitution—born in the Gettysburg Address—puts equality front and center in the American system of values."

Joerg Mueller's hand was up before Adam had finished the sentence. "This is not news to Europeans. We have made the same transition from liberalism to social democracy. Since the Second World War, our Civil War in Europe, we have emphasized human dignity and the equality of all people, men and women, Jews and Christians."

Adam shivered at the implications. He knew that referring to the Second World War as the "European Civil War" was a well-known technique for minimizing German guilt. The conversation with Joerg at the Turkish restaurant had obviously not been enough.

He saw that Aschkin was fidgeting in her seat. He wanted to ask Joerg and the other Europeans in the class about the steadfast failure of the European Union to admit Turkey as its first non-Christian member. Did he not think it had something to do with their being Muslim—outside the Crucifixion club? Aschkin evidently wanted to raise the same question. Their eyes met, but they both held off.

"For Americans," he said, "the great issue has always been race." This was a subject of which he always felt in control. He knew he could expound on the issues of race in America with the appropriate mix of guilt and understanding.

"The Civil War brought us the Fourteenth Amendment. The first victory for equality was the opening sentence: '*All persons born or naturalized in the United States are...citizens of the United States...*' This is a remarkable statement. At a single blow, the new Constitution held that race and blood are irrelevant. You have to see this as a response to the Supreme Court precedent that Lincoln hated most. In 1857 the Court, led by Justice Taney, had held that African-Americans, wherever they were born, could never become citizens. Dred Scott, a slave born in Missouri, could not sue as a citizen. This was one of the factors leading to the Civil War, and this principle establishing equality in birth is the final response."

Marga looked puzzled. "Let me get this straight," she said. "A pregnant woman—my sister—sneaks over the border from Mexico and gives birth here. You're telling me that the child is a citizen."

"Yes," said Adam. "The so-called *jus soli* rule—the idea that the place of birth controls citizenship—crystallized in England when they really thought of themselves as an island cut off from the rest of the world. In fact, with fears of illegal immigration now at new heights all over the world, the English modified this rule that they bequeathed to the English-speaking world. Some people want to change the rule here and limit citizenship to the children of resident or legal immigrants or something along these lines. What do you think?"

Just about everyone in the room had a strong sense of national identity that was based on their parents. The idea that the children of illegal immigrants could become citizens at birth puzzled them.

"I guess I'm in the minority here," said Adam, "but I think that the constitutional principle is right. Yes, we may let in a few people who never become part of American culture, but so what? We complete the great transformation that began in 1787. First the English-Americans constituted the American people, then we added the Germans and the Dutch, then the southern Europeans—the Italians and the Greeks. The waves of immigration constantly expanded our sense of who is an American. Finally, in the process initiated by the Civil War and the Gettysburg Address, we recognized that black and white are equally American. In the process we also ceased talking about the United States as a Christian country."

Holly put up her hand. "You mean the American is something like the 'new Soviet man'? They also claimed that they were getting over the barriers of national identity. I am not sure it is possible." Many in the room nodded. The memories of the dissolving of Yugoslavia and the Soviet Union and the nationalism that had reappeared, still virulent, was fresh in the minds of many.

"Good," replied Adam. "I see we have some tension on these issues. Let's agree to disagree.

"The Fourteenth Amendment addresses equality more explicitly in its final clause: '*No state shall...deny to any person within its jurisdiction the equal protection of the laws.*' Every word in this formulation carries great weight. Let's suppose that the barber shop on the corner refuses to cut the hair of black men. Is this a violation of the Amendment?"

For Grigor the words "no state" screamed off the page. His own Constitution, the German Basic Law, had a similar provision, but with no mention of the state. He argued, "Our Basic Law says 'All human beings are equal before the law.' But...well, I think the American Constitution limits itself here to the action of the state. It does not apply to private discrimination."

"And do you think it would be possible in any case," Adam responded, "to tell people that they cannot discriminate in their choice of friends or lovers?"

Some students looked around the room and caught each other's eyes, as though they had secrets to share.

"Take a look at the so-called civil rights cases decided in 1883. Congress passed a law making it a crime to prohibit discrimination in 'public' accommodations such as transportation facilities and theaters. Several theaters around the country refused admission to blacks. The government prosecuted and the appeals eventually came to the Supreme Court. What was the problem in these cases?"

Ilona, the Romanian judge, privately felt that "some people" were different; but as a trained judge she tried to keep her mind on the legal issue. She argued that if a private theater refused to admit blacks, that would not be considered an action of the state.

"Yes," Adam responded, "but aren't these events open to the public; does not that make them public events? You cannot compare them to private parties in your home. What about this university? Could we close our doors to minorities we do not like?"

Like hell you could, Jaime thought to himself. "Well," he said polishing his sentiments, "technically Regina is a private law school. But it receives state and federal funding in many departments. The land that it owns is tax-exempt. It educates an élite class who will either work in the government or support it in some way. How can you say that the state is not operating here?"

"To tell you the truth, I agree with you," Adam said. "But in 1883 the Supreme Court started to pull back from the moral victory of the Civil War. They interpreted Congress's power narrowly and held that, even after the Fourteenth Amendment, Congress had no power to punish the refusal of private parties to admit black people to their theaters. That was a narrow and strict interpretation, but with an agenda: to put an end to the postbellum campaign to promote the status of African-Americans in the society."

"But surely," Jaime intervened, "there's no way today that Regina could discriminate in its admission policies."

"That's correct," Adam responded. "But you would be surprised at how recently that came to be the law. The history of equality in the United States has had many twists and turns. The 1883 decision signaled the beginning of a half-century of *de facto* apartheid in this country. The federal government would not intervene to prevent the state-sponsored segregation—not to mention the private segregation—of transportation, public schools, even bathrooms in public parks.

"After blacks and whites went to war again, this time all on the same side against the supreme racists of Germany and Japan, the country rediscovered its commitment to social justice. In 1948 the Democrat leader Hubert Humphrey had the courage to get up in front in the Democratic Party Convention and give a short speech that initiated the Civil Rights movement. His rhetorical high point was the line, *'To those who say this civil-rights program is an infringement of states' rights, I say this: The time has arrived in America for the Democratic Party to get out of the shadow of states' rights and to walk forthrightly into the bright sunshine of human rights.'* Six years later the Supreme Court ruled that segregation in public schools was inherently unequal. But these developments still applied only to the states and to their officials. They did not resolve the question of possible discrimination by the Regina Law School and other so-called private institutions."

"How did that change, then?" someone called out.

"Have you heard of the Civil Rights movement in the late 1950s and early 1960s? This was a period of great social upheaval. I was not even here, but I have read about it. African-Americans in the South started engaging in civil disobedience. They were supposed to sit in the back of the bus, the better seats reserved for whites. A little black woman named Rosa Parks boarded a bus in Montgomery, Alabama and sat down in the white section. The driver told her to change her seat but she would not budge. Soon blacks were sitting-in at segregated lunch counters. Finally, in 1964, under the leadership of Lyndon Baines Johnson, Congress enacted another version of the civil rights law that had been declared unconstitutional in 1883."

"But how could they do it?" inquired Ilona. "The law as pronounced by the Supreme Court was against them."

"You're right," said Adam, "But something happened in the 1930s that changed the landscape of American law. Some scholars regard this period as just as revolutionary as the Civil War in the reorientation of the Constitution. What was that?"

"Well," said Joerg, "we had a depression in Germany. I imagine the same thing happened here."

"I think we started the chain reaction around the world here," said Adam. "We had the stock market crash of 1929. For three years the Republican government did little to rectify the collapse of the economy. Then Roosevelt came to power and he sponsored a whole series of public welfare projects to stimulate the economy—to 'prime the pump,' as they put it. The problem was that conservative judges, of the same stripe as those who had blocked the Civil Rights legislation in 1883, declared the new legislation unconstitutional. Roosevelt was furious and he fought back. By 1938, he was pulling out all the stops to support Congress against the Court. He even threatened to 'pack the Court,' that is, to increase the size of the Court by appointing new judges sympathetic to his legislative program.

"Finally the Court caved in. One judge shifted and a new five-to-four majority started voting for public works programs. This is now called 'The switch in time that saved nine.'" Adam realized that this was an inside joke, a play on language, something like one of his favorites—"shift happens."

He wrote on the board, "Nursery rhyme: A stitch in time saves nine." He was beginning to feel that his studied grasp of English was threatening to cut him off from the people he cared about. Immigrants often learned these expressions from books—but Adam usually got them right.

"But I think we have been putting the cart before the horse." He had to write that one on the board too. "Congress intervened rather late in the struggle for racial justice in the United States. The burden remained on the Fourteenth Amendment to ensure that no state deny 'any person within its jurisdiction the equal protection of the laws.' The state need not concern itself with people outside its jurisdiction: there is no burden to ensure equal treatment among everyone in the world—only those under the influence of its government. And note something very important: we say that 'every person' is guaranteed equal treatment by the state to which he or she is subject. It does not say 'every American' or 'every citizen.' If you are a human being, a person, you are entitled to equal treatment—at least to treatment equal to that of everyone else in the same state.

"Of course, every law discriminates. It treats some people worse than others. The law of murder treats murderers worse than those who do not kill. Is this discrimination? Obviously not. We need some general theory to decide when treating people differently amounts to discrimination in violation of 'equal protection of the laws.'

"The story begins with race—black and white. For most of the time from the Civil War to the 1960s, that was the only issue of primary concern to American courts. Some judges thought the exclusive purpose of the Amendment should be to protect former slaves against persecution by the state. But it did not work. Why not?"

In school Holly had heard some denunciations of American discrimination. "Didn't the USA try to exclude all Chinese at a certain point?"

"Yes, Congress passed the Chinese Exclusion Act in 1882, but the Court also intervened to protect resident Chinese against discrimination. Very soon after the Civil War there was a dispute in San Francisco between the local authorities and the Chinese who needed business licenses to open their commercial laundries. The Chinese argued that the local authorities were discriminating against them, and in 1886 they won in the Supreme Court. That meant that the cat was out of the bag." My God, thought Adam, I cannot avoid thinking in these expressions that I had to learn myself from a tutor.

"What does that mean?" blurted out Charlotte, slightly exasperated.

"It means that there was no way to tie the 'equal protection' clause to its historical roots. No one had thought about protecting the Chinese when the states ratified the Fourteenth Amendment in 1868. But racial discrimination is the same, whether directed against black people or against the Chinese. The cat here is the principle of equality applicable to everyone; the bag is the specific concerns of the political leaders in 1868 when they ratified the Fourteenth Amendment."

"How about discrimination against women?" said Chen. "When did the Court begin to take that seriously?"

"The truth," replied Adam, "was that gender discrimination was not even on the Court's radar screen until the social ferment of the 1960s seized the country and we started thinking about all the forms of injustice that had become commonplace in the

United States. All of a sudden we were forced to think about which distinctions were legitimate and which were not. Not only women demanded equality. So did children born out of wedlock, gays and lesbians, the disabled, the aged, foreigners. Who was to receive protection and who not?"

Jaime was excited. "It all goes back to Lincoln's invoking of the Declaration of Independence and proclaiming that 'all men are created equal.' Of course, we have to understand 'all men' to refer to 'all human beings.'"

"So how much guidance does that general clause give us?" Adam queried. "How about separate bathrooms for men and women?"

Charlotte almost jumped out of her seat. "Well, what do you expect?"

Aschkin smiled. Her mind drifted back to the co-ed sauna in Heidelberg. In her daydream, however, she noticed that the figure pressing her to the wall had the outlines of a male body but no interior lines in his face. In her fantasies Peter had lost specificity and become an archetype—a male figure without distinctive features. Aschkin did not have to ask herself who might fill the outline.

Adam was walking in the aisles, tugging at his lapels, turning to one side and the other, reveling in his command over his audience. "What do *you* expect, Charlotte? We all understand that separate bathrooms don't spell discrimination. But then how about separate schools for blacks and whites?"

"The difference," Charlotte said, "is that, apart from in the bathroom, men and women generally want contact with each other." The class began to titter. Aschkin, coming back from her sauna reveries, yearned for Adam's touch.

"I never thought of it that way, Charlotte." Adam was pleased. "What is implied by whites seeking to avoid contact with blacks?"

Joerg knew that in the Nazi period there had been signs all over Germany prohibiting "dogs or Jews" in restaurants and hotels. "It is about contempt and humiliation. There was plenty of that in the Third Reich," he added after a brief pause.

"Yes, but what is this contempt about? Why should whites seek to avoid contact with blacks—or Germans with Jews?" Joerg had emboldened Adam to take a step toward the issue that bound them together in a delicate dance.

Chen could not resist the bait. "Men sometimes feel this way about women. They think that menstruating women are unclean. They do not want to touch them for fear of being contaminated."

Gad Menachem, however, was not going to let the implicitly critical reference to Jewish Orthodoxy pass unnoticed. "Perhaps it started out that way. But no one I know thinks that way now. Everyone now regards the discipline of marital relations"—he was referring to the prohibition against sexual relations during menstruation and for eight days afterwards—"to be a great boon to intimacy and romance."

Mohammed from Senegal concurred. "You do not know how sexy a knee or an elbow can be if it is covered all the time," he said. "Westerners should not assume they understand the sexuality of the East. I am with Gad."

Aschkin felt torn. She wanted to enter this debate, but she was not sure on which side. Was she foremost a Muslim or a modern woman? She would not live by the rules of marital separation. Peter, who was probably ignorant of the whole thing, never raised the subject. Yet there might be something to her tradition that she did not understand. And God knows, she said to herself, she and Peter needed something to revive the mystery and excitement in their relationship. Their sex life had just about run dry. Perhaps an enforced period of separation every month would awaken their interest in one another.

In his adult life, Jaime had known women only as relatives or nuns, yet his theoretical mind did not fail him. "I cannot imagine how men can both have contempt for women and yet seek their mothers in them, fall in love with them, write poetry to them."

It is a mystery how that is possible, thought Adam. "Well, I'm willing to concede that women are different." He was unaware that he was speaking his thoughts aloud.

"So are men," interjected Chen and Charlotte, almost in unison.

"But the whole subject differs from the problems of discrimination in other realms," continued Adam sheepishly after his naïve admission about women. "Let's talk about another famous case in the statute books. This strikes close to home. One Ms. Griffiths—otherwise known as Fré Le Poole—was a graduate student in law just like you. She was from the Netherlands. She fell in love with a young teacher at Yale Law School, John Griffiths..."

"Ahhh...." came the pseudo-swoon from the back of the room.

"Maybe she married just to get a green card," suggested Holly, with a new touch of impishness. The angles for staying in the United States were not far from many of the minds in the room.

"You're right. We really don't know. In any event, she wanted to take the Bar but she would not give up her Dutch citizenship and take American papers, as she easily could have done. The Connecticut Bar would not let her take the exam, solely on the grounds that she was not a citizen of the United States. She got angry and sued—all the way to the Supreme Court. Do you see any difference between her issue and the problems posed by racial and gender discrimination?"

"Yes," said Joerg. "There is no contempt for her here. The Bar was not saying that she was inferior or undesirable in some way, but merely that each nation should govern itself, and that lawyers are important agents of government."

"You mean that she should have gone home to Holland to practice law?"

Joerg had an easy time with this issue. "She had the choice of becoming a naturalized American citizen, she was married to an American, and yet she said no. This is not racism."

The vibrations in the room told Adam that many agreed with Joerg. Germany for the Germans, Spain for the Spanish—each country for its own people. He was going to have an uphill battle to get them to see both sides of the Griffiths case.

"Well, in fact the Supreme Court decided for Ms. Griffiths. They rejected Mr. Mueller's argument. Why did they do that?" This was not the kind of move Adam liked to make in class: it was an appeal not to reason but to authority, yet he needed something to stir the pot of controversy.

"The Court reasoned," responded Jaime, "that the practice of law is a skill like any other profession. Let's take medicine. Would it be fair to exclude foreigners from the practice of medicine? I don't think so."

"It's true," conceded Adam, "that a whole line of cases going back to the early days of the Fourteenth Amendment addresses the issues of economic competition and the creation of an open and free market. In one of the early cases they concluded that the butchers of New Orleans could maintain tight control over the slaughterhouse business at the mouth of the Mississippi. Since then, the courts have struggled to eliminate all restrictions that have the tendency to establish monopolies."

Carlos from Mexico, who had not spoken for a few days, saw an opportunity. He remembered something from school, and offered a comment. "You know, the situation in Buenos Aires was the same, but in the case of silver mining. They controlled the mouth of the Río de la Plata and taxed all the inland shippers who wanted access to the ocean. This was good for you *porteños*."

"Sure," Adam said. "I remember studying that at home. Monopolies always have an immediate good effect for the privileged few, but in the long run they inhibit competition and economic growth. At least this the wisdom we have acquired from the economist Adam Smith. The Bar for lawyers is a kind of monopoly, is it not?"

"You bet," said Grigor, eager to display his knowledge of economics. "We should attack the Bar exam itself. This restricts competition!" The room broke out in applause.

"Many libertarians would agree with you," said Adam, "but rational qualifications are different from qualification based on birth and other irrelevant characteristics."

"But are birth and culture irrelevant to the practice of law?" pressed Joerg. "I think Justice Rehnquist makes a good argument in dissent. You have to be an American to understand the spirit of American law. Savigny, our great jurist, argued the same thing about German law. Each nation has its *Zeitgeist*."

This argument resonated with Adam's Romantic sensibilities. Savigny was among the early German nationalists who had rebelled against Napoleon's imperialism and the supposed universalism of French law and culture. Were the American liberals now preaching the same false universalism by making American law open to all? Now he was torn, just like Aschkin earlier in her thoughts about where she stood on the conflict between Islam and the feminists.

"I said to you at the beginning of this course that we were engaged in a process something like a religious conversion. That is why we spent so much time on the Civil War. The United States Constitution must become an important source of authority in your thinking. I agree that you cannot become a good American lawyer unless you learn these things. But did Fré Le Poole-Griffiths need an *official* conversion to the American 'religion' in order to become a good lawyer in Connecticut?

"Citizenship is a good test for whether you are committed to preserving and cultivating the Constitution," added Grigor, in support of his German colleague.

"Is it not enough to ask new lawyers to take an oath to uphold the Constitution?"

"I would turn the question around," Grigor replied. "Is citizenship really a test of whether you understand the unwritten spirit behind the words on the page?"

"Maybe you should be a native-born American to practice law in the United States. After all, the Constitution says that to be president you have to be native-born. But are we not now verging on racist arguments?" Adam protested, trying to effect a mood of sober rationality. "You know that not too long ago, before the Second World War, departments of English literature in the United States would not hire Jews or atheists. They reasoned that only committed Christians could really understand Milton and Shakespeare, writers who were steeped in Christian thought and symbolism. Don't you think this was nonsense?"

Adam's playing of the Jewish card symbolically drove Joerg back deeply into his seat. He would not reply. Adam sensed too that he had gone too far and wanted to apologize, but he could not do so without appearing foolish. Why had he pressed Joerg so hard when in fact they had so much in common?

There were two parties emerging in the room, as there were in Adam's head. One was the party of the individualists who thought of the practice of law as an intellectual trade that should be open to all who could master it; the other was the party of national mystics who agreed with Joerg that each legal culture expressed a spirit that only natives could grasp. The nativists had been gaining ground, so Adam had thrown himself with additional vigor into the defense of liberal individualism. In the end he admitted, "I find myself in a self-contradictory position. On the one hand I accept the relevance of the national ethos in legal thinking, but on the other I find myself here as the Lone Ranger defending the idea that all men are created and remain equal. The truth is that the decision of the Supreme Court in the Griffiths case was a singular victory for universal equality over group identity. No other country insists on this kind of equal treatment for non-citizens."

This was a overly broad statement, because, as one of the students pointed out, Canada had made a very similar decision. As Adam left the room at the end of the class he felt engaged and exhilarated. This was the way to teach, he thought to himself. To be engaged myself— and not to be afraid of making mistakes.

Walking past the arguing students, he approached the elevator and Aschkin joined him. They entered the private vertical space together, alone. As they ascended, Adam reached over and put his hand around her waist. She said, "I am feeling conflicted."

"I am too. I love the feeling," Adam said, ending his embrace as she slipped out at the first stop. He tried to block the closing doors, but it was too late.

18

The Heat of Battle

PROFESSOR GROSS WAS eager to meet the students that afternoon and start preparing for the confrontation with Julien. As they filed in, he began sifting over the words of the First Amendment: "*Congress shall make no law...abridging the freedom of speech, or of the press.*" How many of these words still had their original meaning? Congress no longer meant just Congress, because all the state legislatures and municipal governments were also bound under the same provision. Did "no law" mean absolutely "no law," as Justice Black had once imagined? And what did "freedom of speech" mean? He would have to explain all these issues to the students and much more: he would have to plant the idea that "free speech" included writing examinations that might offend some people.

He began by setting the stage against the backdrop of the Civil War. "One of my favorite abolitionist preachers was named Theodore Parker." Another one who should have had a statue in his honor on Riverside Drive. "Parker saw the world as a dramatic conflict between opposing forces. I see it the same way. As we have seen so far, the first Constitution stood for freedom—including the freedom to own human beings. The second Constitution stands for equality, as embodied in the Fourteenth Amendment."

Adam's style of thinking appeared to be an application of the agonistic principle. He posed opposites and portrayed them as struggling for supremacy. Jaime whispered to Holly that it reminded him of the way the Church thought about God and the Devil.

But things were not that simple for Adam. He began to speak about Lincoln's Second Inaugural Address, in which the president recognized that both sides had fought for their vision of good; both had believed God was on their side.

"There is a permanent tension," Adam added, "between freedom and equality. Equality surged in the Civil War. Some time afterwards, freedom was due for a comeback. The language of the First Amendment had been there since 1791 but the Courts did not take it seriously until it was time for 'freedom of speech' to assert itself—in the days after the First World War. Note the precise words of the Amendment: *'Congress shall make no law...abridging the freedom of speech, or of the press.'*

"This sounds like an absolute to me—'Congress shall make no law'—and absolutes are a blessing. These words anchor our thinking. There is no room for judgment and discretion. The German Basic Law also begins with an absolute commitment: *'Human dignity is inviolable. The entire power of the state is required to protect it and to respect it.'* Absolutes like these define a culture and tell us where we stand."

Several of the European students looked puzzled. No country in the world protected speech as the United States did. How, they wondered on the basis of their national experience, could there be an absolute commitment to freedom of speech? Joerg's hand shot up.

"Excuse me, professor—you have just mentioned two absolutes. One is a commitment to a form of self-expression. You can say and print anything you want. The other is to respecting human dignity— namely, the human dignity of those you might be talking about. Don't you see these as inconsistent?" Joerg folded his hands after a comment he took to be insightful.

Adam looked pleased. Freedom of expression could indeed infringe upon the sense of dignity of targeted groups. Europeans used the argument of human dignity to limit and control hate speech. "It is a pleasure to be challenged like that right off the bat." He noticed a few students leafing through their dictionaries.

"Sorry," he said. "I think that's a baseball expression. You get up to bat, and someone throws you a fast ball." He was just getting deeper into America and its peculiar idioms.

"I guess that does not help you. Let me put it this way. The First Amendment and its protection of freedom of speech are about as American as you can get. We are aware that other countries are skeptical about the way we enthrone freedom of speech and of the press."

Jaime pursued the challenge, "Does that mean that you are not concerned about the people whose dignity might be injured by free speech? What about Holocaust denial?"

"Actually," responded Adam, "we have no constitutional commitment to human dignity, as Europeans do. The Germans, following Kant, began the post-Second World War trend toward legislating to protect the dignity of all. The Israelis have recently followed the example with their own law based on the same respect for intrinsic dignity. Chen told us about that in our first class."

"The German example is not necessarily so good," Jaime intervened. "They were motivated by guilt for the past and they enacted other policies reflecting the same feelings of guilt—for example, their 1975 Constitutional decision mandating the Parliament to punish abortions. They said they were protecting the right to life. Yes, they had done too much killing in the past, but that is no justification for adopting the Church's position that every fertilized ovum—whether implanted or not—constitutes human life."

Both Adam and Aschkin looked impressed that Jaime knew about the conservative approach of German medicine toward IVF treatment. There must be a story here, they both thought.

Joerg looked uneasy. "What do you mean, German guilt? At the end of the eighteenth century Kant taught that human dignity was beyond all trade-offs; no price could justify demeaning a fellow human being. That is the true origin of the argument on behalf of dignity today."

Gad added, "You do not need Kant to establish the principle of human dignity. It is based as well on the Biblical principles that all men are created in the image of God."

Chen dropped her jaw in puzzlement and frustration but remained speechless. Adam was pleased that the old conflicts still animated the class discussion. He intervened, "For the time being we need not resolve whether it is better to put your chips on freedom or dignity. But we can say this: freedom and equality are in constant tension. Dignity is a good substitute for equality. In the *Dred Scott* case, the Court affirmed the freedom to own another human being. The Civil War established that equality prevailed over that form of freedom. We might also have described this transformation as recognizing that universal human dignity triumphed over the freedom of a few.

"In the American rhetorical tradition, however, the key word is equality, not dignity. The Civil War also introduced the income tax, which favored redistribution and equality over the freedom to earn and keep everything to yourself. Initially the Supreme Court resisted the income tax as 'too much equality.' We needed a constitutional amendment in the early twentieth century to elevate economic equality over economic freedom. As we discussed this morning, Roosevelt carried this development further under his New Deal. But in the law, as in physics, every action produces a reaction."

The students listened intently. Charlotte's toes were again bare, but at rest. Gad was no longer twiddling with his earlocks. Even Aschkin enjoyed this way of presenting the origins of income tax. Her intense gaze betrayed nothing about their drive across the river.

"I have told you that the First Amendment was enacted in 1791 as part of the Bill of Rights. This is true, but the modern, robust, powerful First Amendment emerged as a reaction to the egalitarianism of the New Deal. There were harbingers after the First World War, but in dissenting opinions by Justice Holmes. The leading cases were decided in the early 1940s. Action and reaction. Freedom breeds a commitment to equality. And a strong egalitarian politics produces a reaction in favor of freedom. For us, as Americans, the primary freedom is now freedom of speech."

Charlotte intervened. "It is a shame we don't have any Canadians here because, you know, they share the European attitude about limiting free speech in the social interest."

"That's true—the Canadians limit rights by the all-inclusive principle of their Section 1, which requires that all rights be exercised in a 'free and democratic society.' But they do not restrict the right to speak French. That is important. It is entrenched in the Canadian Charter. So you might think of the American approach to free speech as something like the Québécois right to speak French."

"But speaking French does not hurt anybody," responded Ilona reasonably. "We still believe that some censorship is necessary to protect the vital interests of the society."

"Yes," said Adam, "but when the government starts defining the vital interests that prevail over free speech, they are liable to choose things like the dignity and prestige of the national leaders. Or they will think it necessary to prohibit the burning of the national flag.

In the early 1990s, after some hesitation, the Supreme Court upheld flag-burning as freedom of speech."

Many of the students realized that in their home countries it was still illegal to burn the national flag, and some wondered whether their cultures veered a bit too much in the direction of authoritarian respect for the state.

"Now I understand why the leading Israeli theologian Yeshayahu Leibowitz—I should say late theologian of blessed memory—used to burn the Israeli flag every year!" said Chen. "He was a committed Zionist, but he thought that taking the flag so seriously was a form of idolatry."

"Ah, Ms. Horowitz, are you making a religious argument? And what is that part about 'blessed memory'?"

Embarrassed, Chen replied, "Yes, some religious people are also very liberal. And the expression was just the Hebrew way of saying—what is it? May he sleep in peace?"

Jaime looked at her affectionately.

"May he rest in peace," corrected Adam. "I heard a tape of Leibowitz once. He was very impressive. The usual American arguments for free speech are a bit different. Our culture is infused with a deep anti-authoritarian skepticism: the fear that if you allow the government to gain an inch by censorship, they will take a mile. It's something like 'The power to tax is the power to destroy.' The two things the government wants most are money and respect."

"False gods always need respect," offered Gad sagely.

"This all relates to the Civil War," continued Adam. "Oliver Wendell Holmes, Jr. fought in the war and was injured three times. He was one of the leaders of the pragmatist movement, which rejected all absolutes in favor of solutions tested by whether they worked in practice. About 50 years later, when he was on the Supreme Court, he became the first dissenter advocating freedom of speech for political radicals. The Civil War took place because debate broke down; both sides held firmly to their absolute convictions."

"Everything relates to the Civil War," joked Rodrigo. "Holmes is *your capitán*, my professor."

"Not exactly," said Adam, trying to ignore him as usual.

Joerg picked up the thread. "Oh, I see, you think that wars always occur once debate is no longer possible."

"Right," said Adam triumphantly. "Holmes advocated the marketplace of ideas. If some speech was negative and destructive and disloyal, then it should be countered by more speech. Eventually, he thought, the better opinion would prevail."

Charlotte appeared amused by the discussion and particularly by Adam's slightly naive faith in the marketplace. "*Oui, Professeur.* But the marketplace is subject to the manipulation of the media. *The New York Times* is not a simple consumer or manufacturer. It determines the agenda of discussion. In the case we read for today, *The New York Times* is trying to change the way Southerners think about civil rights. And the Court is obviously on their side."

"Good point, *Mademoiselle*—let us indeed turn to the saga of *The New York Times* in Montgomery, Alabama. What did they do to produce a constitutional crisis?"

Adam decided to focus on the Eastern European students, who were still emerging from the restraints of Communism. They might be relatively more sympathetic to the absolutist tendencies of the American courts on the issue of free speech. He questioned a few of them in order to sketch out the basic facts. *The New York Times* had run an advertisement sponsored by a special committee of civil rights activists to protest at the treatment demonstrators had received from the police force of Montgomery. The advertisement had contained some inaccuracies, such as the complaint that the police had padlocked the dining hall in the college where the demonstration took place, and that Martin Luther King, Jr. had been arrested seven times when in fact it was only four. Although Sullivan, the police chief in Montgomery, had not been mentioned, the jury was permitted to find that the advertisement was 'of and concerning' him and that in principle he could sue for libel under the common law. The libel in question was the implied allegation that his police force had engaged in police brutality. The Alabama jury imposed both general and punitive damages against *The Times*. They delivered an unexplained verdict: liability for a half-million dollars.

"There are lots of problems here." Adam tried to engage the class in methods of questioning the verdict. "What could the Supreme Court do to hold that the law as applied by the Alabama jury was unconstitutional?"

"First," started Ilona, "there is no possibility he could have won in Romania for damage to his reputation. The error by *The Times* was innocent; there was no fault. And I don't think the newspaper is at fault for its advertisements, to begin with. Sullivan should have sued the organization that had paid for the publicity."

"Good points," replied Adam, "but the way libel evolved in the common law, it was a strict liability tort. You could collect automatically for anything that appeared in the paper, including advertisements."

"That's right," said a student from Indiana. "We still have the common law of libel. He could sue for damages in our system."

Charlotte was outraged. "He was not even named in the publicity. And even if he had been identified with critics of the civil rights movement, that would have been good for him in Alabama. What was the Alabama court thinking?

"I think we can guess," said Adam. "It is very clear that *The New York Times*—the most liberal press in the North—was their enemy. They were going to do what they had to do to defend their autonomy. This was the Civil War in another form."

"Everything goes back to the Civil War," jibed Rodrigo again. The Brazilian was getting on Adam's nerves, but there was nothing he could do.

"OK, OK," said Grigor, playing to his strength, which was economics, "but can't the costs of the judgment easily be passed on to the consumers of the paper?"

Adam drew a diagram on the board illustrating the costs of production and the way they influenced the eventual price of goods to the consumer. "True, you could look at this judgment as just another cost of doing business, ultimately expressed in the price of the paper to consumers. Raise the price a penny a day and they would pay it off after the sale of 50 million papers. *The Times* is still cheap relative to European papers because they get so much advertising."

This style of economic reasoning was familiar to Aschkin, and she smiled that Adam was finally getting around to it. Hmm, maybe I am having a subtle influence on him, she thought.

Adam did his best to state the basic conflict in *The New York Times Co. v Sullivan* case. Which side should prevail? The right of the alleged victim to be compensated for supposed harm to his reputation, or the right of *The New York Times* to publish timely political advertisements, even if they contained some false material?

The disagreement in the class was directed more toward the style of argument than the simple question of who should win or lose. Adam had brought them into the thicket of legal argument. At the core of the dispute lay the relevance of economic thinking. Grigor was strongly in favor of the economic approach, but Jaime was opposed. It seemed to him that economic arguments took the soul out of legal thought. To defend his position, he fell back on the explicit language of the Court's opinion. "Why then," he asked, "did the Supreme Court dismiss the economic line of line of argument with the comment, 'The fear of damage awards under a rule such as that invoked by the Alabama courts here may be markedly more inhibiting than the fear of prosecution under a criminal statute'?"

"Bravo," Aschkin called out spontaneously.

Professor Gross recognized that the argument was taking place on many fronts. There was the fight about freedom versus equality, and then, on a totally separate plane, about redistributional economic thinking versus the deterrent effect of harsh financial sanctions. Equality could trump freedom in some cases, and, in others, economic principle could override concern about just sanctions. They were beginning to play the game of legal argument on a multidimensional board. But in the *Sullivan* case, as Adam well knew, the situation was not so complicated: the typically opposing values lined up on the same side.

"In this particular situation, freedom and equality were allied with one another," he said. "In its appeal to the Supreme Court *The Times* claimed freedom of speech, which dovetailed with promoting the civil rights revolution. For the first time in history, the Supreme Court decided that a private judgment in tort law—the decision by the Alabama courts—had violated the Constitution. I'm not sure you realize how radical a step that was. The Supreme Court was saying that the private law of a state, the common law, could violate the 'due process' clause of the Fourteenth Amendment. Why did it happen?"

"In this case," Jaime opined, "the Court could score one for freedom without undermining the post-Civil-War commitment to equality."

"Yes," said Adam, "the interests both lined up on one side, the side of the North against the South, but the decision affects everyone—at least, all public figures, all people who expose themselves to the public eye. Actually, the case has negative consequences for newspapers, more than you might think. There is an exception for cases of 'good faith' mistakes—just as Ms. Romanescu suggested. But the thing no one expected was a procedural consequence of this exception, something unique in our legal system. It is called 'discovery.' To find out whether newspapers have acted in good faith, rather than with what is called 'actual malice,' the plaintiff can force them to open all their files. It costs a lot of money to defend one of these law suits."

Then Adam took a deep breath and let his heart take rein. "Freedom is a complex value. Let us say that in some cases it looks as if all the right interests are arrayed on the same side. If you look more closely, however, you will always find that there are hidden costs to every innovation in the law. Here at Regina we are about to face a conflict of this sort. As you know, the regular undergraduate students are now returning for the beginning of the semester. The law school newspaper, the *Law School Report*, is bringing out its first issue today, and you should find it in the halls as you leave this class. I want you to look at it carefully. They have chosen to run an article that attacks an exam I gave last spring to first-year students in criminal law. There will be controversy. On Wednesday, instead of our classes, there will be a debate about the propriety of the exam, which you should all attend. There is no better way to learn about freedom of speech in America than to witness with your own eyes and ears a conflict about the contours of that freedom. Keep your minds open about who is really winning and who is losing in all this."

The students sat transfixed. "My God, what is this about?" asked Jaime.

"I cannot tell you more now," said Adam. "I want you to think about it for the class tomorrow morning—see if you can get hold of the paper in the meantime. I will explain the exam and we can assess whether the *Report* or I have a greater claim to freedom of speech."

Aschkin was relieved and pleased that Adam had taken steps to turn the potential political disaster into a pedagogical exercise. She was not sure whether he would win, but she shared his pleasure at being on the edge of the board. He had made a novel move, the kind that on the chessboard could lead either to a sudden victory or to forced checkmate.

Leaving the classroom, Adam encountered papers flying in the halls. The student staff of the *Report* were distributing their first issue of the year so aggressively that it seemed as though they were throwing copies as the students passing by. Many of the undergraduates were already back for the start of regular classes; the first years were about to begin their orientation week. Just about everyone paused to glance at the headline. Some sat down to read the lead article. It was all about Adam. It was as if there was no other story in the paper that day.

He felt giddily on a war-footing. He was Lord Byron at Missolonghi, Sigel on horseback, Kossuth in the Hungarian parliament. He was Francis Lieber in the face of enemy fire. When he encountered Aschkin in the halls, she could read the Romantic excess on his face.

"You like being in the headlines?" she asked.

"They spelled my name right. That's something." Adam was reminded of a joke. "Have you heard that Jews love being in the headlines? That is why we own so many newspapers, including *The New York Times*."

"But your nineteenth-century heroes are not Jews. They have something better than headlines. They have statues in their names."

"Yes, except for my beloved Lieber."

She led him around the corner out of sight. Putting her hand gently on his, she said, "I see that you are ready to carry the banner into the field. You are my statue-less, headlined hero. The only problem is your people. Who is riding behind your banner?"

Adam suddenly realized the critical difference between a lawyer for Romantic causes and a Romantic leader in the style of Kossuth. As lawyer for the damned on death row, he did not need anyone to follow him: Gross spoke for his client, and that was enough; his influence depended on the quality of his arguments. In a political conflict however, such as was now engaging the faculty, the quality of argument counted for much less than votes pure and simple. He had to find out who was on his side and who was not.

19

Thoughts of the Father

THAT NIGHT ADAM worked at home alone. He had already taken his steam shower and donned his blue cotton nightshirt. He was relaxed as he worked his way through a pile of law review articles and cases stacked up on his laptop. As he dug more deeply into the meaning of the legal concepts, he suddenly felt the presence of his father looking over his shoulder. He had not thought much recently about Miklós, who had died in Buenos Aires a few years after he emigrated. But now his presence was palpable.

In his student days Adam would sometimes wake up in the middle of the night, wander about the apartment, and then find his father up reading. He would be in undershirt poring over a book, always the same book in Hungarian. It was an irredentist tract: *Greater Hungary from the Carpathians to the Adriatic*. The underlying message was that the Great Powers had betrayed Hungary in the Treaty of Trianon, by which Hungary had been forced to surrender two-thirds of its territory to Slovakia, Croatia, Romania and other surrounding states. Miklós had served as an officer in Franz Jozef's army, the last army to take the field for Greater Hungary. Miklós identified strongly with the faded grandeur of the country whose colors he had once proudly borne.

On those encounters with his father and his book in the small hours of the night, Adam had forged a special bond across time and language. They shared the intimacy of thinking while the world was still, when only their minds were awake and searching together. Now Adam was working on the problem of commuting the death penalty of a poor black Muslim who had killed the owner of a liquor store. This issue itself would have meant nothing to Miklós, but Adam felt instinctively that his father would be proud of him for taking a stand in a case representing an issue of social justice.

Aschkin too was up late and alone. Peter had set off to Philadelphia yesterday to give a paper today at a conference on human dignity at Penn Law School, and he wouldn't be back until tomorrow. Bonded with two men at once, she felt more lonely than ever. But being alone was a small price, she thought, for the easy transition the previous night from the car of one to the house of the other. Am I always to be on a man's turf, she asked herself—sometimes with wheels, sometimes not? Where is my place in all of this?

Her mind was on her daily shots with Dr. Bluestone. She shut her eyes with visions of little dancing embryos across the end of the bed. She felt enormously empowered. Science was serving her as a woman. She could disagree with the doctor about how many embryos or blastocysts would be implanted in her body. She could oppose reductions that he might favor. Not only could she choose life, she could choose how much life she would bring into the world.

She was grateful to Peter for having gone along with the first stages of the consultation with Dr. Bluestone—and for implicitly trusting her with the rest of it—and she was also grateful to him for having secured her her job. Gratitude, she thought, is a beautiful sentiment. But as she was about to doze off she realized that she was beyond indebtedness. She had started to act for herself, to define her own future. She was dubious about whether Peter's sperm was sufficiently "aggressive" for conception even if they were injected into the egg. After all, he had never impregnated a woman. Adam, on the other hand, told her that he already had a daughter. It would make sense to say to him, as Rachel said to Jacob, "Give me a child or I shall die." Aschkin felt her mind spinning—with no firm bonds to reality or moral principle.

She dozed off and slept for half an hour. The sleep cleansed her of her confusions. She awoke with a deep inner pleasure at her sense of command over her own life. She felt an overwhelming impulse to call Adam. She looked up his number on the faculty phone list and dialed. He answered, surprised.

"Is it you?" he asked.

"Yes."

"I was hoping you would call. I can't sleep." Adam spoke pensively. "I'm at my desk thinking about why I'm alive. All of a sudden everything tastes and feels better. I feel connected—to you and to my father."

"Why your father?"

"Because of my case. Did I mention it to you at lunch last week? It was on my mind to see what you would think about it. I am defending a Muslim prisoner on death row."

"Why do you mention that they are Muslim? Because I am?"

"Maybe. I want us to feel like we're on the same side."

"Yesterday we were on the same side of the Nile. It was wonderful in Egyptland. Have you spoken to Julien?" She was less interested in death row than in the *petite mort* that bonded her with Adam.

"Yes," said Adam reluctantly. "Disaster. The debate will happen—on Wednesday."

"Good. It will take your mind off the death penalty. You will think about saving your own skin," she said with a little laugh that made Adam feel close to her.

"I don't underestimate Julien," he said in a serious tone. "He's smart and canny."

"I know, and the whole thing seems to have taken on a life of its own, hasn't it? I'm not even sure who organized the debate—perhaps the *Report*, to boost its distribution. It was a good idea to prepare your students for it by doing that class on freedom of speech, though."

"Yes, and then tomorrow I will spend time on the issues in the exam. The students will become my Jesuits, leading the attack for truth and justice." In the middle of night, he felt totally uninhibited. He could say anything. "I love you," he added.

"*Seni seviyorum.* That's the same in Turkish."

"*Szeretlek. Te amo. Ich liebe Dich.* Do you get the point?"

"Yes, you are a *meshuggenah.*"

"Glory be to Sydney." And he gently hung up the phone.

This, she hoped, would become their habit. They would talk to each other in the middle of the night. The very next morning, before she went to Adam's class, Aschkin bought a dedicated cellphone. She put it on "vibrate" in order to be able to answer without drawing attention to the call. She decided she should be the one to call, because she could more easily pick the right time and place. Their conversations at night would become a private encounter, she hoped, a place in time that they could not find in the crowded spaces of their daily lives.

The consensual bond in the dark would sustain them during the daylight hours.

20

David at War

THE NEXT MORNING, Adam felt secure, refreshed, in harmony with Aschkin. He strode into class, head high, arms full of papers. He distributed the exam to the class. "Let me read the controversial question to you and then we will talk about it. Try to forget the political fight outside. Think of this as an introduction to the style of hypothetical questions used in American law schools. The case presented here is called 'The Revenge of the Big Monkey.'"

The reading took about four minutes. As Adam started to read, he realized that he was semi-consciously imitating the tactic used by his friend Mel when he had argued an important free speech case before the Supreme Court. The case had been about a young man named Cohen who had been convicted of disturbing the peace for walking around the Los Angeles County courthouse wearing a jacket with the words "Fuck the Draft" in large letters on the back. The pro-war prosecutors in California had gone after him and secured a conviction. Cohen then got the backing of the ACLU, which appealed the conviction all the way to the Supreme Court. When Mel had stood up before the nine justices to argue the case, he'd related the facts. When he came to the words written on the jacket, one of the justices had intervened and told him not to utter the obscenity in court. Mel had stood firm and replied, "I'm sorry, Your Honor, I must report the facts that led to Cohen's conviction." His very uttering of the word in court had trivialized the claim of the state that using foul language could constitute disturbing the peace. Showing the banality of these words, Adam thought, should help in discussing the brutal details of his exam. If there was anything shocking or disgusting about his graphic description of David's actions, he was confident that the unembarrassed use of language would defuse the sting. And so he read the question in a level tone.

"David, a part-time security guard, is a member of an anti-fertility cult that worships the Big Monkey. The leaders of the cult, Angie and Barb, have written a credo entitled 'Motherhood is Death.' David, Angie, and Barb regularly play master-slave games, with David as the slave. Angie and Barb tell David to serve them and to commit petty thievery to support the cult. He complies unhesitatingly. They all live together in one communal apartment. David often leaves during the day and fulfills his functions as a security guard without any noticeable problems.

"Angie tells David that the Big Monkey is disturbed by the increasing rate of pregnancy and that David should hunt out pregnant women and kill as many fetuses as he can. If he does not satisfy the Big Monkey, the cult's god will sweep down and kill a million pregnant women in the United States. David expresses some compunctions, but Angie assures him that there is nothing wrong in avoiding unwanted pregnancies, and, as far as the Big Monkey is concerned, all pregnancies are unwanted.

"David sees a pregnant woman walking down the street. He follows her to a deserted spot and pounces on her, telling her to submit to an abortion in the name of the Big Monkey. The woman, named Eve, resists, and David starts hitting her inflated uterus with a steel pipe. The fetus becomes hyperactive, noticeably kicking and protruding, and then falls passive. Fearing that she has lost the child, Eve grabs the steel pipe and begins hitting David over the head. David screams, 'Stop! I meant no harm to you—just to the fetus.' He manages to get the pipe back after having suffered a few cuts to the head. Eve goes to hospital and the fetus is dead on arrival. Two weeks earlier, her doctor had pronounced her expected child healthy and developing normally.

"The next day, David sees a heavy-set woman walking on Broadway. He follows her to an alley and corners her. She pulls a gun on David. David lunges at the gun, and it fires backwards at the woman whose name happens to be Flora. Flora dies from the gun shot wound. It turns out that she was not pregnant at all.

"In a third case, a woman named Gaye is desperately seeking an abortionist to end her pregnancy. All the local clinics are full. She is on the way to her physician's office to plead for help when David spots her and leaps on her from behind. He gags her mouth and proceeds to stomp on her stomach until she falls unconscious. He leaves her on the steps of the emergency room. When she finally awakens in the hospital, the physicians tell her they must remove her dead fetus. Gaye tells the doctors that she wants to write a thank-you note to her assailant, but she does not know where to find him.

"In an interview conducted by a state-employed psychiatrist, David says that he understands that violence is wrong and that his intended victims may have wanted to give birth. Yet at the time of the act he believed fervently in the wrath of the Big Monkey and therefore feared for the life of a million pregnant women. He acted, he claims, to save as many people as he could. The psychiatrist is prepared to testify that David's beliefs in these matters were sincere and deeply held.

"The local jurisdiction defines criminal abortion as the 'willful killing of a fetus by someone other than a licensed physician.' It is punishable by a minimum of five years in prison.

"The local felony murder rule holds: 'All murder committed in the course of committing or attempting to commit [specified felonies including criminal abortion] shall be punished as first-degree murder.'"

Chen raised her hand as soon as he was done reading the question. "Sorry, prof, you say that this is a typical hypothetical question in the United States. Frankly, I do not see anything so shocking about it. But if it is typical, why should so many people object?"

"Bear with me on this one. I will be debating with Julien Wright tomorrow on the faculty's criticism of the exam. For now, I want to use this example to do two things—first, to teach you something about American criminal law, and secondly to instruct you on how to take exams in the United States." Adam's tactic was to get the students absorbed by the ethical issues first, before they confronted the political acceptability of the exam.

At the mention of the word "exam" the class perked up. They knew that before long they would have to sit in competitive examinations along with the American undergraduates, and that would not be easy.

"At the level of exam writing," Adam continued, "you have to have an eye for the interesting issues. Don't waste your time, for example, on David's liability for petty thievery. The exam itself tells you that he committed these minor offenses."

Joerg's hand shot up. "Well, he might have a justification for the acts of stealing. Whatever claim he might make based on the supposed threat of the Big Monkey, he could make both for the assaults against the women and for the petty offenses committed for the same reason." He looked over at Chen. Both were pleased that they had negotiated the first few minutes of the discussion without a problem between them.

"That's true," conceded Adam. "You could say that, in a few words. But there is little point in going into the definitional elements of larceny. The action really begins with the attack on Eve. However, Mr. Mueller, thank you for having introduced the concept of 'justification.' Do you all remember the 1927 German abortion case?"

After a moment's pause and little flurrying through notebooks, the communal response was a nod.

"In that case, the defendant violated the prohibition against abortion. You have to establish that violation even before you get to the issue of justification. Is that true about the killing of Eve's fetus? May I ask you what you think, Ms. Romanescu?"

As he expected, the former Romanian judge answered by referring to the text of the local statute as stipulated in the exam. "Well, this is the 'willful killing of a fetus by someone other than a licensed physician.'"

"Yes," Marga intervened, "but it might be murder, and if you are guilty of murder I cannot believe you would also be guilty of the lesser crime of abortion. Well, even if you are, the more interesting question is liability for murder."

"Now we are at the heart of matter," said Adam, with some satisfaction that the students were leading the way. "Now how do we decide whether the crime is murder?"

Rodrigo was getting very nervous. "But you have skipped what I think is the heart of the matter—namely, your description of an anti-fertility cult, and one that sounds to me like a lesbian one too. Why is that necessary to get to your questions about abortion and murder?"

Though he had few supporters in the class, no one objected to his line of argument. "I suppose you are right," conceded Adam, "though the question does not actually stipulate that Angie and Barb are lesbians. But if they are, would that be relevant to the situation?" He had just violated the first rule of cross-examination by asking without knowing what answer he would get.

"Well," said Rodrigo, who was beginning to think of himself as the serpent in Eden, more cunning than all the other animals of the field, "it all depends on whether you assume that lesbians are likely to be against fertility. If you make that assumption, then their being lesbian makes their hatred of pregnancy more plausible."

Adam was impressed. "Not bad."

"Yes bad!" retorted Rodrigo, "This is like assuming that all male ballet dancers are gay, or that all gays are good at window design." The class tittered at these examples.

"Look, it's just a hypothetical question," Jaime said, coming to Adam's defense.

"Of course it is; if it were real, it would not reveal bias. But we know that my *capitán* wrote it, so we know how he thinks."

Adam was about to lose his cool. But, remembering the incident years ago when he laughed at a student, he kept a straight face. "Let me recommend you to my good friend Julien Wright; I'm sure he will make a much better captain for you than I am. In the meantime, I want to return to the practical question of analysing the facts—not the motives of the professor."

"Back to murder and abortion." Charlotte was happy to join Adam in concentrating on the legal questions raised by the exam. "This is essentially the same question that we discussed last week. Is the fetus a human being? Of course, the Church takes the view that it is."

"Yes," said Adam, "but there is a preliminary issue. Look carefully at the text of the question. Is there some information that suggests some complications about the victim in the attack on Eve?"

"If I were hearing this case," said Ilona, "I would want proof that the fetus was really alive at the time of the attack. Perhaps that is why the text stipulates us that 'the fetus becomes hyperactive, noticeably kicking and protruding, and then falls passive.' If Eve could testify to that fact, a judge or, I guess, a jury could find that the fetus was alive."

Jaime added with a touch of sarcasm, " But of course that would not establish that the fetus was a human being."

Holly turned and stared at him. She had not realized that this was likely to be a point of difficulty between them. She had grown up thinking, as had Chen in the beginning, that the fetus was no more important than a growth on the follicle tubes, but with her conversion she had begun to have more respect for the idea that the fetus represented potential human life—at all stages of its development. She understood that Jaime was bitter about the Church, but how could they continue having a sexual relationship unless they shared a common view about the possible offspring of their passion?

"This is the perpetual and recurrent issue," said Adam. "This form of malicious killing comes up in the courts more often than you would think. There was a recent case of a man who, at the request of his girlfriend, beat her with a baseball bat. But the important precedent occurred in California a couple of decades ago. A man encountered his girlfriend made pregnant by another man. He stomped on her and kicked her with the obvious purpose of killing the fruit of her womb. Lynch—that was his name—was prosecuted for murder, partly because the previous statute on criminal abortion had been declared unconstitutional and the legislature had not passed a replacement. On his appeal to the state Supreme Court, the judges voted four to three that he was not guilty of murder. The majority invoked the common law rule formulated by Blackstone that the fetus is not a human being until born alive. That is, no matter what the evidence that the fetus is alive, if it is not *born* alive, it is not a separate life under the law of homicide."

Mohammed was about to make a quip about the value of pregnant women remaining at home and not venturing into public, but Gad beat him to it. "I can understand why a pre-modern legal system would take this position. According to the Talmud, the fetus becomes a person when the head crowns. Yet you know the famous 'eye for an eye' rule in Exodus. That passage begins by referring to a 'disaster' that befalls a pregnant woman. It means that she loses her child. The point is worth making that the fetus is worth something, even if it is not yet a full person."

Adam noticed that the hour was passing. "We could spend endless amounts of time on this one, and class time and exam time are both limited. So, one final point about the state of the law. After Lynch went free, California amended its definition of murder to hold that the malicious killing of a fetus was murder. This has opened the question for all American jurisdictions whether the better description of the case is murder or abortion. It depends on the local statute because, no matter what you think about the moral status of the fetus, the accusation of murder is applicable only if the statute so provides.

"Now we have to pay attention to the problem of justification. There is much to be learned by applying the balancing theory of the 1927 abortion case. If you did that, what would be the result?"

"Well," answered Joerg, who had reviewed the German case several times, "if the Big Monkey were to make good on his threat, the cost of not killing a few fetuses would be much greater than the cost of killing them. If the threat were real, in other words, the conduct would be justified, based on the balancing theory."

Adam nodded. "This is the law in most states. It follows, according to this language, that the harm to be avoided—namely the wrath of the Big Monkey—must actually be greater than the damage to the fetuses killed. I assume that we do not take the threat seriously, however, so how do we approach the question of David's belief?"

Most of the students could think their way to the right answer, "This is a case of a mistake. David had good faith belief that he was acting in necessity; that is a form of mistake, a good faith mistake," offered Ilona.

"Right," said Adam. "And what kind of defense is a mistake about whether your conduct is justified?"

Grigor had no problem giving the answer under German law. "It is obviously a valid excuse. That is, the claim focuses not on whether the conduct was wrong—we concede that it was unjustified and wrong—but whether you can fairly blame the defendant for doing the wrong thing. The question, however, is whether *any* good faith belief in necessity should excuse an act, or whether the mistake must be reasonable. But I also think it makes a difference whether we classify the mistake as one about law or about fact."

"Yes," said Adam, "all these questions arise under American law as well, and they are all debatable. In fact we need a seminar on each of these issues. But let's look first at the problem of fact and law. This is a classic division in the theory of mistake. Suppose a doctor is mistaken about whether a fetus is threatening the life of the mother—in fact the fetus is in a harmless position—but he goes ahead and aborts it. What kind of mistake it that?"

"Mistake of fact," cried out half a dozen of the students.

"OK. So now what? Should that mistake excuse the doctor in all cases? Or does the doctor have to have made a reasonable mistake— that is, a mistake that a reasonable person would have made?"

"Well," Marga said, picking up the common thread of the argument, "if the doctor is totally incompetent and irrational—a little like our friend David in the hypothetical case—then he should not get the benefit of the mistake. He is guilty of having committed an illegal abortion."

"This is a question debated all over the world," Adam said. "The right answer is not obvious, but I think the better view is that the mistake must be reasonable. If David's mistake is unreasonable then he is to blame for having been careless in believing that he heard the commands of the Big Monkey."

Gad could not resist. "This is what Chen earlier called *meshuggah*. Hearing false gods is clearly crazy."

"Hearing any god is," Chen muttered.

"Well, I see that this word has become a technical part of our conversation. It is Yiddish. Those of you who think that Latin is the basis of the common law, you're wrong," Adam said with a little laugh. "In New York the law is based on Yiddish, but don't think that lawyers in the rest of the country will understand your Yiddish. They will think you have *chutzpah*. I will explain the meaning of that word later." Sydney would be proud, he thought to himself.

"Back to the case. As it actually was tried in Germany, it was based on belief in a false god called the Cat King. In that case, the court refused to find the defendant *meshuggenah* or insane."

"Yes, I know," piped up Joerg. "I know the case. I think they concluded that the defendant was sane and made a mistake of law. Their reasoning is not entirely sound because, under the German code, any good faith mistake about the law, whether avoidable or unavoidable, unreasonable or reasonable, should have some mitigating effect on the sentence. But the judges thought that the mistake was so weird—in the realm of pure fantasy—that the defendant was not entitled to any mitigation of his punishment."

"You know," intervened Chen, "the discussion we are having applies with force to a mistake by soldiers about the lawfulness of the commands they receive from their officers. This is the Nuremberg problem. The only difference here is that the command comes not from an officer but from a mythical being." She tried, behind her hand, to blow Joerg a big kiss, because she was reasoning, in effect, that Germans who followed orders could not get off the hook so easily. They were liable for their mistakes.

"There is a general point here, and it is important for all of you to see it," Adam summed up. "When someone acts in good faith, when he thinks he is doing the right thing, it is hard to punish him to the full extent of the law. But if we do not do that, how do we deal, as Chen says, with the 'good faith' followers of Hitler or of terrorist leaders today?"

Holly thought about the way these things were done at home and was troubled. "At a certain point you have to protect society, whether criminals feel guilt or not. But if that is what you try to do all the time, you end up using force in Tiananmen Square to protect the established order." She felt a shock wave rush through the other Chinese students in the room. No one turned to look at her. She waited, anxious, yet relieved that she finally felt free to speak her beliefs.

Adam recalled her story about the authorities taking away her uncle. "Very courageous thing for you to say." He paused too, looking for the right words—indeed, the right thoughts. "To be honest, I do not know the answer. We must protect ourselves against criminals who pit themselves against everything we believe in. David and his sado-masochistic cult exemplify the political rejection of our culture. The criminal law works best against offenders who deviate from the law for the sake of one crime. The law of crime, guilt and punishment seems not to fit the case of those who reject our society root and branch. At a certain point the criminal law gives way to a form of war against our enemies—I hate to say it—enemies of the state."

"We are entering territory that, as you can imagine, German scholars have thought a lot about," said Joerg, a little condescendingly.

"We have Carl Schmitt bequeathing to us the distinction between friends and enemies, a distinction critical to politics but also in the criminal law. Some forms of criminal law invariably function as special measures to be taken against enemies."

Jaime found himself getting very uneasy. "The Church has its enemies too." He did not want to say so, but he also thought that Israel behaved brutally in detaining anyone they considered a security risk. "Is the criminal law simply brute force, or does it express a form of retributive justice, fitting the punishment to the crime? Obviously," he went on, "the criminal law is supposed to express the justice of punishing people for their crimes. And it is always better to have a trial than to detain alleged terrorists merely on the say-so of a president or parliament."

"Again," said Joerg, "we Germans have had some experience with criminals of this sort. Most of the Nazis were convinced that they were doing the right thing. Then we had terrorists in the late 1960s and 1970s—the Baader-Meinhof gang. Now we have Turkish fathers and brothers who kill their sexually adventurous daughters as a matter of honor. We have to punish them—even though they are, as we say, 'true believer-criminals.' Do you understand my rough translation of *Überzeugungstäter*?"

Aschkin felt slightly offended by the explicit reference to Turkish fathers, but could not deny that these honor killings were a fact of radical Islamic society, in Turkey as well as many other countries.

"Yes, you're referring," replied Adam, "to criminals who are totally convinced that they are doing the right thing. They have no sense of guilt, no qualms about their actions. When we punish them, we treat them as 'enemies' but not as an enemy nation. The use of force is not quite war. Yet the rhetoric of war easily enters into our policies for fighting terrorism both at home and abroad." Adam was delighted to be back on the subject of war, but in this context he felt none of the Romantic excitement he experienced in presenting the Civil War. War is not what it used to be, he thought to himself, self-mockingly.

"If you look at the history of warfare from the time of Civil War," he continued, "you will see that the nations' leaders are always arguing about who is the aggressor and who is acting in self-defense. For Lincoln, the fact that the Southerners first bombarded a federal fort in the middle of Charleston Harbor was critical in justifying his war to save the Union as a war of self-defense. Of course, for the first few years Lincoln was attacking the South, but he still called it self-defense. Just about every war since then has relied on the same rhetoric.

"Self-defense is the key legal idea both in the law of war and in domestic law—that is, in the law that applies to relations between citizens. How does self-defense pose a problem in this hypothetical scenario?"

It was clear to most that Adam was referring to the problem of Eve's snatching the pipe and attacking David in return. Gad, who had studied the variations of self-defense in the Talmud and in Israeli law, responded on point. "The general requirement in self-defense is that the attack be imminent—it must be about to happen. In this case, Eve terminates David's attacks and turns them against him. It is hard to justify that as a matter of self-defense. She is engaged in retaliation, not self-defense."

"But your approach is hard on women," said Chen. "It happens often that after a rape or a sexual attack the woman kills the man. She is not the aggressor. She is still responding to the original attack."

Gad answered, "David is disarmed in this attack. When Eve gets the pipe she is in charge. Why should she be able to justify an attack in revenge?"

"This is the difference between fighting in war and fighting in civil society," explained Adam. "In war you can strike back at your enemy, whether the enemy is actively attacking or not. Provided both sides are actually combatant units wearing uniforms and carrying their arms openly, they are both allowed to kill even while the other side is sleeping. In domestic law—that is, the law between citizens— you lose your right to use force as soon as the attack is over."

Chen wanted to continue the argument but, glancing at the clock, the professor shifted gear. "We have yet to talk about the attack on Flora. This case is different because she is not, in fact, pregnant. She is attacked, she pulls a gun, which is fired against her, and she dies. Can we hold David for homicide?"

Ilona loved these technical exercises because they reminded her of the cases that came before her court in Bucharest. "Well," she said, "the text gives us a tip that the felony murder rule might apply. Could you explain that? We don't have anything like it in Romania."

"This is a relic of the common law," lectured Adam. "The principle is that if you engage in a dangerous felony and death results, there is no need to prove negligence or any form of fault in causing the death. If A rapes B and B commits suicide as a result, A is liable for murder because his felony resulted in the death. Therefore, if David is guilty of an attempted homicide or criminal abortion against Flora, he could be guilty of felony murder. This is a radical result, because he is clearly not at fault for the gun's having fired backwards at Flora. The first question, then, is whether the attack against a non-pregnant woman could be considered an attempted criminal abortion."

"Are we entitled to assume that the assault against Flora alone—regardless of the possibility of her pregnancy—is not a sufficiently dangerous felony in itself?" asked Joerg.

"Yes, I think we have to assume that. If any assault against another person—any blow to his or her body—supported the felony murder rule, then any assault leading to death would be treated as first-degree murder. All the nuances of the law—the distinctions between manslaughter, murder one and murder two would disappear. What would happen to *Law and Order* if the prosecutors could not negotiate these differences of degree?" At that moment a little humor came in handy. The students needed a release from the sustained analytical concentration. "By the way, you should all watch *Law and Order* when you can. It is legally accurate and the best show on television."

"So the felony murder rule circumvents all the distinctions based on actual culpability?" Joerg pressed the point. "That is kind of amazing. American law is still very primitive when it comes to understanding the nuances of guilt."

Adam resisted saying something about the Germans, of course, being more experienced in thinking about guilt. Instead he summarized the logical problem. "This is the logical core of the problem. If attempted criminal abortion is generally a dangerous felony, and if the attempt results in the death of a human being—which it did, because Flora died—then the killing can be classified as first-degree murder."

With all these details to master, thought Adam, how could anyone have time to scrutinize his writing to look for offense given to either women or gays? Rodrigo was quiet for the time being, but Adam knew that the soldier seeking his captain would return to the fight.

"In the abstract, I think you can say that an attempted criminal abortion is dangerous both to the fetus and to the pregnant woman, and therefore," surmised Ilona, "the technical question whether this is an attempted criminal abortion is critical. David's attack is not in fact dangerous to any fetus in existence, and therefore I do not understand how you can treat his attack as attempted criminal abortion."

Chen was not satisfied. "To make the case for conviction," she said, "I would invoke the general rule we learn in Israel that you must judge the actor's attempt according to the facts as he imagines them to be. He thinks she pregnant. That is enough. He is guilty of attempted criminal abortion and, because Flora died as a result of the fight, he is guilty of murder." She felt happy that she had mounted a good prosecutorial argument to defend the interests of women.

"You're right on this point," said Adam. "The general principles of American law concur that the attempt is to be judged from the perspective of the person trying to commit a crime. In this sense David is clearly responsible for an assault against Flora which has the purpose of killing what he believes to be her fetus. Technically, therefore, it looks as though he would be liable for attempted criminal abortion and therefore for felony murder. But still, there is no fetus in this story. It is all in David's imagination. Does anyone think that this is a just result?"

"Definitely," said Chen. "Principles rule." Some students around her nodded.

"I have to disagree," said Joerg. "In some contexts the actions are *per se* dangerous to particular victims and therefore the felony murder makes some sense. But not in this case. Also consider what we just said about the defense of necessity. It does not apply on the basis of David's beliefs alone. There must really be a threat from the Big Monkey. It is not fair to judge David according to his beliefs in attacking Flora, but to refuse him the benefit of his beliefs on the issue of necessity."

"Brilliant argument," said Adam.

"I don't think so," Chen added with an air of deliberate provocation. She was enjoying the intellectual encounter with Joerg. She felt like hugging him because their disagreement was purely theoretical. It had nothing to do with strong personal loyalties—to German or Jews, men or women. "Sometimes you have to take the law as it is," she argued. "The result is good. In general, David is a dangerous guy and if we can convict him, we should."

"Well, that is a good argument too," conceded Adam. "But note that you are relying on his general dangerousness, which I concede, and not on the danger manifested in the specific interaction with Flora."

With that remark Adam sensed it was time to sum up. "Well, I think that covers the basic technical questions for the first two-thirds of the exam. There is a knotty problem I will take up this afternoon, namely whether it would be possible for Gaye, the third woman in the scenario, to consent to the criminal abortion after it happens. In order to assess that controversial question, we need to reflect more on the meaning of consent and how it is given.

"I am very pleased with our ability today to delve into the subtleties of the exam. There is much to be learned from this factual hypothetical. Until this afternoon, then."

As they gradually rose and left the room, teacher and students shared a feeling of work well done, and Adam felt as though he had triumphed over the aura of potential taint that surrounded the exam. His students had engaged with difficult material and they had demonstrated their skills analysing a problem they had never seen before—even without having studied any American law. This, Adam hoped, would be give them confidence in themselves in confronting the American students.

He caught Aschkin's eye on the way out and she gave him an encouraging nod and a thumbs-up. Adam approached her and whispered, "I hope that's not a Turkish way of saying 'screw you.'"

"It might be, but perhaps you got the pronoun wrong," she whispered back, and darted off.

21

Lunch-hour Politics

ADAM REALIZED THAT this was a critical pause. The class on the issue of consent was coming up, and then, tomorrow, the debate with Julien. He had to develop some sense of who was with him and who was not.

He knew that Aschkin, Paul Keskemeny and Ariel Colline were on his side. He thought he could get Nkwame. He wondered about Hans Richter, although he seemed so removed from faculty affairs. Beyond that, he was not sure. As most of the students filed off to the cafeteria for lunch, Adam headed upstairs. He began his tour of the faculty offices by knocking on the door of the man who had once helped him out by taking over part of the class. Pat Graham was sipping a cup of coffee he had brought back from the Aviary to his office. "Pat, have you heard about the article in the *Report*?"

"Don't tell me you're in trouble again, Adam," Pat Graham sighed, leaning against the wall. He stroked his silver-streaked black hair. He was older than Adam but fit and quite the lady's man. His current wife, his fourth, was Korean and a sax player; he'd met her in the one of the clubs he frequented when he was doing research, so he claimed, on jazz and the unwritten law of African-American culture. "I had to fill in for you once and I had no time to practice the drums all semester. Don't tell me I have to do it again."

"No chance." Adam laughed. "I don't make the same mistake twice."

"So what's the mistake this time?"

"I hope there is none, but maybe you heard about my exam last spring."

"Yeah, supposedly with a lot of sex and blood."

"Well, it all depends on what you mean by sex. The Supreme Court has said that abortion is like birth control—both covered the principle of constitutional privacy in the bedroom. So I guess it is about sex, but I see it as about life and death."

"OK," Pat said, trying to end the discussion and get back to the *New York Post*. "Keep me on your mailing list, but I can't promise you anything. I don't make the same mistake twice either."

Adam left, crestfallen. He had used up his chips with Pat and perhaps other members of the faculty. This troubled him. He went back to his office and called Aschkin. "Do you have any ideas? I'm not sure how much support I'm going to get from the people who are not my close friends."

"From what I've heard from a few people in the halls, I'm concerned too. Let me think." She paused for a moment. "Here's a gamble. Why don't you ask Peter to moderate the debate with Julien? Whether he is for or against you, he will at least be neutralized and you will look better. Plant the seed in him this afternoon and I'll work him on tonight."

"Great," said Adam. "I'll email him right away."

While he prepared the email to Peter, Adam asked his assistant, Zetta, to make two hundred copies of the exam question right away.

"*Jawohl, mein Commandant*," she said, saluting him and mocking his tone of urgency. They had worked together for years. A grandmotherly sort, she knew the only way to survive with an intense personality like her Professor Gross was, as she put it, to "humor by humor."

Adam felt disarmed, and laughed, as he often did with her. "And please send an email message to the faculty inviting them to a debate tomorrow morning at 11 a.m. between Julien and myself. The topic will be 'Life and Death in the Criminal Law.'"

"That sounds great," said Zetta. "Can I come too?"

"Yes, of course, I need every clapping hand I can get."

"I remember the exam. At the time I thought it was a bit over-the-top. I didn't dare tell you though."

"Well, if I were always right, your loyalty would not be so important to me."

"Got it. Well, I'm with you."

"It's a shame you don't have a faculty vote," said Adam as he retired to his office to review the exam and think about how he was going to explain the issues of guilt and innocence to his class.

On the way to the cafeteria, Joerg and Grigor stopped off in the men's room. As they were standing next to each in the urinals, Joerg said, "*Ich bin total auf seiner Seite.*'—I am totally on his side.

Grigor nodded. "*Aber wir müssen die anderen auch überzeugen.*"—But we have to persuade the others too.

Rodrigo, who was washing his hands, overheard this exchange and cornered the two as they were leaving. "You know, anti-Semites would have a field day with the *Sullivan* case. Here's an ordinary Irish police chief attacked by a Jewish newspaper that is then defended by a Jewish lawyer."

The two Germans looked at him as though he was a throwback to their grandparents' generation.

"OK, OK," said Rodrigo, "you guys are friends of my *capitán*, I understand. But let us see how the others think." And he led the way to the cafeteria.

After the students had picked up their paper plates and salads or sandwiches wrapped in plastic, and poured drinks into their paper cups, they took seats around a large circular table. Marga was sitting next to Holly, who had Jaime so close to her that he was almost breathing down her neck. Then came Charlotte, Joerg, Grigor and Gad, followed by Mohammed and Chen. There was one empty seat. It seemed odd to the group that Chen and Joerg were not sitting next to each other, because for the last few days they had almost been inseparable.

Grigor looked around and said, "You know, we are the group that speaks out most in class. The others are happy to let us do the brunt of the work. Why not form a club?"

"Great idea," added Charlotte with a smile. "Remember what Chen said this morning—'Principles rule'? Let's call ourselves *Les Principals*. It is a play in English and French on 'principle' and 'principal,' you know—correct standards, and the primary actors."

Mohammed concurred. "*C'est magnifique, Mademoiselle.* We are the Principals with principles."

Just then Rodrigo approached to take the last empty seat. "Well, on second thoughts..." muttered Joerg.

"Listen, guys," the Brazilian said as he sat down, "I am better friends than you know with Ariel Colline."

"OK, we will think about your being in the club." Charlotte disposed of the subject for the time being. "So what about the *Sullivan* case? I am not sure about all the details of Gross's exam, but does it really matter? The *Sullivan* case tells us that free speech is almost absolute. That should cover speech in the classroom."

"I am not sure you are reading the case correctly," intervened Chen. "There are still some values that outweigh free speech. If you are a private figure, if the newspaper is reckless...there are all sorts of ways to defeat newspapers like *The Times*."

"The Jews," added Rodrigo flippantly.

"Sorry," said Joerg. "That is not acceptable here. If you talk like that you will have to leave."

"Ohhh," said Rodrigo, "So there are limits on free speech? I am being offensive, am I? Well, I think my *capitán*'s exam is also offensive. I have seen a copy of the whole exam and there are some parts of it that are even more offensive than the attacks on pregnant women."

"Where did you get a copy of the exam?" demanded several of the Principals.

"Obviously I am not going to tell you, and it is irrelevant. The important thing is that he slandered a lesbian organization by having them organize this David guy's campaign against pregnant women."

"That is ridiculous," said Joerg. "He is the head of the class, and he can ask what he wants in the exam."

"We talked about this last night," murmured Chen demurely. In fact, in a different context, the two of them had talked about Joerg's deference to authority. Her experience in the army had taught her to be suspicious, particularly of male authority. She sensed in Joerg the after-effects of being brought up under a loving but domineering grandfather, a grandfather for whom the *Fuehrerprinzip* was a way of organizing the family as well as society. She had enough affection for Joerg to work with him on his association between love and subordination. Yet the issue was breeding some difficulty between them.

"OK, let me make a different argument," Joerg sidestepped. "He is not right because he is at the head of the class. He is right because, after the constant tension between freedom and equality, freedom has survived the test of history."

"Now you are sounding Burkian," interrupted Charlotte. "History is fine if you catch it at the right time. *Sullivan* was decided in the 1960s, before the United States underwent a revival of sentiments on behalf of women, blacks and other minorities. If the exam offended women and gays, then we have to think seriously whether—in this context at least—we are not up against the limits of free speech."

"Look," said Holly, with the obvious support of Jaime, "I like Professor Gross enough to give him—what is the phrase?—the benefit of the doubt. Let us not prejudge him until we hear more."

Rodrigo enjoyed playing the spoiler in all this. "Oh, my children, don't you see that we are pre-judging either way? We should give him special credit just because he is our only professor at the moment? According to the newspaper, others are opposed."

"I must admit that I have conflicting feelings myself," said Chen. "Personally, I feel loyal to Professor Gross but I am also a committed feminist."

"But maybe feminism means different things in different countries," injected Marga. "In Colombia women are barely let out of the house—particularly if they are *embarazada*—pregnant."

"I will vouch for that," said Mohammed. "Women should not reveal their family status in front of strangers, at least that is my tribal custom."

"Yes, but that means," continued Marga, "that the exam is a good thing if it breaks down taboos about what women are allowed to do and the way they are allowed to appear and feel."

"So why are these American feminists so offended?" inquired Charlotte.

"Let me try this theory from my experience in the Church," Jaime said. "Maybe it is because professional women do not want to be reminded in exams that they are women. They want to be faceless and sexless actors in the legal culture—something like the way that priests and nuns lose their sexuality behind their habits, ornate or simple."

Chen looked at him with interest and puzzlement. "I cannot quite figure it out. In the army we wear the same uniforms and carry the same guns, but everyone is super-conscious of sexual difference."

"Sorry, Chen," mediated Joerg. "I really respect your opinion, but this dispute is beyond our understanding. It is about academic freedom. Does the professor have the right to pose the questions he wishes to? It is in the interest of the students to think about these things, whether they like it or not."

"But women are such delicate creatures," said Mohammed half-mockingly.

Chen jumped in fast. "Get off it, man, you have been around us long enough to know that I am much less delicate than you think." And she laughingly hissed at him with gritted teeth.

Jaime seemed to be lost in deep reflection. "One question I'm concerned about is the context of the exam. Adam is not *The New York Times* fighting for civil rights. He's a professor in a classroom. What does that mean? Does he have special duties to care for his—I almost said 'parishioners'—I mean students, his novitiates in the law?"

"Do you think we are dependent on him? People who are weaker and in need of greater care?" challenged Charlotte.

"Some might think so," he said. "I don't know."

Chen conceded, "I am having trouble too. I would like to think of good arguments to defend the American feminists, but—how do they say?—the argument just won't write."

"I am not having trouble," chimed in Rodrigo. "I know the enemy when I see him. And my *capitán* is my enemy." The rest of the group looked at him as though he was suffering from delusions. He was probably more like Adam than either would have liked to admit. They both enjoyed the scene of battle, the smell of powder in the air. For Rodrigo there seemed to be almost a sexual thrill in pitting himself against the other students. He provoked them toward the final ritual of their meal—collecting his trash and tossing it basketball-style into the huge trash can in the corner of the room.

Chen lingered to talk to Joerg. "I'm touched," she said, "by your sensitivity in this argument." She put her arm around his shoulder.

"I am not sure what my position is," he said. "I am searching. But I want us to be in this together."

"It is difficult for me," said Chen. "I hope the leaders of this faculty movement don't ambush me in a weak movement. My loyalties make me vulnerable to their arguments."

"I understand," said Joerg, "But you are a strong woman. This is why I love you."

Chen did not care whether he was slipping back into home-induced respect for firm leadership. The two had forged an alliance, a worthy side-effect of a faculty caught in conflicting stages of disintegration.

22

Consent

IN THE FEW minutes he had before the afternoon class Adam had only one subject on his mind: the giving of consent. It was one the great mysteries of legal thought, he mused, that the willing participation of a potential victim could convert a wrong into a right, a harm into a good. So if the customer is unwilling to part with his goods, grabbing them constitutes the crime of larceny. If the customer is willing, then the transaction is a sale. The same with sex. If both partners want intercourse, they feel they are creating one of the world's great joys together. If one side does not want it, then the unwanted intercourse becomes rape, one of the most heinous, highly punished crimes on the books.

Everyone understands these consequences of consent, Adam thought. We learn this principle literally with our mother's milk. As babies sucking the breast, one of the first things we learn is when Mother wants to give it to us and when she does not. When she does not, we learn the experience of deprivation and devise ways to persuade her to let us suckle. This is the beginning of all social interaction. In this most universal of all experiences, Adam concluded in his long meditation, we can catch a glimpse of the complexities of consent that befuddle the law. The interaction of baby and mother is model for all subsequent interactions in life. That is, no one ever consents pure and simple, as though he or she were deciding in a vacuum. The giving of consent is always the culmination of a long and subtle dance in which one party makes demands and instills in the other the feeling that he or she is making a free choice.

Peter will probably consent to moderate the debate, Adam thought, but only after Aschkin, as she has promised, interacts with him in the appropriate way tonight. I wouldn't be surprised, he mused, if

Aschkin has to give more than her breasts to get him to agree. Well, it's all in a good cause, he thought, pushing away an unpleasant stab of jealousy. And anyway, nothing they do tonight can come close to the passion we experienced in the car in the New Jersey. He suddenly recalled that they had had great sex in the car but no intercourse. I have not fucked her, he thought; we have never consummated the deal. We never incorporated in a foreign state as we planned to do. How is this possible?

Adam's detours on the topic of sex made it difficult for him to concentrate on the philosophical complexities of consent. He stopped the mental meandering, and began making some notes. For the final class on the exam coming up, he knew he should prepare a little more than usual.

Yet he could not completely get his mind off Aschkin and Peter. OK, he thought, maybe he will consent to sex with Aschkin and as a result will consent to her and my request that he moderate the debate. Perhaps he also has an independent inclination to protect me, perhaps not. Whatever the reason, Peter's passion was likely to carry implications that the dean would not be able to calculate. He would not, in retrospect, have consented to everything that might happen tomorrow or the rest of the week—but he would have consented in bed. And it was not clear to Adam—nor would it be later tonight to Peter—what would follow from that act of intercourse.

When a man consents to sex with a woman, for example, thought Adam, does he thereby agree to fund the potential result—a child's care—for eighteen years? The law assumes that he does. Or perhaps the law simply assumes that biology creates debts. Even if the sperm is stolen—Adam was dreaming up an example for another outrageous exam question—does the father incur a duty of support for the child? The law is surprisingly primitive at times, he mused.

As he approached the classroom, he noticed several couples engaged in intense emotional exchanges. He tried to read their moods. Joerg and Chen were very close and seemed to have carried their relationship well beyond that first dance at the synagogue. Holly and Jaime were pleading with each other, he towering over her as though speaking from the pulpit, she, tough in her political training, and searching for the right emotional note to regain an apparently lost harmony. Adam felt like stroking those to whom he felt close, but he restrained himself. They passed together into the arc of discourse.

He was now ready to confront the core issue of the exam: the sequence in which Gaye tries to consent to David's behavior by telling her doctor that she wants to write him a thank-you note. Adam decided to lay the groundwork in the law before turning to the specific facts in the exam.

"Let us begin by thinking generally about consent as a defense to crime," he opened the lecture. "Why should consent ever constitute a complete defense?"

Charlotte was the first to enter the fray. "Well," she said, "if both sides want it, there is nothing wrong with it." She almost added "provided they are of equal bargaining power." No, she thought, I don't need to say that.

Adam was taken aback by her strong statement because he recalled her email about her affair and abortion in France. Adam could imagine, but presumably no one else could fathom, how long it had taken Charlotte to reach the equanimity expressed in her simple statement that if both sides were willing, there was no foul. After the abortion she had had several years of therapy before she could accept responsibility for the affair with the older professor, her superior in the *Faculté de Droit*. She was now a rigorous libertarian about choice: if you choose it, you own it.

"Sorry," said Adam, sounding more condescending than he intended, "What is the 'it' that both people might want?"

"Most typically sex, but it could be a sado-masochistic beating, or the transfer of property, or a marriage. Just about anything. If you get what you want, you can't complain."

"Keep that last phrase in mind," advised the professor. "We will need it later. For the time being, think about the limits of consent. How about consenting to be killed?"

"That is a problem," countered Gad. "We do not allow people to consent to their own death. I guess the idea is that their lives do not belong to them."

"Yes, and of course, those in favor of assisted suicide say just the opposite," Adam pursued the theme. "They ridicule the theological claim that our lives belong to someone other than ourselves. In the Netherlands, for example, the policy is very liberal. Euthanasia is not exactly legal, but there is an official policy of not prosecuting physician-assisted choices to die. The doctors not only give the terminally ill pills but they actually administer fatal injections, of course with a carefully observed process of consent. You can even schedule a date and time for your state-assisted euthanasia."

"Not in Israel," Gad parried. "Far from it. In many countries you can refuse treatment and die; this is called passive euthanasia. But the religious forces in Israel have convinced the state that allowing someone to die is the same as killing them—that is, the passive is the same as the active. The Dutch ignore the distinction too, but at the opposite extreme—in favor of treating the active the same as the passive and allowing doctors to kill."

"There are good reasons for taking death so seriously," said Adam. "It is irreversible. Unlike slavery, death has no exit."

"Isn't consent to sex irreversible too?" prodded Chen.

"I'm not sure what you mean." Adam looked a bit puzzled.

"Sex changes people's lives forever," she said. "It is not like selling a bushel of tomatoes, a transaction that can be reversed as though nothing had ever happened."

"Precisely," interjected Jaime. "Now you begin to understand why the Church takes such a conservative line, both about euthanasia and about sex outside marriage. It is not consent that legitimizes sexual relations, but marriage." He almost bit his tongue as he said that. He realized that he was embarrassing Holly because just about everyone in the class knew she and Jaime were having an affair. He realized that he was not very good at this "relationship" thing. He looked over at her as if to plead for forgiveness.

Mohammed shared Jaime's and Gad's conservative line. "I am glad to hear these arguments being made. In Islam we regard it as very important to control the sexuality of women."

Aschkin almost fell off her seat. She was waiting for one of the students to correct Mohammed's orthodox line of thought. She was pleased that Chen was waving her hand in the air. How wonderful, she thought, that Israelis and Turks share the same horror of religious fundamentalism.

"If you say that marriage legitimizes sex," said Chen loudly, "then you have a big problem with non-consensual sex in marriage. What happens if a troop commander—I mean a husband—imposes sex on the woman in a relationship with him. Is that not rape?"

"There is a lot of controversy about that today," Adam conceded. "There is little doubt that, in the history of the West, marriage was the framework that legitimized sex. Consent was essential to marriage but not to the consequences of marriage, and sex was one of those consequences. Today I think the weight of secular opinion is clearly on the side of consent as both a necessary and a sufficient condition for sexual relations, whether you are married or not."

"Whew," said Chen. "You had me worried there for a minute."

"I am with Chen on this one," injected Grigor.

"OK. Let's move on to the question at hand, namely the hypothetical case of Gaye and David. The leading precedent for thinking about this problem is a strange case in England that went to the House of Lords in 1975. It's called *Morgan* and, believe me, it caused more controversy than this simple little exam." Adam went over the case, as he had summarized it for Ariel in the museum. "The guys think the wife wants to have sex regardless of her protests. The key point is that the House of Lords said their good faith mistake about consent would operate just like consent. This decision has led to similar holdings where the House of Lords still enjoys influence, notably in Canada and Israel."

A gasp engulfed the room.

"The leading English professors of criminal law supported the decision," Adam continued. "They reasoned that *mens rea*—or a guilty mind—is necessary for criminal liability. If they believed in good faith that they were acting with the consent of the wife, then they did not have a guilty mind."

"This is *meshuggah*," said Charlotte.

"I have written against the decision too," said Adam, as though he needed to establish his credentials with the class. "But let's try to make it more plausible for you by putting it in a cultural context. These airforce guys seem totally perverted. But consider the customs of the Hmong tribe from Laos. They now have large communities in the States, in particular in California and Minnesota. They continue their practice from the home country of marrying off women by negotiating an arrangement between the father and the groom. The groom, with the permission of the father, carries off the bride, who always acts as though she were protesting in order to enhance the manhood and social status of the man who carries her off. Now let's take a case in which a Hmong woman really does detest the prospect of marriage to a particular man. Should we convict the man who is playing by the rules of his culture?"

"We have had this problem with subcultures in Israel," said Chen. "Immigrants think they can do what they did where they came from. Jews from Arab countries think that they can have four wives. As I said earlier, we tolerated this in the early days of the state, but now we demand that minorities conform to the majority culture."

"What about the virtues of multiculturalism?" parried Adam in his professorial mood. "This is sometimes called the 'cultural defense.'" The looks from the class were blank or confused.

"Multiculturalism means that people should be judged according to their own cultural norms. It has become the vogue among the left in the United States. They say you cannot judge minority cultures according to the norms of the dominant society—or it is thought unfair and disrespectful to do so. So can we really condemn the young Hmong man if it is normal in his community to ignore the protests of women being carried off?"

"Of course we can judge him," said Chen. "What do we mean by human rights if you can ignore the rights of women on grounds of conventionally acceptable abusive practices?"

"Be sure you make that argument tomorrow if Dean Levenger is moderating the debate. He will love your invoking human rights in this context. But the issue here is not really whether the conduct of the Hmong or Morgan's airforce guys is right or wrong. We know it's wrong. The question is whether we can blame them for doing the wrong thing."

Joerg felt drawn into this debate. "It all depends on how comprehensive the society is that insulates people from the truth. In some totalitarian societies you cannot really expect individual actors to know that the general world culture holds the view that what they are doing is corrupt and immoral." All of this seemed to most in the class to be slightly too obviously a defense of Nazi actions. "The transient culture of the RAF in the bar is not enough, but when a people live together for generations and inculcate their values in their children, we should be more sympathetic to the errors of those who simply follow like sheep."

When Joerg realized that Chen and others had understood the Nazi subtext, he rushed to qualify his statement by emphasizing that National Socialism was a brief deviation in Germany history and therefore the excuse based on isolation did not really apply. "Slavery in Greece is a better example," he added quickly.

Adam decided to leave the dead with the dead.

"If you read the exam question carefully," he said, "you will see some hints in it of the cultural context that might be relevant in assessing David's culpability in general. He lives within a cult that believes that 'Motherhood is Death.' He is subject to sado-masochistic beatings. The situation makes him dependent on the dominatrices and the beliefs internal to the cult. He does not think for himself. But there is an important fact mentioned in the text that points in the other direction. What is that?"

Ilona, trained in court to look at the precise facts, put her finger on it. "He was a part-time security guard. That means he worked in the outside society. He cannot claim that he suffers total isolation in a community that distorts his judgment."

"What should he have done to find out whether it was rational to follow the Big Monkey?"

"Well, for one thing, he could have inquired at work about what the people there thought about the cult of the Big Monkey. He obviously realized that he was part of a small deviant cult. It was not his whole world."

Jaime wanted to hedge his position. "I have some sympathy for people who live inside religious cults, but typically they have a holy text and a tradition. Here, all David knew was what Angie and Barb said about the attitudes of the Big Monkey. Just two people. He was not relying on a holy text. He *can* be blamed for listening uncritically to what Angie said—in particular when he was potentially exposed to other opinions during the day."

He added a thought that seemed relevant to his own situation. "A priest who leaves the order might be excused for his insensitivities to the world outside, but after a while he bears more responsibility."

"That makes sense to me," said Adam.

"Actually," added Joerg, "there is a connection with the Nuremberg principle that following orders is not an automatic excuse. You have to know whether the order is lawful or not. You can look at Angie's command as an unlawful order. If a military commander were to tell someone to go out and kill all the pregnant women he could find, there is no doubt that the order would be unlawful."

"Yes," said Adam, "this is an effective line of argument. But aren't we forgetting that there is an issue of consent in Gaye's case? If she consented, then there would be no harm. No harm, no foul. It would be as though a military commander ordered his troops to go out and rape women and one of the soldiers found a woman who was eager to have sex with him. You wouldn't convict in that case, would you, Ms. Horowitz?"

Chen was not too happy to have the spotlight on her but she was ready to answer, and she was not going to give Adam what he wanted. "Well, I am not too sure what 'eager' means in a relationship between an occupying officer and a subordinated member of an occupied people. Is consent really possible in cases of domination?" Chen immediately realized the implications of her argument for defending the violent actions of Palestinians resisting Israeli occupation. So did Jaime.

Adam felt pressed to the wall and used a *reductio ad absurdum* as his way out. "Good point," he said. "But maybe consent is never possible; maybe men are always the dominant power, acting like occupying officers. Maybe consent by women is always simply an act of 'eagerly' mollifying the masters. This is the line that Catharine MacKinnon, one of the leading feminists, takes sometimes."

Charlotte almost jumped out of her seat barefoot. "I resent that view very much. It infantilizes women. I know what consent means, and so does every woman who chooses to make love. And we know what excessive pressure means, too."

"All right," said Adam. "If the issue of consent is still alive, then we have the interesting question of whether Gaye consented. What would be the best argument you could make that she did consent?"

"It seems clear to me," offered Mohammed. "She did consent. She wanted it to happen. She tells her doctor afterwards that she was happy that it happened. We have good evidence after the fact that if David had asked her, she would have said yes."

"But is secret consent good enough? asked Jaime. "Suppose in Holland a patient wants to die, and it happens that the doctor wants to get rid of him. The patient leaves behind a letter declaring his wish to die, but the doctor does not see it before he gives him a fatal injection. Is this a case of legally permissible euthanasia?"

"No, no, no," called out several students.

"The point is that the potential victim must do something to indicate consent," said Adam. "Desire is not enough. Some communication is necessary—but between whom, and when?"

As usual, Rodrigo wanted to leave a mischievous mark in the conversation. "Let's supposes a student eats dinner in a Chinese restaurant and gets a Chinese fortune cookie, and it says 'Honorable student, one of your Chinese classmates is dying to have sex with you. Treat him as though he has consented.' The reader of the fortune then rapes one of the Chinese members of the class. In fact, the victim—if you call him that—*had* just told one of his fellow students that he want to have sex with that specific student. Can the reader of the fortune cookie claim good faith?"

"No." The class seemed to respond in unison.

Adam was again unsure how to deal with the Brazilian. "Just to be safe," he said, "let's agree that I will not devise hypothetical cases about students committing crimes and you will not devise cases about professors committing crimes. This is a good deal for me, because I know the crimes of professors are likely to be much worse."

Rodrigo stood and bowed as if to apologize and the class erupted in brief applause.

"But now that we have Rodrigo's hypothetical case, let's stay with it. Surely this is neither consent nor an acceptable mistake about consent. But why not?"

"I know," Ilona volunteered. "I think consent must flow directly from the party consenting. She must want it *and* she must communicate that want herself."

"I see," said Adam. "That, then, is ultimately the problem in the *Morgan* case: the husband cannot do anything that would provide the basis for a legitimate mistake about consent—is that your view?"

"Yes," said Ilona.

"You would admit, though, that if a kinky wife wrote a letter to a neighbor saying that she loved to be taken by force and asked her husband to deliver it, that letter would be consent?" Adam pressed the point.

"I am not so sure," said Chen. "It looks as if she is communicating some kind of desire, but suppose she says no at the time the neighbor starts to force intercourse. Even if it was originally consent, she can revoke at any time. The letter would at most be evidence toward consent. What she actually says at the time of the deed is more important."

Adam resisted the popular example of a woman saying no after penetration had already begun. There was a certain danger, in discussing rape, of going too far with sexual details. Instead he shifted ground. "In sado-masochistic relationships, an ordinary 'no' is not enough to break the prior consent. You need a special code to make it clear you are serious about saying no."

"Yes," said Ilona, "but those are special languages, prearranged systems of communication. This is not true among ordinary people."

Adam backed down. The women in class were outflanking him on these issues. More power to them, he thought. "I agree with you," he said. "There are some things on which prior consent is not binding at the critical moment. Suppose, in the Netherlands, a fatally ill patient agrees that a physician may terminate his life on a certain date. The entire family gathers to bid him goodbye. At the last minute, he says, 'No, I don't want the injection. I will stay alive as long as I can.' Do you all agree there is no way that he can be bound by his prior consent?"

"Obviously," said Jaime in unison with others.

"Similarly, would you agree, Mr. Sullivan, that the nurse could not give consent in place of the patient?"

"Yes, I think that is right. That is another problem with the *Morgan* case. The husband cannot give consent in place of his wife. What he does is no more effective than Rodrigo's example of the fortune cookie. The issue is not only the good-faith mistake, but the source of the mistake. The fortune cookie is not a legitimate source. Nor are the drunken pretensions of an RAF officer in a bar."

"Right," said Adam. "You can think of consent as something like a bequest or a gift. Only the person who actually owns something can give it as a gift. The husband does not own his wife's consent, so he cannot give it. Let call this third-party consent. Do you now see the connection with the saga of Gaye and David?"

"Of course," said Chen. "David has two hurdles to overcome. First she expressed herself to the doctor, not to him; and secondly it was after, not before the fact."

Joerg now felt like provoking Chen. "Yes, but her comments to the doctor are evidence of what she felt at the time of the attack." He added with an air of wisdom, "We have to remember that evidence is not the same as actual consent but is still relevant."

"It does not matter," snapped Chen. "She does not give him consent. He does not get it from her. What she says afterwards is irrelevant." Joerg and Chen acted like a couple that would always be arguing subtle issues of law—about gender and everything else—for as long as they stayed together.

Marga suddenly became agitated. "All this talk about the giving and receiving of consent. Doesn't anyone worry about whether the fetus consents to an abortion?" Holly nodded vigorously.

That was it. They had been round and round on the issue and finally the students had, on their own, reached the nerve center of the modern controversy between the pro-choice and pro-life forces. Marga had articulated the central question that Ann O'Sullivan and Kathy Kong were afraid would be raised by Adam's criminal law exam. How could a woman consent to an abortion in place of the fetus? This was the question they did not want discussed, either directly or indirectly. After all of his years pondering the problem of abortion, Adam felt that he was no closer to an answer than when he was young, Sara had been pregnant, and their family friend Leo had first put the idea of abortion in his mind.

Of course, Ann and Kathy might try various lines of attack, but all of them had already been refuted in the class conversation. Adam began to reflect on the state of the argument. "You could argue that the fetus is just an organ like an appendix, but that was rejected early in the course. You could argue that the mother is somehow the guardian of the fetus and therefore can decide in the fetus's best interests. But is it really in the best interests of the fetus to die? And to die just because the mother wants it to die? Of course, there are many arguments in favor of abortion that have nothing to do with consent. They are based on balancing interests and they were addressed early in the course, in the 1927 abortion case."

Adam sensed that he and his "team" had seen it all. They had been though all the arguments. Paraphrasing a famous line attributed to Sir Thomas More in Robert Bolt's play *A Man for All Seasons*, he continued, "We have cut down all the laws and left the pregnant woman and her fetus alone in the middle of a naked field. They are Hagar and Ishmael sent alone into the desert to await word from God's messenger. This is a frightening moment for them and for us, the theorists of law, the ones whose job it is to ensure that their fate will be based on reasoned discourse."

"And of course," Jaime added, "Thomas More was afraid that at precisely this moment the devil would turn on the couple unprotected by the law, and then what would they do?"

Adam was impressed that Jaime had got the reference. "There are those who would turn on us too, because we have dared to discuss these issues honestly and forthrightly. We have run the issue into the ground. We have exposed the arguments for what they are. The reasoning is naked, and that has left us without protection and without restraint. We are dangerous people."

The students sat stunned. They felt enlisted in a collective intellectual inquiry in which they too were on the line. They were scared and exhilarated. They did not know what to do but to break out in applause. Rodrigo sat alone, defiantly, with his arms folded.

23

The Debate

ADAM AWOKE IN a sweat. There were times, before medical procedures, for example, when he would listen to the tapes he had made of his mother's oral history when she lay dying in the hospital. Her voice soothed him. But any association between the uncertainties of a biopsy and this moment seemed overdramatic. The best thing to do would be to find Aschkin and share a few moments of peace with her. He was not sure how to do that. He tried her new cellphone, but there was no answer. He did not think she would go to the Aviary, because it was too early and it would probably seem too obvious.

He began walking and his steps took him in the direction of Sydney's apartment. He buzzed up and Alice said it was OK to visit for a short time. Maybe, he thought, Sydney would have some advice—he was not sure about what—but in any case, he hoped he might at least have a good laugh.

Sydney was napping but happily roused himself when Adam entered the room. He was in pain and could no longer eat or drink on his own. "I don't know why God is punishing me so much, just because I don't believe in him," he said, proving that his mind was still on top form.

"Let me tell you something, Sydney. I think I'm in love."

"Yeah, yeah."

"Yes, that's right, I think I'm in love with you."

"You said it, not me. Have you had sex with her already?"

"Well, not exactly. Yes and no," said Adam. "It's only ten in the morning."

"Your situation reminds me of the situation in the Bible. It says, 'Do not lie with a man as you would with a woman.' What do you think that means?"

"That's generally taken to be a prohibition of homosexuality."

"You should not read it that way."

"Why not?"

"Well, what it means is, don't just lie there, *do something*. Ten in the morning no excuse."

Adam cramped with guffaws. Alice too heard the joke and came to stroke Sydney on the forehead. "Believe me, he would never have violated the commands of the Bible."

"Me neither," said Adam. "If I get to the point of 'lying there,' I promise I will do something. But right now, I am eager to find her. I have about an hour and a half before a debate with Julien Wright and I need her soft touch on my brow."

"Watch out for Julien," said Sydney. "He's clever and determined. He is the son of a preacher and he knows how to rouse the crowd. He's generally a careful thinker and a good philosopher. You have to find his weak points."

"What are they?"

"You can rattle him by zeroing in on his moral beliefs and then imply, subtly, that he is self-righteous, still unable to emancipate himself from his childhood, listening to his father in church. But now I'm not feeling so good; God has started to punish me again for not believing in one of his preachers."

Adam kissed him on the brow as he always did and eased his way backwards out of the room. This time he did not associate Sydney with his ailing mother. He had another female on his mind and he had to find her. He had to think about where she would have gone on the assumption that she would not want the two of them to be seen together. "Eureka!" he cried out suddenly. "She would go to the place in the neighborhood I hate the most."

The Starbucks chain just beginning to take over the neighborhood. They offered comfortable easy chairs as a come-on but they insisted on serving their coffee in paper cups and they offered pieces of cake in brown bags. Adam had once asked a German friend whether any coffee shop in her home town would serve like that and she said no, it was *ekelhaft*—disgusting. The word came into his mind every time he passed by one of the branches. Starbucks was as American as you could get, and he never set foot in the place.

This time, however, he peered through the window and saw Ariel and Rodrigo sitting together at a table by the window. At the back of the place he saw Aschkin sitting on a sofa, reading. He ran in, nodded at his friend and his potential enemy, and breathlessly rushed to greet Aschkin. She said she had been expecting him. "Remember the joke you told me about the two Jews on the train? One said he was going to Minsk and the other assumed he was going to Pinsk. I had a doctor's appointment today, as every day, on the East Side. This morning I went super-early because I had to spend a little more time there. I decided to take the subway to 59th Street. If you saw me on the train, I thought you might accuse me of deception."

"I would never accuse you of deception—even if I saw you with me on Friday night in the synagogue. Are you all right? Why the doctor?"

"Just some female stuff. Don't worry."

"Well, we're here, thank God. On the sofa. But we can't lie down here."

"You are very conventional, Adam. I could put my briefcase on the floor."

"Not exactly: if we lie down, then we fall under the Biblical command." And he related Sydney's interpretation.

She laughed and said, "I guess this is not the place to continue the process of incorporation."

"Everything is a process, isn't it?" said Adam, mocking the current trends in academic legal jargon.

"Well, if you are going to mock the best and brightest, why not think about having a workshop with a feedback session? I was thinking about your apartment for these purposes, but you have doormen watching the door 24/7 and gossiping even more than that."

"Sorry, my mind right now is on getting through this debate. I admit I'm nervous. It would help to talk about things far away in time and place. Could you help me do that by telling me stories from your childhood? What do you remember most fondly about your early years in Istanbul?"

Aschkin smiled. "When I was little," she began, "we could run down to the Bosporus, jump in and swim in the clean, clear currents. All this was a few blocks from my house. When I was very small, before—you know..." and Adam thought of the lovely parts of her upper body that he had not yet caressed "...I could even swim naked. I had a sense of total freedom and pleasure in the water, the sun, the narrow beach. My friends would meet me there and we would play in the sand, and merchants would pass by and sell us *ayran*, a delicious Turkish drink I will make for you some day. This was the time of innocence, before I even learned that there was anyone in the world who was not Turkish."

"Did you know any Jews as a child?"

"Yes, of course, there was never a difference between us; they spoke the same slang and savored the same pleasures. Only as I got older did I notice that some of them stayed away on Saturdays. And some of them had nightmares about things that happened in the war, things they heard from their families."

"I'm going to start learning Turkish," said Adam. "It will bring me closer to you."

"I've never met a man who wanted to learn my language."

"Tell me how you say 'nice legs.'"

"*Güzel bucuklar*," she said, blushing. "Are you sure you don't want to learn the names of sexual parts first?"

"No, I think about your legs all the time. I can see you running naked into the Bosporus. I can see your *güzel bucuklar*, getting deeper and deeper and disappearing into the water."

Aschkin took his hand secretively behind her briefcase, which formed a kind of barrier between them. "I'm feeling more serene now," said Adam after a few moments. "Your discussion of your childhood reminds me of my best times with my parents as a child. There was no good beach near us, but sometimes we went to Puenta del Este, across the river in Uruguay. We would rent a small apartment there for the summer months. We'd spend the whole day on the beach, my parents and me and my sister Noga. There were a few other Hungarian Jews in the area and somehow we found each other and made our own little camp on the beach. I have special memories of playing in the water with my father. I would go underwater and he would take my arms and swing me under his legs. I still have a warm feeling when I swim underwater."

"It is a special experience: the experience of the womb connected to your father."

Adam felt the same warmth toward her. They enjoyed a few moments of silence, then Adam looked at his watch. "My God, what time is it? I have to go and deal with the likes of Julien Wright."

* * * * *

As Adam and Aschkin were in their private Minsk, the law school was boiling over. They were absorbed with politics of the highest moment. The propriety of Gross's exam was the center of their world—far more important to them than the *desaparecidos* in Argentina or the suicide bombers in Israel. The Lesbian Alliance had first intended to boycott the debate in protest. Then, after it became known that Dean Levenger was to moderate, they changed their tune and exhorted their members to come to expose the anti-lesbian bias of Professor Gross.

Levenger made a pitch to the otherwise uninvolved faculty to come and become informed about the whole dispute. He did not have to worry about whether O'Sullivan and Kong would be there, and he had already had hints that Paul Keskemeny, Nkwame Mavioglu and Ariel Colline were strong supporters of Gross. Yet he knew that the future of the affair would depend on the views of the workaday faculty members, the guys like Pat Graham who did their jobs, read the *New York Post*, never annoyed the students, and rarely had an opinion about politics inside or outside the school. And then there was Aschkin. She, he hoped, would listen to reason, though he already had a sense that she had become in some way intertwined with Adam.

For Peter personally, the debate had several purposes. It was important to him to make sure that an event this big in the little world of Regina Law did not take place without his being perceived as a player in the drama. He also had a strong sense that if someone should emerge as a leader and a peacemaker, it should be him. The debate had also taken on emotional significance for him, the way Aschkin had spun the event in his mind...

She was aware of his suppressed jealousy of Adam—of his gaining attention from the students and, of course, from one faculty member, namely herself. Last night she had, exceptionally, prepared dinner, and over a glass of wine invited Peter to reminisce with her about their more innocent times—their first dinner in Heidelberg, the years spent building their careers together, their trips around the world and the artefacts they had collected along the way. The evening could not but end in a long period of caressing and kissing on the living room sofa, an unusually old-fashioned petting that they had both found very stimulating. They inevitably fell into their long-unpracticed ritual of undressing in front of each other in the bedroom, but this time Aschkin asked Peter to repeat as much as possible the experience they had had in the Heidelberg sauna. He pressed her against the wall of the bedroom and she pretended not to know how to place or move her legs. She felt like a virgin again, but reached a depth of climax that virgins were rarely fortunate enough to enjoy. They fell asleep satisfied, with Peter feeling as though he had re-established himself as her man, her only man, outside the bedroom as well as in.

Peter and Julien arrived at the lecture hall a few minutes early. They both took their seats at the desk on the stage in front. Adam usually avoided the elevation in favor of standing at the lectern in the pit, at the same level as the first row of students. But when he entered this time, along with most of the students, he had no choice but to step up and take his seat on Peter's right. He was less comfortable with the way he related to the students, in this posture of staged superiority, but there seemed no better way than to sit in the pattern already established.

Adam noticed that his assistant Zetta had put a stack of single sheets containing the question by the entrances and also on the desks in the front row. He wondered whether this was a good or bad idea after all, and decided it was basically good—in the spirit of Mel's famous call to "Fuck the Draft" in the Supreme Court.

As Julien, Peter and Adam were conferring about the order of the debate, the students and faculty filed in. His regular participants were there. Among the undergraduate students there were faces Adam did not recognize, mostly female. Many of the faculty sat in the front row. Many tried to remain inconspicuous in the back of the room. Ariel, always eager to show off, sat right up front. Next to him, on the aisle, sat Rodrigo. Aschkin sat in the same seat she always did and assumed an air of normalcy. A few older students or alumnae sat at the side of the room; among them was an attractive young woman in a wheelchair. By 11 a.m. the place was packed, with the crowd still snaking into the hall.

The chatting among the students had long since ceased. They waited. After Peter's preliminary remarks, Julien rose to speak, as if to a congregation. It was a solemn occasion and he was going to explain the meaning of the events to the students.

"I very much regret that I am here today," he began. "But I feel I have no alternative but officially and publicly to call the good judgment of my colleague Professor Adam Gross into question. You will probably hear him claim that this is a question of academic freedom. But it is not. It is a matter of taste and respect for the students, particularly the female students in our school."

Adam could not get his mind off Argentina and the politics of his youth. The dispute about the exam now suddenly struck him as absurd. His worries of last night and this morning seemed to melt away, and he could not take Julien or his faculty supporters seriously. Others in the room were apparently of the same mind. As Julien proceeded to describe the details of the exam, Ariel and Rodrigo jumped up from their seats and stood in the pit below the elevated podium. Ariel put on a blonde wig. Rodrigo knelt before him and pleaded, "My *capitán*, my *capitán*, how shall we worship the Big Monkey?" Ariel told him in a mock falsetto, "Motherhood is death. Go out and kill as many fetuses as you can."

The class erupted in hysterical applause. Peter pounded on the desk with his fist. "Order, order."

Ariel took off his wig and turned to Peter, "Your Honor, we request no more than the traditional right to illustrate the defendant's case with a re-enactment of the alleged crime."

Peter, who thought of himself as fair-minded, could not think of a reason to refuse. "Let Professor Wright finish," he said, "and then, if Adam agrees, you can use *his* time for your demonstration."

Squelching his smile, Adam nodded assent to Peter's view of the two stages of trial. Julien looked perplexed. Peter's ruling was not biased, not obviously wrong, but what should he do? He had already started his sermon, so to speak. Leaving church in the middle of services was not an option he was familiar with, so all he could do was continue. He finished with words invested, he thought, with sinister connotations. "When you read this exam, you get the feeling of slightly sick personalities. This is true of the characters in the exam, David and Gaye in particular. But it might be true of the author of the exam as well. Is there any way to write anything without revealing something of ourselves? Are healthy people so drawn to such perversities? I have heard some students say that this exam must be the only way that some people can get their kicks." He sat down.

Ariel and Rodrigo, spontaneously, put their arms around each other's waists and started kicking, chorus-girl style, in unison. The class started stomping their feat to their beat.

Now Peter was perplexed. "What the hell are you doing?"

"Isn't is obvious?" said Ariel. "We're getting our kicks."

"OK, OK, finish your demonstration."

Ariel and Rodrigo began with the story of David and Eve. Ariel put a pillow under his sweater and acted as though he was walking nonchalantly down the street. Rodrigo crept out beyond the seat and then suddenly leapt on top of him. He pulled out a stick supporting a banner reading "rubber pipe—no offense intended." He started beating Ariel in the mid-section. Ariel screamed and then with left hand under his shirt he started closing and opening his fist, which had the effect of making his puffed-out sweater pop up and down.

Ariel then grabbed the stick from Rodrigo, pulled off the banner and, crying out, "You fetus-killer, you deserve a metal pipe," began hitting him on the shoulder. After a few hits, the two stopped and stood in the front of the class. Rodrigo bowed. The audience was in uproar.

"OK," someone shouted from the back of the room. "It's time for the prosecution's case." For some, this was going to be the leading event of the new academic year.

Peter could not think of a better way to be even-handed than to ask Adam whether he concurred. Adam, who by now was enjoying himself more than he had in months, said, "Absolutely, fair is fair."

Adrienne Fox, the spokeswoman for the Lesbian Alliance, came to the front of the room. "Very funny," she said, looking at Ariel and Rodrigo, "but you are missing the point. Some things about the exam are beyond satire. Look at the names Adam Gross used on this exam. Look at them clearly—Eve, Flora, and Gaye. They appear to be in alphabetical order. But there is a message encoded in each name. Eve is the mother of all the living, so of course she is pregnant and she seeks to defend herself with force. But Flora, the plant-like figure, cannot bear human fruit. And Gaye, of course, is supposedly the most

perverse of them all. Gaye is a very unusual name. Professor Gross
was clearly thinking of something else when he invented a name that
bears close association with the common reference to homosexuals.
So the woman named Gaye thanks her aggressor. We agree with
Professor Wright that you can read this exam as revealing what Adam
Gross really thinks. We in fact believe it tells us what he thinks about
women specifically—and what you discover is not pretty."

The committed feminists stood and applauded. Chen was tempted
to join them. But Joerg, putting his hand on her sleeve, said, "Please,
you have serious issues. This is not one of them."

Fox would not step down. She insisted that Adam give an
explanation for his use of names. In fact, when Adam had been
writing the exam in a moment of pseudo-novelistic fury, his mind
had half-consciously gone back to Gayle, the women he had pined
after when he was a teenager and with whom he'd first danced tango
cheek to check. But in adapting the name to the exam he had dropped
the "l"; the link had been subconscious, the woman of his youth not
fully remembered. Eve and Flora were in fact familiar figures in his
life. Both were common names for Jewish women born after the
Holocaust. Eve or Eva was indeed the most common, and Flora was
popular particularly among Hungarian Jews. "Gaye" was a slip, but
this was not the context in which he expected much understanding
for dropping a letter in the heat of composing a question.

He responded to Adrienne deferentially. "You obviously have
a background in lit-crit and you use your skills well. Very smart,
smarter than I am." But then he could not resist. "I wish your skills
were relevant to the law." At that point his club of supporters, the
Principals, began to applaud.

Another woman whose affiliation was not clear zeroed in on
the slogan. "'Motherhood is Death.' Where did you get this bizarre
slogan?" she demanded. "You must be trying to satirize lesbians and
assuming all lesbians hate children and engage in S-and-M."

If these "interpretative" moves resonated well with the American
students, the graduate students from abroad were less impressed.
Chen muttered under her breath, "If American feminism is an
intellectual game, they can have it." Charlotte said she had had
enough of deconstructionist games from the students in France, and
was not eager to hear more. As usual she was not afraid to speak up.

"Look, people, are you able to get past these abstract displays of brilliance and talk about the neety-greety of the exam?" She and other members of the class felt privileged that they understood the issues underlying the complex fact-patterns.

Since a few students had interrogated Adam directly, Ariel decided that he was himself entitled to direct a few questions to Julien, about the language appropriate for exams.

"So, Professor Wright, tell us about the sublime and the beautiful. Do you the know the work by Bruneau now at the Met—*Happy Mother*—where the Christ child is erect and the Virgin Mary is having a wank?"

"Please don't use that language here," Julien replied.

"Why not?"

"It's offensive—like Professor Gross's exam."

"I see. So anyway how would you have reconstructed *Happy Mother* so that it would not have been offensive?"

"I would have taken God out of it."

"So you would have made it *Unhappy Mother*, with her baby gone?" Some of the students laughed. Ariel was on a roll and he knew it.

Julien was uncomfortably aware that he was somehow being outfenced. "No, it would have been a different work of art," he said in an exasperated tone.

"So would you have taken the fetuses out of Adam's exam?"

"No, but I would described them with greater discretion. I would have chosen words that would protect the weak and sensitive among us."

"Well, should we have guidelines on the faculty that tell us exactly which words are too gory for the innocent ears of our infantile students?"

At this point Julien started puffing up and blurting out his words. "For God's sake, it's not difficult. Oxford standards! Oxford, a better place than this."

Ariel decided to back off lest he generate too much sympathy for a respected professor who was close to making a fool of himself. "I'm sure you're right. I suggest you rewrite the exam and submit it to the student paper for publication. It would teach us all something important."

Adam had done almost nothing, and yet he was coming out on top. He thought he deserved much worse. There were things wrong with the exam, but no one could quite capture the obsessive fetus-orientation in Adam's thinking.

The politics were complicated. Adam's graduate students were lined up strongly behind him, and this was obvious to Peter. Ann O'Sullivan and Kathy Kong and the others on faculty were being suspiciously restrained, allowing the students and Julien to be their stalking horses. Then something unexpected happened, even more unexpected than the farce already playing itself out. The attractive woman in the wheelchair introduced herself as Denise Daniels, an alumna from several years back, now an activist for the rights of the physically challenged. Her target was Julien.

"Here we have the son of a preacher," she said, "who is concerned only with wording—who does not recognize the importance of protecting fetal life against attack, and who refuses to train students to deal with the aggressive arguments made by the camp of death. Here we have the son of a preacher who argues that we should conflate the wishes of the strong with the interests of the weak. Well, we are here to represent the organization Not Dead Yet. We speak for the weak. We do not want the wishes of the strong to determine our fate. If they did, we would all be dead."

Julien felt ashamed that he had suppressed a fundamental Christian teaching in order to carry on his campaign. He had forgotten to consider that fetuses could be consider the "meek," "the sacrificial victims" of modernity. He was flushed and he could barely speak. He was about to say something defiant like, "Well, you think this Jew Adam Gross is any better at understanding the message of Christ?" but he thought better of it. He looked at Ann, who was unable to help him. "Well," he began, both humbly and excitedly, "there are different categories of the weak. Here in the law school, women and people of color deserve special attention. They are our historical legacy. When we are fortunate enough to have disabled students in our classes, of course we should take special care of them. We would not like to see an exam that made the disabled feel uncomfortable."

"First of all, we are not disabled," snapped back Denise. "I am here today going toe-to-toe with you. I am not disadvantaged or incapable of defeating you in argument. What I resist is not your preaching the autonomy of women but your forgetting that every time you advance one group in society, you hurt another. We are hurt by any argument that glorifies the will to end life. We are alive and we choose life."

Peter Levenger found himself deeply moved, and it was like a revelation to him. He had never thought much about the rights of those with disabilities. More importantly, he appreciated Denise's invocation of something like the class struggle. He suddenly realized that, in all apparent struggles for human rights, there were always winners and losers, human rights damaged on both sides. To paraphrase the economists' witticism about the free lunch, there was no such thing as a free human right. This hit Peter now as a truth so fundamental that his failure to recognize it in the past called into question all his habitual styles of thinking and writing.

Ann could not take this line of thought any longer. Obviously angry at Julien and furious at Adam, she got up and finally found the words to explain her campaign against the criminal law exam. "My heart goes out to all those who suffer," she began diplomatically, "but the issue here is not suffering, and it is not mercy-killing. The only question that concerns us is the equality of men and women in the law school. Women have a right not to be gazed upon, not to be scrutinized, not to be reminded all the time of what they have between their legs." The students sat in shocked amazement at the last line.

Emboldened, Ann continued. "They are the ones who bear the children, who run the risk of being attacked by lunatics like David. When they are singled out and then asked to compete in exams, there is no longer a level playing field. This is the question that Adam Gross formulated, perhaps for good but perhaps for bad motives. It has to be judged by its effects. And its effects are the same as asking a math question about how many containers of Zyklon B it would take to kill a thousand Jews in Auschwitz or how much rope it would take to string up a thousand black men in Alabama. No professor has the right to play intellectual games that single out a particular group and make them the target of inquiry."

Ann's supporters, who were many among the faculty and the students, could not help but stamp their feet in approval. Adam was silent. He could not respond because he did not disagree. He recalled his own feelings of unease when he'd felt as though he had zeroed in on Mohammed and expected him to answer a question about racial equality.

No one said anything. Finally, Charlotte got the nerve and raised her hand. "I appreciate the argument of Professor O'Sullivan, but I disagree. Equality between women and men does not mean that women are invisible. We are seen as people with certain kinds of bodies. Most men look at us and they want to make to love to us. And we like it that way. We make sure our hair and our nails are properly done. We wear skirts to show off our legs. Do we really want to enter a profession in which we are treated as androgynous, desexed cogs in the machine of the law. *Vive la différence.*"

This remark provoked both laughter and hisses. Peter concluded that he had to call the meeting to a close. The journalists for the *Report* and the campus newspaper were writing furiously. They started taking photos of the main speakers and all those who had asked questions.

Adam stepped down from the podium, stunned and elated. He had won without swinging a punch—at least it seemed that way to him. Paul Keskemeny buttonholed him and told him not to be so self-satisfied; he had not gained any faculty votes. But he might have swayed an even more important player. Peter approached him toward the rear of the room and put his hand gently over his shoulder. Aschkin saw and joined both of them in a three-way hug. This is the man I fell in love with in Heidelberg, she thought to herself. This is the first woman in my life I have thought I could love with all my heart, thought Adam. And Peter, what did he think? The humor, the argument, the confrontation—it had all had an exhilarating effect on a man who had been pushing papers too long. He felt a new commitment to ideas, to joining the debate himself, even to being as bold as Ariel or Adam. He was holding firm to Adam and Aschkin, but his mind was reaching beyond them.

Julien had a large group of young women around him, but he felt dejected. He had been personally attacked as the son of a minister. Ann was furious at his failure to sound the right note. He had mounted an attack against a colleague and he was unsure whether he had succeeded. His only thought upon the leaving the room was, I have lunged at a prince and I have not slain him.

24

Nightmare and Normalcy

THE AFTERNOON DRIFTED away in ongoing discussions, maneuvers, and retellings of the great debate. Adam tried to get out of there was early as he could. He recalled Wittgenstein's habit of running out to a movie in order to get his mind off the intensity of class discussion. He left the building without knowing where he was going. He ended up in the first row of the first cinema he could find, an art house one. The film turned out an old one from the early 1980s, *Whose Life Is It Anyway?*, which Adam had heard about but never seen. In a hospital room, a sculptor called Ken, played by Richard Dreyfuss, is lying, paralysed from the neck down after a car accident. All he can do is talk, and he comes across as a bright, witty, living mind trapped in a tomb of a body. Ken becomes determined to be allowed to die, and he makes friends with some of the hospital staff and gradually persuades them of his right to do so, so that they support him at trial. The point of the film was to present a sympathetic portrait of death by choice (with "dignity" as it was often described). It was full of the clichés that one heard so often in the discussion about terminal patients choosing to end their lives. It made the argument that life was a right, not a duty, and the title itself was a popular anti-clerical slogan. In the view of the film-maker, Ken had no duty to bear his suffering and stay alive only to permit those who loved him to be with him longer. But the film examined both sides of the moral argument, as well as asking to what extent government should be allowed to interfere in the decisions of a private citizen. It was an argument that was still raging today in most so-called civilized countries of the world.

As Adam left the theater he thought about how euthanasia might be carried out—by taking pills? Or by lethal injection, like

when an animal was put down? Imagining it, he was disturbed by
the similarity between that method and capital executions in the
United States, where people would be strapped down on a gurney
before the needle entered their veins. He started thinking about the
last years of his mother's life as an invalid. She had talked about
"checking out" and had been worried constantly about the costs
of her care to the family. Adam realized that he would have been
deeply hurt if she had chosen an "early exit." The same with Sydney,
even though he was not related to him. Although Sydney could
make jokes about God punishing him for his atheism, Sydney never
seemed to think that his life was solely his own, to dispose of as he
wished. For Sydney, and, Adam thought, for himself also, a choice
for death would be in violation of the most basic Jewish values.

He walked home, depressed and confused by the film but
elated by the paradoxical way in which the struggles of the day
had brought him closer to Peter as well as Aschkin. The hug at the
conclusion of the debate was one of those surprising turns that
humbled him in the face of unexpected human emotions. Wouldn't
it be ironic, he thought, if his political fight were to win him a male
friend intrigued by his ideas, but at the same time render him more
ambivalent about trying to take Aschkin away from her husband?
As for Aschkin, he wondered, what was the bond that mattered to
her most? If she had to choose, would she side with him? If there
was a triangle among them, what was the path of life and what was
the path of death?

These thoughts still occupied Adam as he undressed and
ritualistically entered his steam shower. He loved sitting in the
shower and staring at the subtle differences in the lines engraved
in the blue and grey tiles. He was proud of the way he had designed
the flowery border traversing the four walls. Adam stretched out
and lay prone on his wooden bench. When the shower filled with
steam he could barely see the wall on the other side. He was totally
relaxed. Then he felt that he might be falling asleep so he quickly
turned the shower handle and rinsed himself in cold water. He dried
himself luxuriously with a rack-heated towel, donned his blue night
shift, took half an Ambien to help him fall asleep, and then sat back
on the flowered sofa sipping a glass of red wine. He had barely put
the glass down before he dozed off.

Some time in the middle of the night he had a dream—a set of unforgettable images that constituted not just a nightmare but the *cauchemar* of his life. He was in a closed room with other people. They were all naked and expecting to take a shower. But there was no shower handle. The steam came out and filled the room and it was hard to inhale. Then it became harder and harder to get air. There was no way to turn on the cold water and rinse down the mist. He could no longer see the people next to him. They started screaming and banging on the door. And then the image changed. He was still in a closed room, this time naked and alone. There was no shower, he was floating in a liquid, and he inhaled and exhaled only the liquid. Suddenly he felt pins jabbing at him. And then there was an enormous hit, a shock to the room. He reeled and felt as though the roof was caving in on him. He looked for a place to hide but there was none. He was tied down, unable to maneuver.

When he awoke, drenched as though he were still swimming in liquid, he realized immediately the association he must have made with the film and his subsequent imaginings. In the hands of the Nazis, as Adam interpreted the associations of his own dream, the practice of euthanasia had led eventually to Auschwitz. He told himself that he must have felt personally threatened by the possibility that some man stricken with quadriplegia could enlist the state in his private decision to die.

But why, he tried to reason, should the voluntary decision of a terminal patient lead him to fear the use of gas chambers in an attempt to commit genocide against the Jewish people? This, he sensed, was the role of the second part of the dream. In his unconscious he had made the leap from the systematic war against the Jews to the practice of abortion—his own abortion. But wasn't this just a little paranoid? he tried to convince himself. Then something came back to him, a memory he had repressed for at least 40 years. When he was a child, his mother had told him that she had had two abortions before he was born. Economic conditions had been hard, and they could not afford a child. This meant that he was truly wanted, his mother had explained to him. Nonetheless, he felt at the time that he had narrowly escaped the knife.

He realized for the first time why his mother had supported him so strongly when Sara Kalvermann was pregnant and they had had to confer with Leo to find a way out of the situation. I guess it was her thing, he said to himself, and then rebuked himself for being so snide even in his private thoughts. "My God, she's been dead for ten years," he said out loud. "And she still shapes the way I think."

He paced the apartment for an hour, looking for his absent father immersed in his irredentist book on "the greater Hungary." He tried to call Aschkin, but apparently she was asleep and had shut off her phone. Finally he fell asleep again and got up after 9 a.m., dressed languidly in his favorite blue linen suit and white silk shirt; with heavy steps, as though he were still living in liquid, he made his way to the law school.

As he approached his office, he saw a small group of his students gathered at the door. Chen, Joerg, Jaime and Holly formed the core of what they called a "delegation" from the class. He invited them into his office to talk. He felt a warmth toward this core four in particular. They had been though several stages of intellectual evolution together. His feelings toward them were almost familial.

"We wanted to see how you were holding up after the debate yesterday," Chen began.

"To tell you the truth," Adam said, "I had a ball. But my feelings changed afterwards. I guess it was a let-down. Now, just between us, I feel like apologizing to the criminal law students from last spring for having foisted my anxieties about abortion on them."

"Listen," said Chen, with the others nodding, "those two guys, the prof and Rodrigo, had the right idea. There is nothing here that is worth more than a laugh."

"But I have realized now that I have a special history with the issue of abortion and all the problems of life and death that the question raises." He felt that with this group he could be more self-revelatory. "I have special sensitivities both as a Jew and as the particular child I was. What right do I have inflict my *meshuggas* on innocent first-year students who barely know the difference between murder and larceny?"

"Professor," Joerg intervened, "you don't have to tell me about carrying around guilt for having a special history. Every day of my life I have to deal with me being German, of recognizing who my grandfather was, of falling in love with a Jew. *Gott im Himmel*, sometimes it is more than I can bear."

"But," said Adam, "I am guilty, as Ann O'Sullivan claims, of having made the women in the class feel uncomfortable. I should apologize to them at least for that."

"Don't be ridiculous." Jaime spoke as if his turn had been scripted. "I know about real conflict—having lived through the struggle between the Pope and the liberation theologists. Do you think that John Paul II ever apologized for his wrongs? He forgave the wrongs of others because that gave him Christian power—remember the Turk who tried to assassinate him?—but he never humbled himself and he never recognized his own guilt for the assassination of Bishop Romero." In the midst of his account Jaime burst out laughing. "Excuse me, professor, but suddenly I was struck by the image of Job in his misery surrounded by his visitors who seek to explain the mysteries of God's way in the world. But we are not visitors to a stricken man, and you are not Job."

Chen added, "Jaime is right. This entire episode has been overdramatized. You are not Job, and you should not think of yourself as being on the defensive. I think some very strange things are going on in this law school. It is as though, when you don't have a real enemy, as we do in Israel, you have to make one up. You and Ann O'Sullivan are not enemies. You just think you are."

"I wish you could convince her of that, and try a few other members of the faculty while you're at it."

"Perhaps we will. In the meantime we would like to ask you to drop this stuff about fetuses and sado-masochism and get back to the central subjects of the course. Don't misunderstand me, it has been interesting and valuable to go over the issues in the exam. But we want to continue on the high road you were on before this controversy hit the fan, as they say."

"This is good. I want to do the same thing, and we will, in about half an hour," said Adam reassuringly.

"We are looking forward to it," said the students as they left the office. Adam closed the drawer on his nightmare and turned toward his books.

25

The Return to Trust

"THE FIRST THING I want to do today," Adam began, "is to thank my young captain for his brilliant performance." The class stood and applauded as Rodrigo feigned embarrassment, crossing his arms to hide himself in mock humility.

Ariel, nonchalantly hanging around outside, darted into the room and said, "What about me?" The class stood again, turned and applauded even more loudly. Ariel backed out of the same door, arms extended, his gaunt fingers waving their tips to the crowd.

"We did a lot of technical work on the criminal law exam," Adam continued. "You know the stuff well, very well. Now I want to remind you that we are more than technicians. I have been telling you that since the very beginning of this course. The entire first part of our study of constitutional law was about the conflict between freedom and equality. These are values embedded in our conflicting constitutional texts. These are the ultimate questions that will not go away.

"Now I want to take you back into the value conflicts that defined the history of the common law. And this story is told primarily by recounting the struggles of the great hero of early common law, Sir Edward Coke. His name was spelt C-O-K-E, like the soft drink, but pronounced 'Cook.' He was born in the mid-16th century into a privileged family of lawyers. He initially had a career in politics and rose to hold the office of Speaker of the House of Commons. In the early 1600s he rose to power as the prosecutor of the Catholic conspirators who tried to blow up the House of Commons and kill King James I. Their plan had been to replace the Protestant king with his daughter, a Catholic. This was the famous Guy Fawkes conspiracy, which was frustrated on 5 November and ever since that date has been celebrated in Commonwealth countries as Guy Fawkes Day, a festivity of relief that the plotters did not succeed.

"Even more notable was Coke's prosecution of the great literary figure Sir Walter Raleigh, the romantic figure of the time, probably a lover of Queen ElizaAnn I. The charge was 'treason by compassing'—which meant plotting—'the death of King James.' This was sufficient to trigger the death penalty without any proof of action in furtherance of the malicious intent. The remarkable feature of this case in 1603 was the primitive level of the procedural protections available to Raleigh. He could not have a lawyer to defend him. He could not confront the witnesses against him. He could not call witnesses on his behalf. It is hard to recreate the mindset that drove this procedural system. They must have assumed that if someone was charged with a really terrible crime, a crime like treason, then the accused should have fewer rights at trial.

"Do you see anything wrong with this way of thinking?"

"Obviously," said Charlotte. "This violates the presumption of innocence as recognized in the 1789 French Declaration of Human Rights. He is being punished prior to the conviction."

"That is a good way of putting it," reflected the professor. "You're saying that the denial of procedural rights is itself a form of punishment for being a suspected traitor. Excellent idea. I usually read the French Declaration to prohibit imprisonment and other harsh treatment prior to conviction, but your argument is better."

"So what finally happened?" asked Jaime. "How did the legal system evolve so that we treat all suspected criminals in the same way, with the same rights?"

"I'm not sure," responded Adam. "The Sixth Amendment now recognizes the three fundamental procedural rights that were absent in the prosecution, or should I say persecution, of Sir Walter Raleigh. Today a criminal defendant—no matter how evil he is thought to be—has a right, as the Amendment says, '*to be confronted with the witnesses against him.*' The Sixth Amendment also guarantees that the defendant has '*compulsory process for obtaining witnesses in his favor.*' And, most importantly, the defendant is today entitled '*to have the Assistance of Counsel for his defense.*' It is incredible to think that in 1603 Raleigh had none of these rights. The critical witness did not appear at trial. Raleigh was not able to cross-examine him. He could not call witnesses of his own, and he had no lawyer to assist him.

"Coke argued that the law of his time was based on reason. He wrote in his first Institute, 'Reason is the life of the law; nay, the common law itself is nothing else but reason... The law which is perfection of reason.' This sounds good, but it had nothing to do with the criminal procedure of the time, which was based exclusively on the interests of the state. It is hard to believe that the law could enjoy so much grandeur while the systems of criminal procedure enjoyed the level of refinement you might expect from a London street market.

"But interestingly, in 1610, things began to change. Coke himself undertook to reform some features of the procedural system. You have read Dr. Bonham's case. What is it about? Marga, may I call on you?"

"Sure. Dr. Bonham was practicing medicine without a license, or the College of Physicians said so. They charged him, tried him, and imposed a fine. Dr. Bonham objected. He felt railroaded."

Adam added, "Under its charter from Parliament, the Royal College had the authority to do this—they were entitled to supervise the medical profession."

"Yes," Ilona intervened excitedly, "but this is a perfect model of an inquisitorial system. It reminds me of justice under Ceaucescu. The College is police officer, prosecutor and judge all rolled into one body."

"Right, and this was what Coke was going to change. But what authority did he have to revise the law?" queried Adam.

"Here's the rub," said Joerg, now enjoying his command of English idioms. "Coke appealed to a European concept of law. He said that the statute was *Gesetz*, but not *Recht*. If it violated higher principles, it was null and void. In effect, he anticipated the reasoning in the 1927 German abortion case."

"Absolutely right," said Adam. "He asked the question whether the statute conformed to the principles of 'common right or reason.' The common law is interpreted as the higher law of reason, as principles of right, precisely as the German law of abortion is embedded in higher principles of law in the 1927 case. You remember our discussion of the alternative word for law in all the European languages: *derecho*, *droit*, *diritto*, *Recht*, *prava*, and I will throw in the Hungarian counterpart *jog*. What is the point here? Law has a higher reality. Right has its own principles, above the law of Parliament. And if Parliament's law conflicts with the principles of right, it is null and void. This is a revolutionary argument."

"Yes," countered Jaime, "but there was not much in the law to be proud of. Perhaps the substantive law was based on reason. This was Coke's Madonna. But the law of procedure was his whore, to use as he saw fit to convict enemies of the state."

"I agree," said Adam, "but in Bonham's case, he began to have a change of heart. He argued that one rule of procedural justice particularly was inherent in the common law. What was that?"

"No person should be a judge in his own case," replied several students in unison.

"Right," said Adam. "The College of Physicians in London could not simultaneously prosecute the case, judge liability and collect the fine. You can read this as a way of the common law's seeking its identity opposed to the civil law's inquisitorial system."

Joerg was taken aback. "We no longer do that—have prosecutor and judge wrapped up in one person."

"I understand," conceded Adam. "With the French Revolution things changed in Europe too. But we are talking about the early seventeenth century in Coke's case. This was the beginning of the liberalization of procedure—there followed the Petition of Right in 1628. This was a demand to King Charles I to recognize the basic principles of due process in criminal procedure."

"I thought the big date was 1215, and wasn't it the Magna Carta?" queried Gad.

"Yes," replied Adam, "for the barons. They got the right to trial by a jury of their peers and some kind of due process. But it did not help poor Walter Raleigh very much. The interesting thing about this period in the early seventeenth century was that all the basic institutions of the English tradition were in conflict. In 1613 we encounter a knock-down, drag-out fight between Coke's courts of the common law and the Chancellor's court of equity."

This was a totally new idea for the students from outside the common law world. They knew about equity as general principles of fairness but they did not know there were two distinct systems of courts, one in law, one in equity. As Adam explained it, the Chancellor, as officer of the King and the Church, sought to supplement the common law with rules requiring the "just enforcement" of the simple rules of the common law. For example, if someone entered a contract under duress or fraud, the law courts would do nothing to provide relief from the contract. The disadvantaged party had to plead in equity to get an injunction requiring the stronger party not to enforce the unfair contract. "Equity worked solely on the person—by commanding performance, with the threat of imprisonment in the case of disobedience, called civil contempt. There was no jury at all—ever." Adam pointed to the ongoing influence of equity by getting the students to read out the Seventh Amendment, which guaranteed a jury trial solely in "suits at common law." Suits in equity were implicitly excluded from the scope of the Amendment.

When Chen realized the way equity worked, with its power to compel imprisonment of those who disobeyed its orders, she called out, "My God, that is the way our religious courts work at home. They will not cancel a marriage or grant a divorce, but they will order the husband to grant a *get* or bill of divorce."

"And if the husband does not do it?"

"Well, the rabbinical courts can put him in jail until he complies—just like the Chancellor."

"Interesting," reflected Adam. "I wonder whether there is a connection between reliance on God's authority and the capacity to imprison the recalcitrant parties until they comply. In any event, the aspect of all this that interests me is Coke's personal battle against equity. He won against Parliament in 1610, but now in 1613 he had a tougher fight—against the Chancellor's power to imprison. You have in your materials the case that brought the fight to a climax. A jeweler named Glanvil cheated a customer called Courtney by selling him a stone worth much less than the price. He had the *chutzpah* to insist on security for the purchase price. He got this from a third party named Hampton, who issued a bond to Glanvil to pay if Courtney did not."

"*Chutzpah*?" asked one of the Chinese students.

"You already know *meshuggah*—now for your second word in Yiddish, the secret language of the law. *Chutzpah* is usually defined by the case of the children who kill their parents and then plead for mercy because they are orphans. This case is just as bad. Glanvil cheated the buyer and then wanted an innocent third party to put cash on the line to secure the fraudulent price. He even tried to collect the bond from Hampton."

"Yes," continued Marga, looking at her papers, "then Courtney went to equity to get an injunction against Glanvil. Recognizing the fraud, the Chancellor's court of equity ordered Glanvil to release everybody from their debts."

Ilona could not resist. "The Chancellor orders him to be put into jail. I love that. I could not do that when I was a judge in Communist Romania. But it is better than seizing his property. Particularly if he does not have any property."

"Well, I am not so happy about it," said Grigor. "Judges are not always right. Glanvil did not commit a crime. He should not be put in jail."

"He didn't think so either," said the professor. "He tried to test the legality of his confinement by bringing a writ of habeas corpus in the common law courts. The writ requires the warden to explain why he is holding the body, namely the *corpus*. Now we have a full-blown conflict between law and equity. Equity says put him in jail. Coke says, 'You have to justify the confinement to me under a writ of habeas.' How would you have liked to be the warden in this situation? You would not know who was your boss."

Holly was dubious. "I don't like the idea that judges can order disobedient people to go to jail. That is too tyrannical. I put my faith in habeas corpus and Coke's law."

Jaime looked puzzled. "I have doubts about ecclesiastical authority, but the Chancellor speaks in the name of the same religious values that support the authority of the king. There are no democratic institutions at stake in Coke's time. I think the Church had an innate advantage, given the values of the time."

"My God," Holly fired back, "you should be ashamed of yourself. Our loyalties now should be to the secular legal institutions, not to the Church."

Law versus equity, the courts versus Congress—the students were beginning to grasp the great dramas of power that played themselves out behind the scenes of legal conflicts. The legal issues were but camouflage for deep battles for supremacy in the structure of government.

Adam stressed the essential point. "These are not cases about whether the College of Physicians can collect fines or whether the jeweler can collect his bond. These are cases that are ultimately about the structure of government. In the end, the result is that Coke won one and lost one. The courts of law triumphed over Parliament, but the king intervened and decided that Chancellor's courts would prevail over Coke. This was a defeat for the writ of habeas corpus."

Jaime was deep in thought. "I think the Pope would have decided the same way. If there was a difference among the cardinals he would resolve the difference and claim that it was his princely office to do so and that he was answerable only to God. Maybe their system of authority is all make-believe, but when God enters the legal argument, God trumps."

"Maybe you're right," said Adam, feeling as though he had now become the student. "Equity won because, although Coke could claim that law stood for tradition and for sound principles of justice, equity could claim God on its side. And historically this was true. The branch of the law that drew more religious sources eventually triumphed over the common law."

"God forbid," called out Chen, appreciating the irony of her expression of dismay.

"In my view, Coke should be seen as a great Romantic lawyer fighting for the supremacy of his values. In the end, however, he lost. But did he lose in history? A few decades after the dispute, Thomas Hobbes wrote a little book called *A Dialogue between a Philosopher and a Student of the Common Laws of England*. In the book Hobbes portrays an argument between a philosopher (himself) and a lawyer, representing Coke. Hobbes defends the power of the king and of Parliament. Coke argues for the superiority of reason and the common law. Part of the argument is about the meaning of the word 'law.' The gist of the exchange is in your class materials. 'La' refers to Coke, the lawyer, and 'Ph' to Hobbes, the philosopher."

The students looked it up.

> La: This Legal Reason is Summa Ratio; and therefore, if all the Reason that is dispersed into so many heads were united into one, yet he could not make such a Law as the Law of England is, because by so many successions of Ages it hath been fined and refined by an infinite number of Grave and Learned Men.

> Ph: [...] None can make a Law but he that hath the Legislative Power. That the Law hath been fined by

refined and Learned Men, meaning the Professors of Law, is manifestly untrue, for all the Law of England have been made by the Kings of England, consulting the Nobility and Commons in Parliament, of which not one of twenty was a Learned Lawyer.

La: You speak of the Statu[t]e Law, and I speak of the Common Law.

Ph: I speak generally of Law.

Adam waited until they had all read it. "Do you see what is going on here? The word 'law' has two different senses. In one sense it means statutory law—the law laid down by the legislator. In the other sense, it means Law as a set of higher principles—the common law as a moral order. When the courts perceive that a statute violates this moral order, they can declare it null and void. Thus in Hobbes' fictionalized version the lawyer tries to distinguish between statutory law and the common law. The philosopher—representing the power of the king in Parliament—says, No, no, no. All law is the same. It is all like statutory law. Therefore Dr. Bonham's case is wrong."

"But this is complicated," injected Jaime; "there are many different versions of this 'moral order' that trumps the statutory law. It could be the principles of the common law. But it could equally be equity—which also stands for higher principles of reason. It could also be the Constitution."

"You are right. Parliament has many enemies. There are many forces seeking to be superior to the statutory law."

Jaime was entranced. "There is no clear winner here. Hobbes obviously rejects the relevance of Dr. Bonham's case. He portrays the law as positive law dependent on authority. Yet the king as ultimate authority can favor equity as a system, ameliorating what appeared to be the strict rules of law."

"I agree," said Adam, "but in history there was a winner. And the winner is..." Adam pretended to be opening an envelope. "The winner is the Constitution—at least for the United States. The Constitution is the higher law that matters. If there is a conflict between the statutory law and the Constitution, as Chief Justice Marshall ruled in 1803, the Constitution must prevail. Thus the American judges acquired the power to declare statutes unconstitutional. But that is nothing more, really, than what Lord Coke said in 1610—the courts can rules statutes null and void when they conflict with higher principles of law.

"The 'war'—if I can call it that—between law and equity was a little different," continued Adam. "There were two systems of courts at odds with each other. With the king's support, the courts of equity won, and in the next class we shall see how that influences the shape of modern corporate law.

"But I want to leave you today with one point. The constant pressure from these higher sources of law makes the law morally sensitive. The law must stand for decency. It must punish fraud and coercion. It must uphold the rights of the innocents—such as the innocents who suffered at the hands of a fraudulent jeweler.

'The reason this is so fascinating is that the characters are all Romantic figures. They put their lives on the line. Coke was willing to risk all for the sake of the law. Raleigh was in and out of prison his entire life—just like my favorite characters from the Revolution of 1848. Ellesmere, Bacon and King James himself –they were characters to remember. I have one class left. I want to talk to you about your future lives as lawyers and why it is important to emulate these great Romantic figures in the common law tradition."

Adam ended, exhausted. It had been one of the most intense hours of the course. He would have much to talk about in the final hour tomorrow. He walked out of the room, books under his arm, muttering to himself, "I have yet to tell them about bonds, equity, and the heart of it—the trust."

26

Insurance

WHEN THEY ENCOUNTERED each other in the hall right after class, Aschkin overheard his mumbling and whispered to him, "I loved the lecture—I even want to work with you on some cases posing questions of freedom and equality."

"Can we talk about his privately?" he said with a grin.

"I feel the same need," she said. "*Do I dare to eat a peach*?, to quote your favourite poet. The closest place I can think of to a secret garden is a room in the basement of the library. No one goes there. Look for the books on Turkish law—no kidding—and then turn to the left. Meet me in half an hour."

Adam returned to his office and waited in a state of great excitement. Was it better to be a Romantic at law or a romantic in life? The inner garden of the law school library might be the place where their bond would be sealed.

After an achingly slow 30 minutes, Adam took the faculty elevator down to the lowest level of stacks, a place he had used to visit when he did research in European law. He wandered around among the country collections looking for books with vowel signs that could be the language of Atatürk. There were lots of dusty books collected under the headings of Romania and Yugoslavia and other countries unlikely to find many takers.

He turned a corner and there, standing near a collection of nineteenth-century books written in Arabic script, was Aschkin. Her hair was down as though she was ready for bed. She led him down the row of books to a barely visible metal door, which she opened with one of the keys on her chain. In contrast to the spare stacks of the library, the room inside was comfortably furnished with a desk on one side, an easy chair and a couch in the corner. There was even a Ficus in the corner that managed to survive in the interior light with occasional care by the night janitor. "The former dean installed this room years ago as a special retreat for women in times of their monthly stress," she said softly. "It is barely used any more."

"Are Ann and Kathy likely to come here?"

"I don't think so. They are too *machista*," said Aschkin. "They wouldn't want to be caught in a special place for women who admit their weakness. There's something wonderfully old-fashioned about this place. I like it."

"This is exciting. My fantasy is to get caught *in flagrante* by Ann and Kathy when they're armed and doing shore patrol. They start shooting at us and we have to duck for cover."

"They won't be armed down here. I think I need to comfort you and help you relax." Aschkin took Adam in her arms and stroked his back, and then lightly massaged his shoulders. He took her head in his hands and kissed her gently on the lips. She responded with her tongue, and her gestures indicated to Adam that whatever he did, she would one-up him on the teenage scale of sexual exploration. If he stayed above the waist, she would slip her hands down toward his crotch.

Adam reached inside Aschkin's shirt and felt her firm, pointed breasts. "I cannot tell you how long I have been fantasizing about this."

"Do you think they are made in the image of God?" she said impiously.

"If not, then God is not perfect."

"In Judaism this is known to be true," she said. Adam let the line go because he was so intent on kissing Aschkin's nipples. She began squirming and moaning as she had in the car down in what they had come to call "Egyptland."

"I want to fuck you," he said.

"Ohhh, how naughty! But let's wait until we can spend the night."

Adam felt slightly more relieved than he wanted to admit. His ability to satisfy Aschkin in intercourse would remain an open question. He feigned disappointment and threw her down hard on the padded couch. He landed on top of her, kissing her cheeks and forehead.

"That will be soon, I promise you." She swooned and reached for Adam's urgent hardness, unzipping his fly and sliding her hand in, around and then cupping the most delicate part, underneath. He fell back into a posture of feigned helplessness. She pulled off his underpants and grasped him fully and firmly. Adam felt bound to respond but he could barely move his body. He could massage her with his hand but could not reach her with his tongue. His fingers went in and she started to vibrate in a way that excited Adam even more. "I'm not going to last long," he said through gritted teeth.

Aschkin turned slightly and reached down to her purse, which she had left next to the couch. Adam asked her what she was doing.

"I don't want to leave to leave any traces here. Remember Clinton and Monica's dress. Not for us. Wait a moment...I should have something here that will keep our secret for us." Rummaging with her free hand, her other hand continuing its hypnotic movements on his body, she produced a small resealable plastic bag. Kissing him, she whipped his maleness several times very fast. Adam cried out and started to come. She was tempted to put her hand over his mouth. He grabbed the little bag from her, held it firmly against himself and caught the ample spurts as his whole body shuddered.

"That was smart," he said. "But I feel so incomplete." And he pulled her closer to him.

"And I am beginning to feel more complete," Aschkin said softly, and smiled.

He lay back on the couch and she cuddled next to him, his hand still massaging her womanhood. "It feels good," she said, "but I don't have to come. It is not necessary for me every time."

They lay together for about ten minutes. There didn't seem much to talk about. Then Aschkin said, "I'm sorry, I have to go—perhaps it is better if we leave separately. I'll take the bag; my purse is large and you have nowhere to put anything if you meet anyone outside." She got up and dressed, as Adam admired her dark skin and graceful curves.

"Next time we spend the night together," he said. "Promise?"

"Promise," she replied, as she kissed him several times and then took her purse and darted out of the door. Adam felt that part of his spirit was gone.

Aschkin was moving fast. Once she left the library she sped to the nearest ladies' room, checked it was empty, shut herself in a cubicle and then reached into her purse. She pulled out the plastic bag, plus a long, thin bottle from her collection at home. It looked like a test tube with a wide mouth and a lid. Carefully she unscrewed the top, opened the plastic bag and poured the still-warm contents into it, shutting the vial with its firm-fitting lid. The empty bag was resealed, to throw away somewhere well away from campus or home.

Outside on the street, she hailed a cab and told the driver, "Take me to East 76th Street."

* * * * *

Adam spent the afternoon and evening alone forlorn, working on his death penalty case. It was becoming urgent now, and he had put off his final class until tomorrow to make time to work on the case. He fell asleep, half expecting his nightmares of the past few days past to revisit him. He dreamt of a room, much like the secret spot in the library, but it was full of liquid, and he and a woman, presumably Aschkin, were swimming toward the room but only he could enter. He stayed alone, anchored to the couch as much as a fish/man could be. There was no pain, no discomfort. Adam awoke in the middle of the night with a distinct sense that the world was a friendly and enveloping place. He felt connected in a way he had always wanted.

The phone rang. Aschkin's soft voice cooed on the other end, "How are you, my love?"

"Better," replied Adam. "Hearing you, better."

"I can't bear to sleep with Peter tonight. I'm still up working in the living room. He has gone to bed."

"What shall we do?" inquired Adam.

"Not much we can do right now," she said, and fell silent. "I want to ask you something. Let's suppose there are three wheels of fortune. On the first there are three possible outcomes, each with a probability of one in three. Get it so far?"

"Yes, I know something about math," said Adam, laughing at Aschkin's slight condescension.

"OK. Now, wheel A has the following payoff scheme: minus-$40, plus-$30, or plus-$100. How much would it would be worth to play the wheel once?"

Adam thought for a second. "Well, other things being equal, I would say $30."

"Right," said Aschkin. "Now suppose there are two other wheels. On one the pay scheme is zero, plus-$30 and plus-$60. On the other the payoff is always $30. Among the three wheels, which one do you prefer?"

"I would take the first; there is a bigger potential on the upside."

"Yes, but also more risk on the downside."

"That's life," replied Adam.

"Good for you. I love you. You know what the right answer is in finance?"

"Actually, I don't."

"The right answer is the third wheel. No risk, no upside, no downside. But you are willing to take risks. You are a Romantic, my dear."

"Now I know what I am."

"Yes, and I love you for it. Our life is like the first wheel. To tell you the truth, I prefer it to the third one too, even though I'm not supposed to."

"How do you feel right now," queried Adam.

"I feel plus-100. How about you? Marriage is the third wheel."

"I always thought Peter was the third wheel in all this," punned Adam.

"Well, maybe he is forcing us to keep our balance. I always thought your third wheel was your daughter, your loyalty to Abigail."

Adam fell silent.

"Are you there?" she asked.

"Yes, I'm thinking. There is something I have to tell you. Something happened today—I'm not sure what it was—that compensated for a great misfortune in my life over 30 years ago. It was in Argentina. I lost a child when I agreed that my girlfriend Sara would have an abortion. I felt very guilty about this and it influenced my life in many ways. I developed a kind of obsessive interest in issues relating to the beginning of life and the end of life. The truth is that Abigail was never born. I made up the relationship as a way of pretending that the whole thing never happened."

Now Aschkin was silent. Finally, she said hesitantly, "But you did get her pregnant, didn't you? You were the father?"

"I always assumed so. Frankly, I never thought about it. I always felt guilt for the abortion as though it were my child."

"This is kind of amazing. And you had me believing the whole story, too." Aschkin's voice had gone very quiet. "I thought for sure you had a child."

"Is this important for you? Why do you care so much?"

"I don't know what to say. I'm a little confused right now. I think I have to go. The wheels are spinning in my head."

They tried to smooth out the end of the conversation with affectionate words but Adam felt that something was missing. He had confessed the truth about the child he had never had, and he felt relieved and burdened at the same time. He'd known she would be hurt by his lie, but Aschkin seemed disappointed in ways that he did not understand. "I think the wheel might have come out minus-40," were Aschkin's final words as she hung up the phone.

27

The Star Chamber

THE NEXT DAY Adam felt the wheels had already spun and were about to indicate his fortune. The faculty was to convene in the morning to discuss their response to his exam, and in the afternoon he would have to give his final lecture of the course. This was the day, the day he must go forth into battle—or at least explain to the students the meaning of taking risks both in life and in the law.

Occupied as he was with his death penalty brief and Aschkin, he had neglected his planning for the meeting. He didn't know how many votes were on his side, nor who they were. He would have to cope with Julian and his other enemies and wait to see who, besides Ariel, would speak up for him. He had hoped to call the students from his current class to testify that they found nothing objectionable in the exam. It would be better if he'd had students from the class that had taken the exam, but he had done no research to find out their names. In any case, he felt the need to have his foreign students with him, the regulars, the leaders of the class who had convinced him that he was not Job and there was no reason for pity. But this was a faculty-only event. Even though the complaints about the exam had originated with students, none would be present at the critical hearing.

As the faculty filed into the seminar room, Peter, as dean, took a seat in the middle of the long edge of the oblong table. He put down a yellow legal-sized pad in front of him. On his right were Pat Graham, reading the *Post* as ever; Hans Richter, with some architectural plans; and Ariel, with nothing in hand, taking a seat at the narrow end of the table near the window, the better to see his potential opponents and ridicule their arguments. Aschkin took the seat next to him. At the other end of the table Ann and Kathy sat together. On the side facing the dean were arrayed Julien, and several of his colleagues from the Commonwealth countries, some of whom Adam had rarely seen. He recognized Jill Andrews from the UK and Alexandra Rogers from New Zealand, but that was the extent of his personal knowledge of them. Nkwame was there, quiet in his seat opposite the dean. Paul took his place on the dean's left side, dressed as usual in his green sports jacket, white shirt and black scarf. Adam noted his air of indifference and sat next to him in the hope that he could move him clearly into his camp. Interspersed around the table were others distant from Adam both professionally and personally. They did corporate law and taxation and limited their research to the word product of the American courts and the regulatory agencies. They did not know any languages but English, and were suspicious of projects that went beyond the needs of the big firms downtown. He knew that he had little chance with this group, largely because he never socialized with them, never took them to lunch—and they, of course, reciprocated the distance.

As soon as Peter called the meeting to order, one of the colleagues who knew Adam least well suggested that Adam absent himself from the discussion. This came as a surprise. It was like asking the defendant in a criminal trial to leave the courtroom. Ann immediately objected, much to Adam's surprise. Paul immediately passed a note to Adam. *"This is dangerous, it means she probably already has the votes."* Other joined the chorus for exclusion. Before waiting to see whether there was a majority against him, Adam announced that he would not leave under any circumstances. He said it was "a matter of personal honor" for him to attend and to hear what was said about his exam and about him.

Pat exploded and threw his paper to the floor. He was so furious that he started to bang his fist, but caught himself in mid-air. "That is so like you, Adam! You're like one of the Southern white gentlemen always concerned about their 'honor' and their 'tradition'—just code words for keeping us folks in their place." Adam felt chagrined and knew that he had lost a few votes—and not necessarily from those sympathetic to African-Americans.

Pat continued, "I've always wanted to say this. I resented that I had to take over a class of yours simply because you laughed at a student, they revolted against you, and you asked them whether they preferred to leave the class. Was that too a matter of honor?"

Adam was hoping that someone would object that the past incident had nothing to do with the exam. No one did. Pat's comment set the tone for the ensuing discussion. Julian recalled the incident Peter had privately told Aschkin about, when Adam had used vulgarity with a female secretary. "When she was late with a project, he said, 'When the fuck are you going to get this done?' This is the kind of thing a well-trained Oxford professor would not say," Julien concluded. The Commonwealth group seemed to nod in agreement.

"Is that all he said?" laughed Ariel from the end of the table.

"It is clear that Adam has a problem with women in this school," said Julien.

"Julien, shame on you, that you talk like that," Ariel threw in. "You would probably would have wanted to impeach Clinton for having an affair with an intern in the White House."

"You bet I would."

"But I thought," argued Ariel, "that this meeting was called to discuss the exam. And I frankly see nothing wrong with it."

Ann was silent. Kathy Kong, too.

Julien did their bidding. "I have here a petition signed by 60 students in the class, all complaining that they were offended by the exam."

"That's good," intervened Adam. "Give me their names so that I can interview them and we can talk to them here."

"No," Peter said. "We cannot do that. I have seen the names and I know the list is valid, but we have to protect the privacy of the students. They would not have signed if they'd thought they would come under cross-examination."

"Excuse me," said Ariel, "have you ever heard of the Sixth Amendment and the right to cross-examine the witnesses against you?"

"Sorry," said Peter, "this is not a criminal prosecution. We are not the state, and, even if we were, our purpose is not to punish. It is only to decide what is good for our community."

"My dear dean, have you heard about due process?" Ariel smiled.

"'The road to hell is paved with due process'—have you never heard that, my dear Colline? This is a collegial process."

Ariel broke out laughing. "Collegial my ass. I would call this a kangaroo court but I wouldn't want to insult kangaroos."

"Well," responded Adam, "can I at least call the students of the current class to have them testify about the exam? They understand the issues very well and not one of them, so far as I know, thinks there is anything to be offended about."

Pat objected. "I don't see the relevance of what these students say. They didn't take the exam. They were not under time pressure. Perhaps as foreign students they have different attitudes anyway."

Peter concurred. "I'm afraid that's right."

Adam started laughing. "Do you realize that I am now in the situation of Sir Walter Raleigh when he was being tried for treason in the early seventeenth century? He couldn't confront the witness against him and he couldn't call his own witnesses. Not much has changed in the last four hundred years. The situation is rounded out by neither of us having a lawyer to represent us."

"Oh, Sir Walter," gloated Ariel. "No wonder Rodrigo calls you his captain."

"What was that?" asked a few colleagues spontaneously.

"Nothing," said Ariel, sitting up straight. "I think Adam is right. His situation is as bad as someone being tried for treason in the time before we began to recognize the basic rights of due process."

Peter had little patience for this line of argument. "Look, I respect due process as much as the next man. But do you follow the due process rule when you're grading exams? No, you don't. You look at the paper and evaluate it yourself."

"I guess you're right," conceded Adam. "So let's look at the exam and evaluate it ourselves. By your own argument, though, the petition Julian submitted is totally irrelevant."

Peter had to agree. Adam expected Ann to object but she did not, which worried him more than ever. It obviously worried Paul too; he leaned over and whispered, "There's something fishy here. Your enemies have a card up their sleeve."

Julian had the debater's skill to turn the consensus to his advantage. "Yes, I agree to look at the exam and read it in context—the context of Adam's life as a scholar and teacher. It *is* relevant, therefore, that he used foul language with a secretary. I also feel bound to report that, when I had an office next to Adam's, he had a constant string of attractive females coming to see him. He would typically close the door, and I often wondered what was going on inside."

"If you had these runaway erotic thoughts, we should be prosecuting you," snapped Ariel.

Julian huffed. He recognized that his fantasies revealed more about him than about Adam.

Paul objected in Adam's place. "This reminds me of the old Commie ethic of judging the whole person in every criminal case. I thought that in this legal culture we assessed acts, not persons. Everyone has the right to be judged on the basis of specific acts—or, in this case, specific exams."

Kathy Kong broke her silence. "The exam speaks for itself. *Res ipsa loquitur*." This line got a few smiles from her colleagues; they always found the half-appropriate use of legal jargon amusing. She invoked the example Ann had used in the debate a few days ago. "Suppose a math professor examined his students on the number of gas ovens of a certain dimension it would take to kill a thousand Jews a day?"

"In an exam like that, the professor would display a prurient interest in the process of killing Jews," said Adam. "The excessive interest reveals a latent anti-Semitism."

This was the wrong thing to say. Ann just stared at him, and the rest of the faculty got the message. They were beginning to think he had an equally prurient interest in the killing of fetuses.

The faculty would not relent about Adam's personal sexual history. On the pretext of reading the exam in context, they mentioned every rumor they had ever heard. There was, for example, the episode in which he had been dating an Orthodox Jewish student, a mother with five children. Then there was another case in which a student had met him in Los Angeles, slept with him, and then received a good grade in his class. Peter was beginning to wonder how the faculty could dig up so much dirt about Adam. Was the gossip mill that effective?

Kong went on the attack. "What I want to know is where you got that slogan that 'Motherhood is Death.' Now that lesbian women are pressing hard for the right to parenthood, I find the use of that slogan to have to have unfortunate implications. It undermines parenthood and therefore indirectly reduces the status of lesbians and all women. Wasn't that choice of words entirely gratuitous in the exam?"

"I think you're right, Kathy, I didn't need to make up the slogan, but I wanted to make the motivations of the cult more believable. I think there is something of the frustrated novelist in me."

This level of honesty and self-criticism generated some sympathy among the undecided members of the faculty—mostly the women from the UK and New Zealand. Most of the faculty, however, continued to press Adam about incidents with women in the past. They wanted to know what these amorous adventures told them about the true purpose of the exam.

"Did you not have an affair with Dean Rachel White before she left?" Julien pressed him.

"That is none of your business," responded Adam.

"And what about the abortion you convinced your girlfriend to have when you were in Argentina?"

Adam went ashen. The room fell eerily silent. Finally, Aschkin came to his rescue. "I thought you all believed in the right to abortion? This is the problem with the exam: you think he is campaigning for the rights of the fetus. I think this whole conversation is beneath the dignity of this faculty."

"Bravo," said Ariel. Paul nodded. A few of the other women expressed support with their body language.

"By the way, Julien," asked Ariel, "do you mind if I start inquiring about your love life? That will tell us a lot about how to interpret your remarks at this meeting."

Julien looked aghast. "You would be just guessing. We have hard facts about you, Professor Gross."

That was precisely the point that disturbed Peter. How could the faculty, many of whom were newcomers like himself, dig up all this personal dirt against Adam, about the way he had spoken to secretaries, about his love life from at least a decade ago? How could they know about the alleged abortion in Argentina? He knew about these things because there were notations in Adam's personnel file about complaints made against him—as well as notes about his accomplishments. He also knew that the university conducted a background check on foreign-born faculty members and would have found out something of Adam's personal history before he came to the States. But only the dean had access to these files.

Disturbed, he called a recess, ostensibly for everyone to use the rest rooms or grab a cup of coffee. He ran back up to his office to see whether the file had been tampered with. It was there, in the correct drawer, but filed out of order. It looked as though someone had taken it out and returned it. But he and his secretary were the only people authorized to do that. He asked around. No one on his staff knew anything about it.

Returning to the meeting, Peter announced that he had strong personal reasons for ruling that Adam's past was out of bounds in the discussion of the exam. He could not give his reasons at that time, but asked the faculty to trust him that there were sufficient grounds for his decision. "I do not want to say any more for fear of making a false accusation." The faculty were told to focus on the words of the exams or he would dismiss the meeting.

Julien and Pat disregarded the dean's ruling and continue to press the attack. After ten minutes of efforts to control the meeting, Peter gave up and left the room. Aschkin got up to leave with him but then, noting that he was already out of the door, she returned to her seat.

As soon as the dean stepped out of the room, Ann declared that unless there were objections she would chair the session, but she would not vote one way or the other on a resolution of censure. With Peter gone and Ann not voting, there was a total of 18 professors remaining at the table. When the hand vote was finally taken, 12 supported a motion of censure and six opposed. The six dissenters were Adam himself, Paul, Nkwame, Ariel, Aschkin and, surprisingly, Hans. The Regina Six, as they immediately dubbed themselves, decided to go out for lunch and a drink together to mock the faculty vote. They immediately made a statement to the *Law School Report* that the vote meant nothing. It would not affect Gross's tenure or teaching responsibilities. Aschkin was torn between her loyalty to the dissenters and to Peter, who was locked in his office not taking calls. Finally she joined Adam and the others for a celebratory glass of wine. She insisted only that they keep Hans off the subject of plumbing and Ariel turned off, period. Adam hugged her and they walked out together.

28
Glory

ADAM APPROACHED HIS final class feeling giddy. The solidarity of the Regina Six had infused in him more of a sense of community than he had ever had at this or any other law school. The five other people of the Six were now his friends. They were a bloc on the faculty. After all, had not all his heroes been unjustly persecuted? The famous immigrants of 1848—Franz Sigel and Lajos Kossuth—had they not gone through the same thing? Woe unto those, he thought, who were always treated fairly in life.

He had visions of a new alliance in the law school—his Principals in class joined by the Six dissenters. They could become an influential bloc. But now, he reminded himself, I have serious business. I must motivate the students to be ready to devote themselves to the great issues of law that will present themselves in their lifetimes, in their countries. Now, at the end of the course, he had come to think of the students as his colleagues. He had visions of them all working together on some great crises that would loom in the new millennium.

"The first thing I have to tell you is something about the vocabulary you are going to use for the rest of your professional lives. Contrary to popular suspicion, it is not enough in New York to know a few words of Yiddish. *Meshuggah* and *chutzpah* but that's about it. You will have to do business with your English-speaking clients."

This was obvious to everyone. The students sat back and let the familiar become the present. "Tell us, my *capitán*, my *capitán*." Everyone laughed with Rodrigo.

"You buy a house, right, you pay money, you get legal title?"

"*Ja, ja, ja,*" butted in Joerg.

"But suppose you don't have enough money. So you borrow from the bank. You have to give the bank security. Now you get the whole story of law and equity but in practical terms. You give the bank legal title to the house and you retain the protection of equity."

"Oh, thank God," said Jaime. "The law associated with God and the king comes out against the banks and in favor of the little guys."

Adam wondered who would be the next student to mock him.

"In a nutshell, you have all of modern finance in this transaction. The common law created two kinds of title, legal and equitable: one goes to the bank, one is retained by the home-owner. Both are protected. This is the modern mortgage. We say that home-owner—or the mortgagor—has an 'equity' in his house. That is the total value minus the debt to the bank. If the value is a million dollars and he owes \$200,000 to the bank, he has an equity of \$800,000. Notice that debt is relatively fixed but equity varies with the real estate market. If the market goes down, the home-owner's equity may go down to \$700,000 or \$600,000.

"This is the same as the modern corporation. The shareholders start with a certain capital. Then their management raises more money by borrowing from bond-holders. The creditors have a bond in place of their money. The shareholders own what is left over—their original capital plus earnings, as both are affected by the market. They are just like the home-owner. This is called the equity in the corporation. Shares of stock are equity. They are bought and sold in the equity markets downtown.

"One more point. Those who own stock have votes in the management of the corporation. They are thought of as the real owners. They have the power to hire and fire the managers. In this case, I think, Jaime, equity is on the side of the rich and powerful.

"So there you have it. We need bonds with others, because we give them money and other valuables. We have equities because others have to respect the value we have in our homes and in our businesses.

"And the most important of all is trust. We call it the trust, but without trust pure and simple none of this would work. The trust is simply like a mortgage. You give legal title to the trustee who holds it for the benefit of a third person, the beneficiary. Think of it as a triangle. The trustor conveys legal title to the trustee, but by a separate vector in the triangle he conveys equitable title to the beneficiary.

"All these institutions are possible because of the peculiarities of the common law—in particular, that we had courts of law and of equity. Civilian countries can imitate what we do, but it is not the same. They have to use contracts and provide special legislation to generate institutions that function the same way as those that grow naturally from the oddities of the common law.

"I could have told you that in the beginning when Joerg asked me about the dogmas of the common law. But then we would not have had all this fun.

"In one sense, my message to you is to cherish your bonds, fight for your equities, and preserve trust at all time. Without trust the legal system would not function. You cannot have a policeman backing up every law and enforcing every contract. We need to cultivate good faith and trust to make the law work.

"We should not forget what we have been through together. The fight about the exam is a microcosm of the war that engaged us in the middle of the course. We had to struggle through all the issues of religion and the rights of women, we had to face up to the one-sided nature of the Constitution before the Civil War, we had to learn about the necessity of the Romantic struggle to make the law complete.

"Now I hope we all meet again in a much greater struggle. We know that conflicts are brewing with the Arab world. There was one war ten years ago and talk of another some day. We will be challenged again. Then we should remember Oliver Wendell Holmes, Jr. He would have loved our little disquisition on equity and bonds; he would insist that we learn more economics than I taught you; but in the end he was a Romantic living in the wake of the Civil War. He was an American version of the European heroes, Franz Sigel, Lajos Kossuth and Francis Lieber. He would urge us to become warriors of the law, fighters in the courtroom, champions of free speech, defenders of civil liberties. Wherever the risk was, wherever we could be wounded, we should fight. In the last paragraph of his famous article 'The Path of the Law,' he argues that the practice of law is not about money and power. Quoting Hegel, he says, '[It is] not the appetite but the opinion [or the mind] which has to be satisfied.' He praises Leslie Stephen, the historian of English criminal law, as having shown how, and I quote, 'a hundred years after his death the abstract speculations of Descartes had become a practical force controlling the conduct of men.' And then we encounter my favorite sentence in his entire body of work.

'Read the work of the great German jurists, and see how much more the world is governed today by Kant than by Bonaparte.' We cannot all be Descartes or Kant, Holmes conceded—or Francis Lieber, let me add—but we should aspire to the kind of happiness that comes not from money but from an engagement with the law on a spiritual level. In his final sentence Holmes counsels the students whom he was addressing to immerse themselves in the 'remoter and more general aspects of law [...] It is through them,' he concludes, 'that you will not only become a great master in your calling, but connect your subject with the universe and catch an echo of the infinite, a glimpse of its unfathomable process, a hint of the universal law.'"

With these words, Adam knew that he was done. He gathered his papers. The students stood and began to applaud. Rodrigo cried out from the back, "My *capitán*, my *capitán*!" Everyone present, Adam most of all, was torn between tears and cries of satisfaction.

29

New Lives

IT WAS 4 P.M. and Peter was still locked in his office. He was dejected, and felt betrayed by his own faculty. He was composing a memo declaring the vote illegal, and sufficiently hostile toward him for him to treat it as a vote of no confidence in his deanship. He explained that the reasons for his ruling would soon become clear. He added that Adam had been denied the basic elements of due process in a way that differed little from the unjust trial of Sir Walter Raleigh, and declared that he would have no part of it. His resignation would be effective two weeks later, on Labor Day.

Adam and Aschkin smiled knowingly when they read of Peter's adopting of the Sir Walter Raleigh argument. "Ah, my shining knight," she mocked.

"Once a night is good enough for me," jibed Adam, recalling an old joke. "He came out on the right side nonetheless."

Yes, for the moment, we are all on the same side, she thought.

The president of the university, who rarely interfered in decisions of the law school, accepted Peter's resignation and asked the faculty to choose an interim dean immediately. They convened the following week and elected Ann O'Sullivan. She would serve for one year while the faculty engaged in a nationwide search. If the committee was properly stacked, they would find no one better suited than Ann.

Now Adam understood why Ann had always said that none of this was personal.

In law schools in most parts of the world, resigning and retiring deans received a sabbatical leave for a semester in order to give the new person in charge an opportunity to lead without the *Ancien Régime* overlooking every step. In this case, the leave was especially urgent. Ariel suggested to Peter that he spend some time in Israel investigating the legal status of Palestinians on the West Bank. Peter liked the idea, so Ariel made a few calls and landed Peter a spot at B'Tselem, an Israeli centre for human rights in the occupied territories, in Ramallah, the unofficial capital of the Palestinian National Authority, in the occupied West Bank six miles north of Jersualem. B'Tselem was short for *B'Tselem Elohim* or "*Imago Dei*"— made in the image of God.

Aschkin was amused that Peter wanted to work for an organization bespeaking a religious message. She felt conflicted about whether to join him, but in the end decided that, if she were not prepared to leave him right then and there, as she was not, then her choice was made for her. The newly installed Ann granted her leave without pay for the fall semester, and they were off for Jerusalem.

Aschkin's sudden departure hit Adam like a distended version of her leaving him alone in the secret room of the library. He fell into a depression. He told people, with a wry smile, that of course it was about the official censure. Though no one knew the details of his relationship with Aschkin, Ariel, Paul and others close to him intuited that his depression was about Aschkin's leaving.

It was October before Aschkin sent him her first email from Jerusalem. They were settled and she had found an *ulpan* where she could start learning Hebrew along with the new immigrants. She was thrilled by the architecture and spirituality of the city. She was also close to home and could hop over for weekends to visit her parents and family. Then she repeated the line from one of their earlier conversations. "*Istanbul'u dinliyorum, gözlerim kapalı.* 'I am listening to Istanbul, my eyes closed.' Will you learn some Turkish in my absence?"

Adam wrote that he felt very satisfied by his work and his connection to her, which he was confident would survive their separation. Their correspondence broadened his interests. He said he would start learning Turkish so they could compare notes about their respective languages. They also started writing about the Biblical sites that Aschkin was seeing for the first time, about the books they were reading, about their feelings toward one another. It was as though they had just begun courting.

Peter was apparently happy, though he had a constant hassle passing through checkpoints in order to visit Ramallah. He too wrote an occasional note to Adam. The three of them felt close to each other. It was as though there were three independent, strong bars of iron surrounding a soft core of deception.

Aschkin's experiences in Israel dampened any thoughts she might have had about converting to Judaism. She had expected to find men and women dancing during services, as she experienced in the synagogue in New York, and she was invariably disappointed by the conventional style of Orthodox religious life in Jerusalem. The separation of men and women in services, the taboos about menstruation, the constant repetition of the same prayers—it reminded her too much of the mosques she had visited as a child. She would learn, she would speak the language, but she would remain herself—caught, like Adam, between different cultures.

For his part, Adam took some solace in greater religious observance. He went regularly to the spot where Aschkin had joined him, he started learning the prayers, and he learned to merge his recurrent loneliness with the comfort of engaging in a collective ritual. The local rabbis—both of whom happened to be from Buenos Aires—were very sensitive about political issues. They made a point of including a prayer for all the people suffering of the world, not just for the people of Israel. They asked Adam to speak a few times on the political situation brewing in the Arab world. He found a supportive connection between his political commitments and the teachings of the prophets to bring justice to the entire world.

Also, perhaps because of his commitment to outside causes, he had never felt better among his colleagues. The Regina Six—sans Aschkin—met from time to time to discuss the political future of the school, and it turned out they had good reason to do so. About three weeks into the fall semester they experienced a twist of fortune. The two Latina cleaning ladies—who happened to be on cordial terms with their fellow Latino Adam Gross—discovered a photocopy of Adam's personnel file under the carpet in Kathy Kong's office. When they confronted her with the file, Kathy claimed it was a plant and immediately turned the file over to Dean O'Sullivan and disclaimed any responsibility for possession. Ann kept the matter secret for a few days. When the president of the university finally heard of the incident, he began a formal inquiry. The focus of course was on Ann, but, so far as Adam knew, there was no hard evidence against her.

As the semester passed, Adam and Aschkin seemed to grow closer. But the question of the future never came up. Adam sensed that there was a major gap in their intimacy, some huge issue that was not being discussed. He assumed that the impediment was the triangle with Peter.

Just a few days before Christmas Peter and Aschkin returned to New York. Adam suggested that the three of them—two Jews and a Muslim—meet for dinner on Christmas Eve. That morning, unexpectedly, Adam and Aschkin met at the market near 110th Street and Broadway. There were people standing around, but Adam rushed to hug her, devil be hanged. She held back, but he put his arms around her and drew her close. At once he felt a bulge in her mid-section. He reached down and felt the shape. This was not a newly arrived *panza* from eating too much humus and falafel.

"My God, you're pregnant!" he blurted out.

"Yes, I am."

"From Israel?"

"No, from August in New York."

"Is Peter's middle name August? He must very pleased."

"Yes, and surprised too, and he has accepted our new beginning."

Aschkin was acutely conscious of treading a thin line between deception and overt lying. She knew that she was deceiving both Peter and Adam, but she did not how to correct the situation and was not sure whether she had to. She recited a story to herself that went something like this: I did what I had to do. Both Peter and Adam consented to sex with me—even if it never acually happened with Adam, he was willing. For generations a woman's consent to intercourse has been taken as consent to having a child. Why should not the same be true for men? And I love both of them. Why should I create jealousy and conflict? They now seem to like each other. I cannot say anything now.

"Does this mean that you're committed now to a *ménage à trois*? Am I the third wheel?"

"Yes, my third wheel of fortune. I love you and I find in you many things that I have nowhere else in my life, and I feel I make a difference in yours. I cherished the email correspondence between us last semester. I would get up every morning hoping there was a message from you. And I would spend the whole day composing my reply. I want that to continue in person."

Adam examined his own feelings and tried to answer honestly. "That is enough for me, for now. And I'm thrilled about the birth. The child is in good health?"

"Yes, totally. I've had blood tests, ultrasound, the works. Hadassah Hospital treated me like a heroine of the state. They know the value of motherhood—even for Muslims who are not citizens."

"We should all celebrate tonight," said Adam happily.

"Yes. And Adam—you know now that motherhood is life, right?"

"Yes, the cult of the Big Monkey had it totally wrong." And he took her in his arms again.